On Becoming Homeless

The Shelterization Process for Homeless Families

Ione Y. DeOllos

University Press of America, Inc.
Lanham • New York • Oxford

Copyright © 1997 by
University Press of America,® Inc.
4720 Boston Way
Lanham, Maryland 20706

12 Hid's Copse Rd.
Cummor Hill, Oxford OX2 9JJ

Library of Congress Cataloging-in-Publication Data

DeOllos, Ione Y.
On becoming homeless : the shelterization process for homeless
families / Ione Y. DeOllos.
p. cm.
Includes bibliographical references and index.
l. Shelters for the homeless--United States. 2. Family social work--
United States. 3. Social work with the homeless--United States. I.
Title.
HV4505.D46 1997 363.5'85'0973--dc21 97-13285 CIP

ISBN 0-7618-0838-8 (cloth: alk. ppr.)
ISBN 0-7618-0839-6 (pbk: alk. ppr.)

♾™ The paper used in this publication meets the minimum
requirements of American National Standard for information
Sciences—Permanence of Paper for Printed Library Materials,
ANSI Z39.48—1984

To my husband,

Peter Ernest

CONTENTS

LIST OF FIGURES

LIST OF TABLES

FOREWORD

Originally written as a doctoral dissertation in sociology, this monograph by Ione DeOllos focuses upon the problems of homelessness and the role of shelters in dealing with homeless families. In one sense, the monograph is descriptive. But in another sense, it refers to what goes on besides the obvious flow of daily events. The DeOllos findings are rich and provocative. When I was asked to prepare this Foreword, these findings stimulated me to speculate freely about their implications.

Certainly, homelessness is an ancient phenomenon. However, the establishment of shelters devoted only to house families who are temporarily without domiciles is of relatively recent origin. One of the major concerns of the DeOllos monograph is to examine the role of shelters in the life of the homeless family. The temporary shelter, whether run by a public or private welfare agency, attempts to do more than simply warehouse and feed undomiciled individuals and families until they can find housing. Functioning as a welfare agency, it usually assists people not only in finding such housing (especially for families) but also in rehabilitating them in order to minimize the chances of their becoming undomiciled again.

Historically, homeless populations have been regarded by resident communities ambivalently, that is, simultaneously as romantic free spirits and as disreputable intruders. Gypsy families are often seen as a universal exemplar of permanent homelessness.

On the one hand, the romantic view identifies homeless individuals as free souls outside the constraints of community life--in addition to gypsies are the itinerant cowboy of the movies, the hobo, the sailor wandering the seven seas, among others. In romantic fantasy, these free souls experience exciting adventures, rectify injustices in settled communities, and travel the open road.

On the other hand, unconstrained by "normal" community life, homeless people are viewed with distrust, suspicion, and often disdain--besides gypsies are European bombed-out families in World War Two who had to leave their community (Larney 1994), the Hooverville residents of the Thirties economic depression, the displaced Okies of the Thirties, people living on the streets (such as "shopping bag ladies"), the inhabitants of Skid Row, and so on (e.g., Anderson 1940).

But seen either romantically or as deviants, homeless families as well as individuals are considered to be a threat to the ongoing patterns of living in the community. In the seventeenth century American colonies, all unmarried persons were required to reside in the households of families--as boarders, apprentices, bonded servants, slaves, and so on. Likewise, families who were identified as unfit to govern their own affairs or who were "strangers" without their own domiciles had to live in households of resident families. As time went on, the homeless population grew too large to control by enforced household membership. Other techniques of control were established: workhouses, wholesale ordering the poor out of town, wide scale use of apprenticeships to control the deviant, dependent, and poverty-stricken (often to the detriment of poor families).

In recent times, the temporary shelter came into existence as another means for controlling the homeless population--again expressing an ambivalence of the domiciled community toward homeless people. On the one hand, there is a belief that territoriality--a sense of home--is inherent and necessary for effective child rearing. Hence, even a temporary haven is better than none in meeting the human need for "homefulness," particularly when there are children involved. To lack a home is not merely an absence of shelter; to be homeless is comparable to an illness, a lack of well-being, and it is the duty of the community to bring the undomiciled back to health. On the other hand, there is the mistrust of the homeless poor, and one must protect the community from them. The temporary shelter permits surveillance and control over the lives of the homeless poor.

The perception that homefulness is an element of human nature implies that homelessness should be treated like an illness. Dealing with the homeless poor thereby evokes a model of rehabilitative treatment: Homelessness is a kind of sickness. The shelter is seen as a sort of hospital; the shelter staff is like a medical staff dedicated to bringing the homeless back to a normal state of being; the homeless are the patients. In short, what is known as the medical model is invoked by the agencies of the community.

In the medical model, there is a normative role to be carried out by the patients (what sociologist Talcott Parsons and his associates have called the sick role). This role permits the patient to hold normal obligations of everyday life in abeyance in order to devote all attention to regaining a state of health and well-being. According to this model, the successful patient is supposed to cooperate with the physician (especially to follow the physician's instructions) and supporting staff in achieving a state of normality.

The rehabilitative role of the temporary shelter hence requires that homeless "patients" in the shelter follow the instructions of staff in attaining the normal state of homeful well-being. These instructions involve various "medicines," such as how to get and retain a job, how to maintain a household, proper parenting, and so on. To the extent that the staff of the temporary shelter fails to provide appropriate instructions to their "patients," the agency has failed in its rehabilitative role.

The performance of the temporary-shelter staff in "rehabilitating" the homeless cannot be properly assessed without an examination of the role of shelter inhabitants. The medical model "works" in accurately describing the treatment process only when there is a consensus between "physician" and "patient" on their appropriate roles. Implicitly, the model assumes that there is complete trust between the healer and the sick. However, given the element of mistrust in perceptions of the homeless (evoking a comparable mistrust by the homeless themselves), one can question how well the medical model "works" in institutions like the temporary shelter. In one sense, the DeOllos monograph can be seen as an examination of the influence of mistrust on the effective operation of the temporary shelter.

The DeOllos monograph deals with the perspective of homeless inhabitants of temporary shelters with regard to their prospects for the future. Her analysis is based upon participatory field research, during which time she became intimately acquainted with staff and homeless inhabitants at two temporary shelters. In this monograph she describes the phases of reaction that ensue over time of dwelling among parents residing with their children in a temporary shelter. Following Sutherland and Locke (1936), she identifies the phases of this development as the shelterization process. However, in order to apply the development to sheltered families, DeOllos has had to introduce modifications into the description of the process.

The DeOllos version of the shelterization process is briefly outlined below. (This capsulization omits many significant elements and perhaps distorts the description. The reader is urged to refer to the text in order to understand properly just what this process is, how it may vary, and what qualifications must be understood.) In reformulating this process, DeOllos draws in particular upon the work of Daniel Glaser (1964) on prisons, Erving Goffman (1961) on mental hospitals, and Sutherland and Locke (1936) on homeless men. The stages of parental shelterization process include:

Stage 1: Compliance, uncertainty, and feelings of humiliation
Stage 2: Anger, frustration, and resentment
Stage 3: Hope, goal setting, and planning
Stage 4: Frustration and resignation
Stage 5: Hopelessness, alienation, repeated episodes of homelessness

If one compares the stages in parental shelterization described by DeOllos with the attributes of the medical model, it is apparent that there is a clash between the perspectives of the staff and residents of the shelter. Only in Stage 3--hope, goal setting and planning--is there consensus upon the expected performance of shelter residents. Otherwise the shelter experience appears to widen the perceptual chasm between staff and homeless inhabitants.

The alienation of shelter residents is particularly significant for homeless families. The absence of permanent domiciles may well be an acceptable state for single adults. In fact the freedom of movement afforded by this fluid state of existence may even be of advantage in facilitating upward mobility or at least in seeking economic stability. However, for families with children, the home provides an anchor for stabilizing socialization patterns and for routinizing everyday activities. The alienation of the parents directly affects their relationship to their children and further destabilizes the socialization of the children. Hence, the alienation associated with the later stages of shelterization is of particular significance in its effects upon homeless families. For this reason (as well as others), the formulation of the shelterization process by DeOllos is important for understanding what happens to families in temporary shelters.

The study by Dr. DeOllos has dealt with the torturous course of experiences of the residents of temporary shelters. Her findings evoke parallel questions about the staff in these shelters: How do these experiences stimulate changes in the perceptions and activities of the staff of temporary shelters in response to the residents' shelterization process? Changes in staff perception would undoubtedly in turn reflect upon the ensuing interaction between staff and residents, and thereby have a lasting effect on the rehabilitation of homeless families.

The DeOllos analysis may also be useful in gaining an understanding of other phenomena as well. For example, recent legislation by Congress for "reforming" the way the national welfare system functions seems to operate under assumptions of the rehabilitation (or medical) model. This legislation replaces such programs as Aid to Families with Dependent Children with a rehabilitation plan that confines eligibility to a limited period.

Receiving monetary payment is coupled with participation in rehabilitation activities.

Like the temporary shelters for homeless people, the revised welfare system is seen as (a) rehabilitative, (b) demanding that dependent persons take responsibility for facilitating their "recovery," and (c) defining the entitlement as temporary. Each of these stipulations conforms to the medical model as formulated by Parsons and his associates. Except for the action of collecting the "sickly," dependent families in a single location, many of the same elements of the process seem pertinent.

The above similarities between shelterization and welfare rehabilitation suggest comparabilities between their stages (or phases) of development. Given these putative similarities, one would anticipate that parents beginning the "reformed" welfare program would initially exhibit compliance in the face of uncertainty at their entrance into the program (Stage 1). As they take part in the routines preparing them for employment, they would show frustration and resentment at being forced to undertake rehabilitation activities as a condition for receiving welfare payments (Stage 2). But with the passage of time they would connect these activities with potential employment and self-sufficiency; then they would actively participate in goal setting and planning (Stage 3). However, if the training and job searches are fraught with difficulties, frustration and resentment may take over (Stage 4). Finally, failure in their job search (or inability to hold a job) might lead eventually to a sense of alienation and hopelessness (Stage 5).

If these hypothetical stages occur for parents in the "reformed" welfare programs, one would anticipate a general lack of consensus between welfare staff members and welfare clients similar to that between shelter staff and the family-residents of temporary shelters. Hence, the analysis by DeOllos may also provide insights into problems that may emerge in rehabilitation programs associated with "welfare reform."

In addition, the DeOllos monograph evokes questions pertinent to policy making that would avoid the shelterization process. In recent years suggestions have been made regarding universal healthcare insurance; these suggestions may have a bearing upon the homeless population as well. Like state of health, housing is vital to the well-being of families and their members. That being the case, one might consider the establishment of a universal insurance program that would cover rent and mortgage payments in emergencies. Such a program would permit families to remain in their existing housing during periods of unemployment or to occupy comparable housing in the aftermath of natural or personal disasters. Since most families would not face such emergencies, premiums would be sufficiently low to permit families with low incomes to participate.

Such a housing insurance program would allow families in dire straits to continue living a normal existence. They would be spared the stigma attached to homelessness and residing in a temporary shelter. While the housing-insurance scheme may seem far-fetched at first glance, it suggests that there is at least one less expensive alternative to temporary shelter programs to accommodate families that are vulnerable to homelessness.

Although the investigation undertaken by Dr. DeOllos might not fall under the rubric of evaluation research, her analysis stimulates one to speculate upon the policy implications of her findings. At times staff and residents seem to be working against each other--and mistrust one another. In this atmosphere of mutual mistrust, sometimes it seems to be miraculous that the shelter can accomplish its mission. The analysis by Dr. DeOllos provides us with much insight into the shelter's operation. With this insight, we can then impose our own assessment of the functioning of staff and homeless residents. This assessment may stimulate us to formulate putative alternatives to the existing state of affairs.

The suggestions presented in this Foreword are only offhand speculations evoked by the DeOllos findings. With serious effort, no doubt numerous, more-profound implications can be drawn from them. Perhaps, after contemplation about the analysis in the monograph, each reader will be motivated to prepare a personal Epilogue cataloging additional implications.

BERNARD FARBER
PROFESSOR EMERITUS

ARIZONA STATE UNIVERSITY

PREFACE

Homeless individuals and families must meet the basic human needs
for food, shelter, and clothing through charitable organizations,
governmental agencies, and/or private agencies, or scrounging for
them on the streets. In Arid Acropolis,[1] the need for shelter may be
met by seeking out the aid of Baghdad Inn, an emergency homeless
shelter located at the intersection of two major streets. This shelter
was originally managed by a charitable organization. In the 1980s,
amid charges of mismanagement, it was removed from the control of
the charitable organization and placed under control of a board of
directors (Annual Report 1989; Findaroom 1989). At the time of the
study the shelter received funding from United Way, private
donations, and Federal, State, and Local governments (Annual Report
1989).

The Neighborhood

The shelter is bordered by a cemetery, railroad tracks, and medium-
sized supply businesses. Generally, the buildings which house these
supply businesses arc in need of repairs. Interspersed among
businesses are rental houses and apartments. Most of these residences
sport sloping porches with rotted railings, broken steps, and sagging
doors. Most of the paint has peeled from the outside walls and the
screens are missing from many of the windows.

Some agencies specifically designed to provide aid to the homeless are centrally located a few blocks from the shelter. Among these is a soup kitchen, funded by St. Vincent de Paul Society, which provides lunches to the shelter for women and children residing in the family dorm. Store-front buildings adjacent to the soup kitchen house an adult education center, a public-health outreach office, a State welfare office, and a mental-health outreach office.

Adjacent to Baghdad Inn is a Free Clinic which is used extensively by residents of the shelter. The Clinic receives funding from the State and Federal governments. This clinic is staffed by a doctor, a psychiatrist, four or five nurses, and several security guards. It provides non-emergency medical assistance for shelter residents as well as for individuals living on the streets. The clinic can provide most treatments required by clients except for surgery. On the average the clinic handles 1,200 cases a month (Typesalot 1989).

The Shelter's Physical Structure

Baghdad Inn is a large concrete block, sandstone-colored building. The front door consists of a single glass door with two narrow windows on either side. This door leads into the lobby of the shelter and is normally inhabited by several individuals loitering in the shade provided by the small awning above the door. The building has two windows on the ground floor, one of which is shuttered and at one time served as a mail window. The second floor has two sets of three windows breaking the monotony of the facade. The back wall of the building is broken by two windows on the second floor and two doors on the ground floor. These windows and doors, the only breaks in the stucco-covered walls, provide an image of an impenetrable monolith. The sidewalks in front of the shelter and along the side of the Free Clinic are inhabited by homeless men and women. Since the shelter is closed during the day (except for the day room) these people await the time they can re-enter the shelter by sitting on the steps of the Clinic or standing on the street corner.

In back of the Clinic and separated from it is a smaller building which houses the offices of the case managers. Seven case managers worked with 376 single individuals, up to 200 residents of Tent City (discussed earlier), and 30 mother/child families. Case managers assist residents in determining their needs and developing a plan aimed at accomplishing their goals. In addition, case managers supervise residents making certain residents work toward their goals and taking steps to get out of the shelter (Typesalot 1989).

Tent City

Behind the main building is a large grassy area officially called the Park but known to the residents as "Tent City." Tent City has two cement areas with four picnic tables each and a covering which provides the only shade in the compound. The entire Tent City area is surrounded by a six-foot high hurricane fence.

The grassy area of Tent City is ringed with small tents made of blue plastic tarp draped over wooden supports. The fronts and backs of the tents are open. In order to have some privacy, individuals living in these tents use scrap lumber and plastic to form a back wall and a door. Men and women are allowed to live together in this area, making it desirable for couples.[2] The residents of Tent City are allowed to cook for themselves. Hence, old grills, hibachis, and campfire ashes can be seen next to many of the tents. This area is home to as many as 200 individuals at any one time (Annual Report 1989; Typesalot 1989).

Residents of Tent City told of frequent knifings and rapes that occurred in the encampment at night. Some homeless individuals living on the streets in the vicinity commented they preferred living on the streets to living in Tent City because of the danger. In 1990 Tent City was closed and individuals residing there were relocated to other shelters, resettled into subsidized housing, or chose to move into the street or under river bridges.

Baghdad Inn

The two floors of the main building shelters single men, single women, and women with children. Upon entering the shelter visitors are struck with its physical condition. Lack of windows, which becomes increasingly depressing once inside, makes the halls and rooms dark and dreary. Rooms and corridors are painted in pale colors and have become smudged over the years. Floors are covered with dark tiles which only adds to the morose feeling. Most of the rooms and hall on the second floor are cluttered with shelves and boxes. Walls and ceilings of the bathrooms have peeling paint and the shower stalls are moldy. Residents shuffle along the corridors, further adding to the oppressive sight.

First Floor

The first floor of the main building is primarily occupied by administrative offices for staff of the shelter. Doors to these offices remain closed throughout the day and are locked when left.

A day room is located at the rear of the first floor. This room is a large tiled room with tables and a television. When entering the day room the deafening jumble of noise from several competing conversations and the television is at once noticeable. The tile floors and bare walls add to the commotion by echoing the noise back onto the crowd. It is difficult to hear a person who is not talking in a loud voice when in this room.

Until 1990 the day room was available for use by all homeless people, street people as well as shelter residents. Homeless people living on the streets were able to enter the day room during the day to rest, get out of the heat, or use the shower and restroom facilities. Additionally, morning meals and evening meals were served out of the day room to all homeless individuals. In 1990 the day room was closed to all but individuals residing at Baghdad Inn.[3]

The first floor also houses the single men's dorm with a wing which serves as the sleeping area for working men and men with male children over the age of seven. The single non-working men's area has beds for 244 men (Annual Report 1989; Typesalot 1989). Single men sleep in bunk beds arranged in rows extending the length of the room. There is no privacy for any of the men in this area of the shelter. During the day when the men must leave the shelter, their possessions are placed on their beds. This procedure does lead to loss of personal items through theft. Single men complain of the dangers of the single men's dorm. They relate incidents of being threatened with weapons, i.e., knives and guns, when they are unfortunate enough not to have cigarettes to share. The shelter has rules restricting possession of weapons while in the shelter but has not been able to enforce them.

The room for the working men with male children is separated from the main men's shelter by locker units which were placed there to provide more privacy. The working men's area has 88 beds (Annual Report 1989; Typesalot 1989). These are single beds rather than the bunk beds of the single men's dorm. Locked trunks are provided to each man in the working men's dorm to provide security for their possessions. Children, who can hear arguments and threats of violence in the single men's dorm, are generally too frightened to sleep and often ask their fathers to stay awake to protect them.

Second Floor

The second floor houses a daycare, job search office, single women's dorms, and families' dorm, and a long narrow conference room. The conference room is used for staff meetings and staff training sessions. This room is not available for use by residents of Baghdad Inn.

The job search office helps residents of Baghdad Inn obtain employment. The office provides daily employment announcements from two major area newspapers as well as free use of four telephones from which they can call to make interview appointments or make followup calls to check on the status of applications (Annual Report 1989; Typesalot 1989).

The daycare center is close to the family dorm. This center takes children of residents for up to eleven hours a day for five days a week in order for parents to have time to seek employment, apply for welfare and housing, or search for housing. The daycare center is able to provide for children aged zero to five; however, sometimes children as old as sixteen stay there (Annual Report 1989; Typesalot 1989).[4] Daycare teachers are never sure how many children they will have at the center each day with numbers ranging from five to twenty-five. Daycare takes place in a single room that has been divided into areas by using short bookcases. The room is decorated in bright colors with large cartoon figures and alphabet cards painted on the walls. The children are provided with creative, developmental activities throughout most of the day (Apple 1989).

A large L-shaped room with a single window accommodates a school for homeless children. The school is an accredited school providing grades one through eight. In the 1980s the school moved from the shelter to a local church basement in order to have more space. At this time the room was converted into a play room and family room for the families. This provided a much needed indoor space where children could play freely and safely. Additionally, this room provides a place where mothers can watch television with their children. The single women's day room does not allow children in the room which means mothers can watch television only after their children are in bed.

Single women are placed in one of two dorms. The single women's shelter has a total of 44 beds (Annual Report 1989). The beds in Dorm A are of bunk-bed style while the beds in Dorm B are single beds. Dorm B is used primarily for working women who are allowed to sleep days if they work evening or late night shifts. Each woman is given a locker for possessions in Dorm A or a dresser in Dorm B. Dorm B may be used to house women who are suspected of suffering from mental illness. Dorm B can also house occasional mothers with children if need for emergency sheltering arises. Mothers temporarily housed in Dorm B complained they and their children were awakened in the night by screams of mentally ill women. These mothers struggled to get their frightened children back to sleep that night and several nights thereafter.

The single women's day room has a snack machine, soda machine, microwave, and television. The tattered furniture in the day room includes sofa, five tables, stuffed chairs, and a number of other chairs. Additionally, two bookcases have twenty to thirty books ranging from out-of-date textbooks on Psychology, Astronomy, and History to novels (most frequently westerns or romance novels). At times there are several children's books; however, these are often removed to the family dorm.

The women's and children's donated clothing bank is entered through a door from the single women's day room. The clothing bank is open two afternoons a week. During the rest of the week the room is locked. When women have job interviews or are beginning new jobs, they are allowed into the room at other than the posted times in order to find appropriate clothing. The clothing bank is staffed by volunteers who sort the clothing and straighten the room. In spite of their attempts, the room often has a rather chaotic look brought on by frantic scrounging by the women. It is rumored that mice seen in the shelter through the day have built their nests in this room.

The family dorm is one large room which has 30 beds and cribs in it (Annual Report 1989). Mothers with male children under the age of seven and female children of all ages are assigned to this dorm.[5] Each family is assigned a bed which is in actuality two twin beds pushed together and covered by sheets and a blanket for a double bed. Mothers sleep in this bed with their children other than infants, who are given a crib which is positioned next to the mother's bed. Each family is provided with a dresser which does not lock for its possessions. Normally, the area around a family's bed is cluttered with trash bags filled with possessions brought to the shelter or collected during the family's stay. There are no partitions between individual sleeping areas, but mothers attempt to respect each others' areas by not intruding into space immediately around each family's bed. The openness of the room presents problems for mothers as they try to agree upon a time to put their children in bed. Often, as a mother tries to quiet her children at night, another mother's children are still running and playing in the room, making bedtime even more stressful.

Families have a kitchen area on the second floor. This area is a very small room with two small shelf units, refrigerator, and kitchen table. Mothers are not allowed to cook in the shelter but may bring foods designed for the microwave, cereal, milk, soda, crackers, and so forth. Except for milk, cereal, juice, and formula, all foods brought into the shelter must be consumed that day. This rule is necessary in order to control the constant problem of mice and roaches. Hence, mothers must use a large portion of their welfare check to purchase food in order to feed their children.[6]

Laundry facilities, which consist of a single heavy duty washer and dryer are shared by the shelter staff (for washing sheets and blankets), single women, and women with children. Use of the facility requires signing up for a particular day and time. Arguments among mothers, single women, and shelter staff frequently occur when assigned times are not closely followed or when staff must use the laundry facilities during times set aside for family use.

Starlight Inn

In 1990 Starlight Inn opened its doors in a newly acquired hotel in Arid Acropolis. The hotel was converted into a shelter which could accommodate families without requiring men to live apart from their wives and children.

Starlight Inn is located on a street dominated by closed hotels and businesses. Those hotels that have remained open need repair. The neighborhood around the hotel has predominately run-down apartments or single-family dwellings. The strip of land on which the shelter is located is neutral ground between the territories of two juvenile gangs. Random automatic-weapon fire in the parking lot of the hotel was a continual nuisance on New Years Eve in 1990 (Question 1991). The street in front of the shelter is used by local prostitutes to solicit paying customers. Homeless mothers often complain they are approached by men during the day as they walk to the grocery store or the bus stop.

The hotel office was converted into the main offices for Starlight Inn. A small round reception area, referred to as the "fish bowl" by residents, serves as a meeting room for board meetings and classroom for parenting classes provided by Arid Acropolis Homeless Outreach office. The walls of this area have floor-to-ceiling glass panels which look out onto the grassy area in the center of the shelter and provide a view of most of the rooms. This means that while classes are in session anyone coming into the office or walking through the grassy area can observe it. Lack of privacy interfered with interactions between families attending classes and class leaders so, after three months, classes were moved into the dining room of the restaurant. However, when the smell of the sewer became overwhelming classes were moved to individual rooms.

Rooms at Starlight Inn, like other hotel rooms, have small bathrooms with a toilet and shower/tub, separate vanity, and one large room with double beds and dresser. Some of the rooms have television. One family is assigned per room except in cases of larger families where the adjoining room is opened and the family given the use of two rooms.

Families at Starlight Inn are served lunch and dinner by St. Vincent de Paul Society's soup kitchen in the hotel's restaurant. Since the hotel had been empty for some time prior to becoming a shelter, there was a great deal of repair required to the rooms and restaurant. Initially plumbing in the restaurant area was faulty resulting in a sewer odor permeating the entire building. The odor was so offensive that parenting classes had to abandon the area and search for other places in which to hold classes on several occasions.

Parenting Classes

During the course of the study parenting classes were initially held only at Baghdad Inn. When Starlight Inn was opened in 1990, an additional parenting class was taught to the parents who lived there. Classes were similar in content with only a few differences which are discussed below.

The County homeless outreach office provides a facilitator to present parenting classes for families with children in the Baghdad Inn shelter. Classes were begun in the late 1980s and continued under the direction of the same facilitator for the study's duration. Baghdad Inn staff requested these classes to meet special needs of families with children. Stress of living in homeless shelters may lead families to resort to severe physical punishment in order to control children exhibiting behaviors created out of stress. To this end the shelter has a rule against corporal punishment and provides parenting classes in efforts to afford parents with alternative methods for disciplining their children.

In order to insure that parents would attend classes, parenting classes are a required part of case management plans[7] developed for every parent living in the shelter. Failure to attend classes may result in eviction from the shelter for failure to work on the case plan (Pinstripe 1990). However, the importance of classes, and thereby the importance placed on attendance, varies with the case manager. Some case managers are very strict about attendance while other managers show little interest in attendance records of their clients.

Classes have been held at Baghdad Inn in a variety of rooms. When classes began they were held in the conference room on the second floor. However, staff complained classes had not cleaned up the room when finished and requested the conference room be closed to classes. Classes moved to the single women's day room. During class time single women were required to vacate the room and the television was turned off. This created tense moments at the beginning of classes when single women refused to turn off the television and leave the room. Also, because of mental health problems, a single woman would return to the room shortly after she had been removed, seating herself in a chair in front of the now-blank television and initiate conversations with the screen.

After several months classes moved into the playroom. This resolved problems of removing single women from their day room and, since classes were no longer sharing space with the soda machine or microwave, traffic into the room was eliminated. When the play room became too dirty to hold class, classes were moved into the mothers' kitchen. It was held in the kitchen for only a few classes until the play room was once again clean. The day classes returned to the play room was one of relief since the kitchen was uncomfortably small.

Structure of the Classes

Parenting classes at Baghdad Inn meet one afternoon a week for three hours. During the first hour attendance was restricted to women so that problems of several families attempting to live in the same room could be presented. This first hour allowed mothers to complain about shelter staff, rules, administration, boyfriends or husbands, and each other. Problem-solving methods were investigated for each problem presented in efforts to demonstrate utility of non-combative forms of problem resolution. Methods have included (a) having various staff members or administrators come into class to answer specific complaints and explain rules which applied and alternatives available to the mothers; (b) having mothers confront each other with particular problems in settings with an impartial judge (the facilitator) pointing out areas where there is lack of communication and presenting possible ways of resolving differences; (c) having mothers make suggestions on how to deal with particular problems regarding children, boyfriends, husbands, or any other individuals; (d) sharing alternative sources of information or aid; and (e) strongly urging mothers to call Child Protective Services if they felt a child was being abused or neglected.

The second and third hours of class were used for presentation of various projects and topics related to child rearing. Husbands, boyfriends, and men with children were encouraged to attend during these hours. Attendance of men at classes was rare. If problems presented the first hour had not been resolved, discussion continued until a resolution was obtained. Mothers often brought up topics discussed at night amongst themselves. They wanted input from the facilitator to aid in understanding their problems. During classes mothers often spoke of abuse, physical and emotional, endured at the hands of family members. They also discussed relationships with parents and siblings, expressed frustrations at being homeless, and expressed concern for their children's future.

Parenting classes at Starlight Inn, like at Baghdad Inn, met one afternoon a week for three hours. However, unlike classes at Baghdad Inn, men attended all three hours of Starlight Inn classes. It was commonplace to have one male present at classes. Classes at Starlight Inn also were more focused on child-rearing topics and less concerned with stresses of shelter living. This was likely due to the greater sense of privacy at Starlight Inn.

Topics presented at both shelters by facilitators focused on areas specific to raising children and areas related more specifically to adult parents. Classes focused on children included (a) alternative forms of discipline; (b) child development issues, i.e., at what age to expect certain types of behavior from children; (c) how children think differently from adults to demonstrate communication with children must be handled carefully; (d) goals of children's behaviors; (e) how to talk to your children about sex; (f) child abuse prevention; and (g) parents' role in children's education. Classes focused on the adult included (a) information regarding sexually transmitted diseases; (b) problem-solving techniques; (c) alternative reactions to various life situations and how to identify them; (d) goal setting, how to attain goals, and importance of attaining goals; (e) fashion and make-up lessons; (f) information regarding health issues, i.e., pregnancy prevention; (g) information regarding welfare programs; and (h) information regarding adult relationships, i.e., difference between love and lust. Classes prior to holidays generally focused on making something for the children, i.e., Easter baskets, Valentine's Day cards, or Christmas stockings.

During breaks between the first and second hour, snacks were served to the mothers. The homeless-outreach office provided these snacks as means of supplementing nutritional intake of mothers by offering foods they were unlikely to receive from soup kitchens. Snacks included fresh fruits and vegetables, crackers, cheese, and nuts. Sweets were included but represented a small proportion of the total amount of food. On special occasions, i.e., baby showers or mothers' graduations from parenting classes, special foods were provided. These were generally selected by mothers being honored and often consisted of pizza or submarine sandwiches and Pepsi.

Notes

1. Names of locations and shelter staff and residents have been changed to protect identities of homeless families who participated in this study.

2. Children are not allowed to remain in this area because of the danger. Thus, families with children are not allowed to stay in Tent City but must instead live inside the main shelter (Typesalot 1989).

3. This meant that individuals not residing at the shelter could no longer use the showers, restrooms, and upstairs laundry facilities (Annual Report 1990).

4. Children older than five are expected to attend either Arid Acropolis public school or the school for homeless children (see below). Parents are encouraged to keep older children in school so that they do not fall behind in their studies (Apple 1989; Typesalot 1989).

5. Male children over the age of seven and fathers are required to stay in the working men's dorm on the first floor. If mothers have male children over the age of seven but no adult male is present in the family, they are not allowed to stay in the shelter. In such cases efforts are made to locate another shelter in which they may stay (Typesalot 1989).

6. Mothers generally complain about the quality of food supplied by the soup kitchen and often report their children will not eat the food provided.

Therefore, they prefer to cook food they have purchased in order to accommodate their children's preferences.

7. Case management plans are developed for every individual living in the shelter. The purpose of the plan is to provide a blueprint as to the steps of obtaining housing and independent living. In order to remain in the shelter individuals or families must be taking steps to achieve each of the prescribed goals.

ACKNOWLEDGMENTS

A work such as the book you have in your hands is not done without a great deal of assistance and support from others. Over the four years it took to bring this book to completion, I have had to rely on many kind and generous people. To say that any one of these individuals was more or less important to the process than any other would be a misrepresentation of the true nature of the process.

First, I would like to express my gratitude to the families who spent time sharing their lives, hopes, dreams, and sorrows with me. Homeless individuals generally reach a homeless shelter with little to call their own. One of their prized possessions is their personal life story. The families who appear within this book graciously allowed me to glimpse into their most private possession, themselves. On one particularly hot afternoon I sat in the single women's lounge at the Baghdad Inn holding a three day old baby while listening to stories about the difficulties and dangers of living in a homeless shelter. Suddenly, the mother of the baby I was holding turned to me, tears in her eyes, and requested, "Tell them our story, help them to understand that we are people who love our children and want the best for them. We just need a little help." Hopefully, I have discharged my duty and have told the stories of the mothers and their families in a way that allows the reader to know they are caring, loving people who want the best for their children. With help from others hopefully the baby I was holding that day will not have to know the pain felt by families living in homelessness.

I would also like to express my gratitude to the agency personnel who kindly allowed me to invade their shelters, their parenting classes, and their routines. Without their assistance I could not have met and interacted with the families in a manner that allowed me to build the trust needed for participant observation. I am also grateful to Babette Pinstripe, Ron Askagrant, Georgette Apple, and the many nurses at the Homeless Health Outreach office who provided a source of information and support. They frequently furnished me with a different viewpoint on many of the problems the families faced. By doing so they contributed another dimension to the understanding of the field setting.

I wish to express my appreciation to Dr. Bernard Farber whose patience, guidance, and encouragement helped make this effort possible. Dr. Farber has been a friend, mentor, and task master depending on what I needed most to inspire me to move forward in my efforts. His quiet reassurance sustained me during difficult times when it seemed as if this study would never see the light of day. I would like to thank him for the endless hours he sat and patiently listened to me as I struggled with concepts, methods, and the difficulties of field work. His steadfast confidence in me served to refocus and revitalize me providing the strength I needed to complete the project. In addition, Professor Farber's patient editing of countless drafts provided much of the clarity that exists within the book. The knowledge I have gained through my collaboration with Professor Farber will surely assist me in all of my future endeavors.

I would also like to thank Dr. Leonard Gordon, Dr. José Cobas, and Dr. Jill K. Kiecolt for the many hours they spent reading early drafts, making suggestions concerning all aspects of the study, and providing editorial comments that helped to focus the concepts discussed throughout the book. A special note of thanks goes to Professor Fred Lindstrom and Mrs. Laura Lindstrom for their patient listening when I needed to talk and their hours of editing of early drafts which helped make this project readable. A note of gratitude goes to Dr. Angela J. Hattery for her help in editing the final draft. I would like to express my appreciation to Sandra Balistreri and Dr. Debra Edwards whose friendship supported me through the dark hours when I thought I would never get finished with field work and writing.

The kudos for the final, and certainly painstaking, editing and formatting goes to Nancy Annis and the office staff (Joyce Scott, Jennifer Scales, Kara Combs, Lesley Francis, Vanessa Schooley, and Justin Rummel) in the Department of Sociology at Ball State University. When involved in a project such as this book, I frequently got caught up in the broad brush strokes forgetting the small but significant details. I want to especially express my appreciation to Nancy Annis, the individual who kept bringing me back to the details. Without her kind assistance this book would not be in the professional style or quality of presentation that it currently enjoys. Many thanks, Nancy.

Finally, and most significantly, I would like to express my appreciation to my family. A note of appreciation goes to my parents, Harvey and Marj Nelsen for their encouragement of everything I have attempted. My love and gratitude goes to my husband, P. Ernest DeOllos. If anyone has had to live with this book as I have it has been Ernie. He patiently listened while I argued with myself over passages and concepts, while I cried as I dealt with the pain of the families, and when I fumed over each rewrite. I also appreciate that he knew of the potential danger that existed at the shelters but never once suggested that I quit even though I am sure there were times when he wanted me to. He truly became a part of the endeavor enduring countless hours of boiling eggs for coloring for Easter, shopping for the least expensive Christmas candy, and remaining calm when the refrigerator was overloaded with fruit and vegetables for the next day's parenting class. Sometimes it is easy to forget what family members must endure while researchers are off searching for answers. I want to thank Ernie for supporting me throughout this project even though it was often burdensome to him as well.

CHAPTER 1

Introduction

During the 1980s and early 1990s homelessness was a social issue of growing concern to social scientists, social workers, policy makers, and the general public. The increase in the numbers of homeless individuals present on the streets of the cities in the United States has stimulated a number of studies attempting to determine who these people are and how they became homeless (e.g., Appelbaum 1988; Hope and Young 1986; HUD 1984; Maza and Hall 1988; Peroff 1987; Robertson and Greenblatt 1992; Ropers 1988; Rossi 1989a, 1989b; Wright 1989). These studies have shown that individuals within the homeless population are most likely to be young males with an average age in the mid-30's. Minorities, particularly blacks and Hispanics, are over-represented in the current homeless population. Women, a rapidly growing segment, represent an estimated 20 percent of the homeless population (Appelbaum 1988; Peroff 1987; Ropers 1988). Homeless people of the 1980s tended to be recently undomiciled, many without homes for less than one year (HUD 1984; Ropers 1988). Finally, Maza and Hall (1988) and Ropers (1988) have shown that families who are homeless represent an estimated one-third of the total homeless population.

Numerous studies provide the reader with a demographic description of the homeless populations found in specific areas, cities, states, or shelters (e.g., Baker and Snow 1989; Garrett and Schutt 1989; Gioglio 1989; Kivisto 1989; La Gory et al. 1989; Ropers 1988; Rossi 1989b). Additionally they provide a discussion of the antecedents to the homeless condition. Homeless populations are generally broken into categories of single men, single women, unattended children, and families. However, less frequent are descriptions of changes in identity and relationships to extended families that homeless families experience as they struggle to extricate themselves from homelessness. Changes begin with the loss of the family house or apartment and continue until the family is once again stably housed. It is essential to gather information concerning experiences of homeless families, problems they face while homeless, and impacts of these experiences and problems on the likelihood of acquiring and sustaining a future home so the needs of homeless families may be adequately addressed.

The Study

This study utilizing data collected from participant observation is designed to address some of these issues. It provides a description of some of the problems faced by homeless families while living in two homeless shelters, Baghdad Inn and Starlight Inn.[1,2] The methods used by these families in their struggle to keep their family units intact are investigated as well as the forces that serve to separate the family members. Additionally, this study discusses how residing at homeless shelters effects survival of family units as well as effects on the quality of relationships between homeless families and their kin. Finally, relationships between families' experiences during residence in shelters and their ability to maintain independent domiciles once they move from the shelters is discussed.

The results of this study provide awareness of the effects of crowded conditions which exist in shelters like Baghdad Inn, the strains that the loss of a home places on family and kin ties, and impacts of homelessness on ways in which families are able to perform their functions. Additionally, this study discusses how experiences, i.e., humiliation of being labeled homeless, frustration of searching for homes or apartments which meet housing programs' requirements, and feelings of rejection by family, friends, and agency personnel, operate to change the families' sense of identity. Finally, this study discusses the effects of shelterization (a term used by Sutherland and Locke (1936)) on family relationships and future successes of families in maintaining homes or apartments.

In 1936 Sutherland and Locke observed that new residents of a homeless men's shelter adopted an identity similar to men who had been homeless for longer periods of time. These men gradually adopted the unique language, values, and beliefs of long-term residents. Data acquired in this study suggests homeless families experience a series of stages during their stay in homeless shelters that closely resembles the experiences of the men in Sutherland and

Locke's study. As a result this study expands Sutherland and Locke's concept of shelterization by describing the shelterization process experienced by adult members of homeless families.

Additionally, Glaser (1964) and Goffman (1961) suggest that ties with relatives and friends weaken with isolation brought about by entering a total institution. As ties to relatives and friends weaken, new ties are made with people residing in the same institution. Data in this study was gathered in homeless shelters which do not totally isolate individuals from relatives or friends so therefore these cannot be considered total institutions. However, in spite of the fact these homeless families are not isolated from their relatives, data in this study suggests that ties with relatives and domiciled friends weakened over time and that new ties developed with other homeless families and homeless individuals to replace those lost. Therefore, this study using a different population supports the findings of Glaser and Goffman.

What is a Home?

For most people a house or apartment represents a place where an individual may retreat at the end of the day and feel the comfort and support of other family members: a place where all members of the family can gain a sense of security and safety. A house also represents a place of privacy where the family may carry out family rituals and interactions that take place in intimate relationships which are characteristic of family life. A home under these circumstances becomes more than four physical walls which surround a space, it takes on meaning which relates closely with functions of the family as a social institution. Home "is the center of a web of human relationships" (Harrington 1984, 101). At least as an ideal, home permits individual family members to step away from the rigors of daily interaction with people outside the family and to receive emotional support from other family members (Lasch 1977). In this way the physical structure of the house becomes a functioning part of the family as an institution serving as a warehouse for family possessions and memorabilia, a safe retreat from the community, and a private place in which to perform the rituals and interactions associated with family life, i.e., a place where the family can perform its functions in safety and privacy (Jahiel 1987; Rivlin 1986; Walsh 1992).

Homelessness represents more than the loss of the physical structure consisting of walls, ceiling, and floor. As Robertson and Greenblatt (1992) suggest, homelessness is increasingly being viewed by researchers as an experience rather than a personal attribute. Loss of a person's house represents loss of place in the community and loss of physical space in which families may function in their most intimate manner in privacy. Loss of house then places family members in situations where they are unable to perform appropriate functions in the "normal" domiciled manner. Homelessness places stress on families as members attempt to interact with extended families and to perform reciprocal functions while living on the streets or in shelters. Without the physical structure of the house homeless families must adopt other methods of meeting these functional needs. As a result of the inability to reciprocate, extended families may decide to cease offering assistance or limit amount of assistance available. Moreover, homeless families may become reluctant to ask for further assistance. Changes in a family's status as domiciled as well as potentially deteriorating kinship relationships and the stresses produced may serve to alter a family's sense of identity.

Prior to presenting the study in more detail, a common view regarding who may become participants in this study as well as understanding their situation is necessary. To this end definitions for homeless people and homeless families is presented.

Definition of Homelessness

The term homeless has been defined in a variety of ways with the primary focus of the definition being either nighttime residence of individuals, specific identifying personal characteristics of individuals, or combinations of both. An overview of these definitions is provided in an effort to develop a definition of homeless families for this study which attempts to avoid the limitations of the other definitions.

Definitions based on nighttime residence include some combination of a variety of characteristics:

1. Persons living at missions or at public, private, or emergency shelters (Committee 1988; Hope and Young 1986; HUD 1984, 1986; La Gory et al. 1989);
2. Persons living on the streets, in public or private places not designated to be used as sleeping accommodations such as cars, parks, subways, and bus or train terminals (Committee 1988; Hope and Young 1986; HUD 1984; HUD 1986; La Gory et al. 1989; Rossi 1989b; Wright 1989);
3. People who lack a fixed regular and adequate nighttime residence (Committee 1988; Gioglio 1989; Rivlin 1986);
4. People who live in "cheap hotels or motels when the actual length of stay, or intent of stay is forty-five days or less" (Hope and Young 1986, 19);
5. People living with friends or family, in tent cities, or in institutions "the actual length of stay or intent of stay is forty-five days or less" (Hope and Young 1986, 19);

6. People having a tenuous hold on housing of the lowest quality; precariously housed (Rossi 1989b; Rossi and Wright 1989; Rossi et al. 1987); and

7. People who "have a more or less reasonable claim to a more or less stable housing situation of more or less minimal adequacy, being closer to the 'less' than the 'more' on one or all criteria" (Wright 1989, 20).

These definitions suffer from limitations of having excluded some groups of homeless people by selection or elimination of particular nighttime residences. Most frequently those homeless individuals residing in other families' homes, cheap hotels or motels, or long-term shelters have been excluded from study (Appelbaum 1990). Ambiguity in terms, i.e., "adequate" nighttime residences used by the McKinney Homeless Assistance Act (Committee 1988), "customary,' regular access to conventional dwelling" (Rossi 1989a), or "more or less" in describing adequacy of shelters available (Wright 1989) creates confusion concerning which groups are included in the definition. Additionally, time limits placed on certain categories of housing by Hope and Young (1986) tend to exclude those groups found in long-term shelters.

Murie and Forrest (1988) defined homeless population as one symptom of multidimensional exclusion from social consumption norms of the majority of the population. This definition utilizes a person's characteristic in addition to one's identification with a particular set of economic characteristics as a means of labeling a person homeless. This definition, however accurate, is imprecise. Questions remain as to which social consumption norms are most important for identification or are all norms of equal importance, and finally, at what level individuals become disadvantaged and therefore homeless?

Patton (1988) used a combination of personal characteristics of the individual and the individual's place of residence to determine the condition of homelessness. In discussing rural homelessness, he developed five major groups of homeless individuals: (a) the traditional homeless person--street persons who suffer from substance abuse, personal tragedy, or mental or physical disabilities, unattached to the current labor force, and unable to maintain a permanent address; (b) the new poor--working poor who move in with friends or family when savings dwindle away; (c) the new hermits who can be found living off the land; (d) the mentally ill; and (e) the displaced farmers and farm-workers. Patton's definition may function in rural settings but has grave limitations when applied to urban settings. The majority of urban homeless would fall into the first category which is far too broad to be of much use since it automatically eliminates homeless individuals who reside in shelters or missions, cheap hotels/motels, or in Single Room Occupancy dwellings.

For the purposes of this study, the definition of Hope and Young (1986) was utilized with some adjustment in an effort to overcome its limitations. Families were considered homeless if they slept or lived in (a) public or private places not designed to provide sleeping accommodations for any length of time, i.e., street people or unsheltered homeless families; (b) shelters or missions provided for this purpose for 45 days or less, i.e., families residing in emergency shelters; (c) shelters or missions provided for this purpose for any length of time, i.e., families residing in transitional (or long-term) housing; (d) cheap hotels, motels, or Single Room Occupancy dwellings for 30 days or less; (e) cheap hotels or motels where rent is paid through public funding or private funding of charities; (f) other unique situations, such as living in homes of friends or relatives for a period of 3 months or less, i.e., short-term or new homeless families; (g) other unique situations such as living in the homes of friends or relatives for a combined period of indefinite length, i.e., long-term homeless families; and/or (h) any series of these possible living conditions.

Homeless families who were the focus of this study were those who fell into the second and third categories. However, it was possible for families who participated in this study to have had histories of homelessness which included any or all of the categories within the definition. Prior experiences with any of the living arrangements described produced changes within the families. As John Steinbeck wrote, "The movement changed them; the highways, the camps along the road, the fear of hunger and the hunger itself, changed them. The children without dinner changed them, the endless moving changed them" (1991, 362). The stresses families endured prior to entry into the shelters must be evaluated in order to determine changes which resulted from living in shelters. As a result the definition of homelessness utilized in this study needed to include all the potential living arrangements families had experienced.

The Investigation

Chapter 2 presents discussion of the history of homelessness. The discussion begins with a short presentation of the history of homelessness in England since many of the attitudes and policies of the American Colonies began with English policies and attitudes. The history of homelessness in the United States is then traced beginning with the early American colonies until present day. A more complete description of the contemporary homeless population is given along with a discussion of ties current homeless individuals have with family and friends, antecedents to current homelessness, reactions of private charities and governmental agencies, and legal reactions to the homeless population.

As suggested by Steinbeck (1991), families underwent changes due to their homeless condition. The purpose of this study was to investigate changes that occurred to the families' identity and their ability to perform prescribed family functions while living in shelters for homeless people. The effect of shelter life on family ties and reciprocal relationships with extended family members was investigated. Knowledge of the importance of assistance given by kin to family members during a crisis as well as when and why limits were placed on amounts of assistance provided aids in understanding assistance provided to homeless family members by their relatives. It was important to understand how aid to homeless families was limited and how that influenced homeless families' sense of identity. Thus, Chapter 3 discusses the role of reciprocity, how reciprocal relationships were effected by personalities and ability to provide assistance, and what happened when kin assistance failed to provide for families' needs. The study's developmental process informs the reader of steps taken in the course of the study, obstacles encountered throughout the study, and solutions for each of these difficulties.

The physical structure of the shelters in which families lived limited the abilities of families to perform normal functions, i.e., observing family rituals, celebrating special occasions, and discussing issues of concern to the family. Sensitivity to the obstacles homeless families faced as they attempted to maintain family activities while searching for employment and housing, aids the reader in understanding stresses family members faced during their stay at the shelters. Description of the shelters and their neighborhoods is provided in the Preface, so the reader may understand obstacles presented by the physical structure and location of the shelters. Chapter 5 provides a demographic description of individuals and families who resided at the shelters of Baghdad Inn and Starlight Inn during the time of the study. Additionally, demographic profiles of the mothers and fathers who participated in the study is presented. The reader will find parents participating in the study were not demographically different from the rest of the shelter population except that they were parents.

Following these chapters the various pathways taken by families in getting to shelters are discussed in Chapter 6. This discussion demonstrates the move from being domiciled to being homeless is not a direct one-step path for most families in the study. Rather, families proceeded through a series of steps before coming to the shelters for assistance. Some of these steps involved assistance of kin. This chapter additionally discusses the impact of receiving kinship assistance in attempting to avoid homelessness on the availability of kin assistance after moving into shelters.

Using data collected from the families, Chapter 7 describes the effect of living in homeless shelters had on the families. As families attempted to deal with stresses of being homeless and attempting to find employment and housing, they proceeded through a series of stages.   Each stage can be identified by characteristic behaviors exhibited by adult family members.   The length of time spent homeless in conjunction with experiences of being homeless served to progress families through the stages.   Chapter 7 investigates how families progressed through the stages as well as the family's potential of becoming domiciled and remaining domiciled at each stage. Chapter 8 provides a description of the shelterization process using hypothetical families.   These families presented descriptions of how adult family members encountered obstacles at each stage and how identity of the family as homeless or domiciled was affected by the experiences at each stage.   Additionally, hypothetical descriptions discuss the potential for families to remain domiciled after moving from shelters and how shelterization influenced families' potential for remaining domiciled.

In Chapters 7 and 8 the shelterization process is described in ideal terms and through use of hypothetical families.   However, not all families experienced the shelterization process as a linear movement from one stage to the next.   Rather, they skipped stages or regressed to previous stages.   Chapter 9 discusses fluctuations in progression through stages as presented by families in the study.   Additionally, Chapter 9 presents discussion of the effects of the shelterization process on homeless families and their relationships with extended families as potential sources of assistance and support.   The conclusions that can be drawn from the study are offered and examined.   Policy implications of this study are discussed in Chapter 10.   Additionally, questions left unanswered by the study are enumerated thereby suggesting areas that need further investigation.

Summary

This study provides more than a demographic description of families who find themselves living in homeless shelters.   Rather, data collected provides a picture of problems faced by homeless families in their attempts to maintain family units, find new housing, and continue reciprocal relationships with their kin.   Thus, this study describes a series of stages through which homeless families progress as they struggle to regain a domiciled lifestyle.   By providing information concerning special needs and problems of homeless families, this study is useful in designing programs to assist families to regain a stable life in a home of their own.

In order to begin investigation of experiences of homeless families, a history of homelessness, past arrangements of assistance, the reactions of private charities and governmental agencies, and legal restrictions to the homeless population required examination.   We take up this discussion in the next chapter, Homelessness Through Time.

Notes

1. A complete description of Baghdad Inn and Starlight Inn can be found in the Preface.

2. Names of locations and shelter staff and residents have been changed to protect identities of homeless families who participated in this study.

CHAPTER 2

Homelessness Through Time

Throughout history there have been people in varying numbers who are not affiliated with a particular group and who lack permanent housing, known today as the homeless population. The types of aid provided, individuals or agencies providing the aid, attitudes toward homeless individuals, and government policies have undergone changes as societies have experienced disruptions brought about by war, famine, plague, and industrialization.

This chapter focuses first on the history of homelessness within the United States. However, much of the early law dealing with vagrants was transplanted from English law and many attitudes held by the populace can be traced back to England. To understand current views of the homeless population and efforts to provide aid, it is necessary to include early English history in the discussion. The chapter includes a discussion of England from the 1300s until the mid-1800s and the United States from 1700 to the present. The historical perspective of the United States focuses on particular time periods, the 1700s until the Civil War, post-Civil War until the Great Depression, the Great Depression, and World War II through the 1970s. The final section discusses such aspects of contemporaneous homelessness as the characteristics of the homeless population, current theories regarding causes of homelessness, and reactions to homelessness by charities, governments, the courts, and homeless people.

Background Influences: England

In antiquity as societies experienced social and economic disorganization, people were displaced from their land and their families and were left to roam the country looking for jobs or begging to survive. Vagabonds, wandering artisans, beggars, and religious mendicants are found in historical records dating back to the writings of the Greeks and Athenians. Homer (Butcher and Lang 1906) writes how Odysseus disguised himself as a beggar in order to enter Ithaca. In Classical Greece, beggars could be found on the streets, and Athens had a form of state aid for the needy (Bahr 1973). In order to control wandering strangers, Kings Hlothoere and Eadric of Kent (673-686) instituted laws whereby the host took responsibility for any stranger who had spent three nights in his home (Axelson and Dail 1988). When faced with an overwhelming demand by wandering monks for aid from the church, Ecgbert, Archbishop of York (732-767) tried to restrict the movement of monks by ruling that monks should remain where they were at the time of their conversion (Axelson and Dail 1988).

Traditionally, the family was charged with caring for an individual in times of need. However, with disruption of economic or social institutions (such as families and religious groups) created by wars and famines, the family was not always available to provide aid. In Rome and medieval Europe, hapless vagrants, especially hunchbacks, cripples and mentally ill, were often able to find a place in the entourage of nobility. During this early history hospitality was extended to strangers since they often brought news of other places. Additionally, Catholicism directed Catholics to extend charity to strangers (Cohen and Sokolovsky 1989).

By the fourteenth century, begging had become well established and generally tolerated (Cohen and Sokolovsky 1989). Vagrancy had not yet been defined as a crime, and came to be idealized in the form of such people as St. Francis of Assisi (Miller 1991). Cohen and Sokolovsky (1989) list several classes of beggars which existed in Europe during the late Middle Ages and the Renaissance: (a) gypsies who first appeared in Europe during the Middle Ages; (b) sturdy beggars, beggars who were able-bodied; (c) impotent beggars, individuals who were unable to work because of an infirmity such as mental illness, physical deformity, or old age; (d) mendicant friars, monks taking their vows of poverty seriously, wandered Europe in emulation of Jesus and the Apostles; (e) university scholars, students and sometimes their professors who resorted to begging to pay their fees (these individuals were included in the category of sturdy beggars by 1600); and (f) bands of thieves and robbers. Men were dominant within all of these groups of vagrants. However, there were many women, children, and elderly among their ranks (Cohen and Sokolovsky 1989).

The Black Plague

In 1349 Europe was ravaged by the Black Death (Cohen and Sokolovsky 1989; Miller 1991), which decimated an estimated 30 to 40 percent of the population (Miller 1991). This loss of life meant a shortage of laborers. The feudal system, which was beginning to crumble prior to the Black Death, was unable to recover after the plague. Many laborers left feudal estates looking for work at higher wages. In efforts to keep laborers or attract new laborers, feudal lords were forced into paying ever-increasing wages. In efforts to save the feudal system and the feudal lords' hold on the land, Edward III passed The Statute of Laborers in 1351 (Cohen and Sokolovsky 1989; Miller 1991). This legislation which rolled back wages to the levels prevailing prior to the Black Death, compelled laborers to accept employment when offered to them, punishing those who refused with imprisonment, penalized laborers who accepted higher wages than specified, declared food to be sold at reasonable prices, and disallowed giving aid to able-bodied beggars (Cohen and Sokolovsky 1989). This law provided prototype for vagrancy laws that would be enacted in the Colonies in that it distinguished between impotent or worthy poor and able-bodied vagrant or unworthy poor (Miller 1991).

Wage levels set by the Statute of Laborers were low in comparison to the cost of food making it difficult to meet daily needs. Therefore, many vagrants in rural communities chose to flee the countryside in efforts to avoid job offers. Many of these laborers flocked to the city where the law was less likely to be enforced, thus creating a large number of urban vagrants. In 1359, in efforts to control the influx of rural vagrants, authorities in London ordered country laborers to leave the city or risk the penalty of being placed in the stocks (Cohen and Sokolovsky 1989).

England: 1400-1700

For the next two decades vagrancy laws were repressive and severe. At the same time, a never-ending series of wars created recurring cohorts of homeless vagrants with which officials had to cope (Cohen and Sokolovsky 1989). In 1547 Edward VI made tough new laws in efforts to eliminate vagrants and beggars. The new laws attempted to exempt impotent poor from the harsh penalties enforced on the able-bodied. Thus, we see the development of a means test whereby a person's ability and willingness to work are utilized to calculate their level of need (Miller 1991).

The Poor Law of Elizabeth in 1602 required that able-bodied vagrants be sent to workhouses. If able-bodied vagrants did not perform work provided, they could be sent to the galleys or banished

(Axelson and Dail 1988; Cohen and Sokolovsky 1989). Elizabeth I provided for transportation of vagrants to the American colonies where they could be indentured for a specified period of time (Miller 1991).

During periods of labor surplus, the government would diminish the amount of relief provided hoping the poor would leave the community or the country. In 1613 King James minted the farthing; a newer smaller coin; so smaller alms could be given to beggars (Miller 1991). Additionally, a residency requirement was enacted making vagrants the responsibility of the community of origin. One such act, the Act of Settlement of 1662, was enacted partly in response to the masses of soldiers who were wandering the countryside seeking work. This act authorized the city and town authorities to return newcomers who may become a public charge back to the community of last domicile (Miller 1991). Under this act, persons could be passed from community to community until they arrived back at their community of origin which had the responsibility of providing aid.

Summary

In summary, the waves of wandering able-bodied laborers released from ties to the feudal system, orphans, widows, impotent beggars, as well as soldiers released from duty after war, threatened the elite power structure of England and drained resources of the cities. In response to demands of the nobility and community authorities, English monarchy set down a series of laws whereby vagrants went from being tolerated wanderers bearing news to criminals being charged with vagrancy. The Protestant Reformation provided philosophical and religious justification for harsh treatment often prescribed as a cure for vagrants by claiming that work was a religious duty (Cohen and Sokolovsky 1989). By refusing to work, vagrants were rebelling against God and needed harsh punishment in order to atone for their sins and be returned to pious lives. At the same time laws and religious enactments attempted to diminish the numbers of vagrants, the economic system was changing in a way that increased the numbers. The Industrial Revolution in its development required free movement of labor, destruction of old occupation categories, and growth of large cities. These changes helped to increase the numbers of wandering laborers as they left rural areas for the developing cities in search of work (Cohen and Sokolovsky 1989). This development ushered in the urban vagrant (Miller 1991).

The United States: 1700-1980

At the time England was attempting to deal with waves of vagrants the American colonies were in the early stages of development. As mentioned earlier, the colonies became dumping grounds for many English vagrants when workhouses could no longer deal with them. The Colonies had few idle poor and the few worthy[1] poor present received aid by being rotated among families of the community (Hoch 1987; Miller 1991). Vagrant men would move from north to south, from south to north, or, most frequently, west into the frontier. As the need arose, the colonies developed vagrancy laws by adopting such English laws as the Statute of Laborers and the Act of Settlement (Erickson and Wilhelm 1986; Miller 1991). The laws enacted attempted to limit the movement of idle men and to make the community of legal residence responsible for providing aid (Miller 1991; Rossi 1989a).

Communities had a procedure by which they "warned out" strangers who might become burdens on the community. A "warning out" was an order by local courts to remove vagrants from the city limits. In 1675 the refugee stream from the Indian uprisings in Rhode Island became so great that record numbers of people had to be "warned out" and expelled from Boston and Newport (Miller 1991).

Massachusetts of 1700s

Jones (1975) wrote an historical description of transiency in eighteenth century Massachusetts. In 1692 the Province of Massachusetts enacted a law whereby persons not warned out-of-town within three months of settlement became inhabitants of the town and entitled to relief (Jones 1975). By the 1760s towns in Massachusetts were experiencing increasing numbers of transients. Even more important, these transients were in need of economic assistance. In efforts to control the drain on the town's ability to provide aid, increased number of young single people were being warned out-of-town before they could establish residency. Others being warned out included mothers with illegitimate children and families.

Rising numbers of transients prompted eighteenth century Massachusetts towns to attempt to control numbers of poor to which they must give aid. Local institutions such as churches and schools reported the arrival of a new family and would refuse entrance into the institution. If this family had employment they were allowed to stay. However, if the family appeared needy and a possible candidate for welfare, the town took measures to assure the family moved on (Jones 1975).

By 1750 workhouses were so widespread in Massachusetts that the General Court was required to regulate their operations (Jones 1975).

In 1794 a statute was enacted which ended the warnings-out system and replaced it with a system whereby transients were returned to their legal residences (Hoch 1987; Jones 1975).   Thus, Jones demonstrates that as towns in Massachusetts went through various waves of transients, new procedures were adopted in efforts to protect the town from the financially draining business of supplying aid to dependent transients.

In response, private charity efforts began to arise to help aid vagrants.   In 1735 the first almshouse was established in New York City.   The first soup kitchen made a brief appearance in New York City in 1802 and then reappeared during the economic downturns of 1808, 1812, and 1817 (Cohen and Sokolovsky 1989).

Post-Civil War

Waves of homeless "tramps" trudging the roads of the United States occurred at the end of the Civil War.   Union and Confederate soldiers, released from active duty, had only their own resources to use for their attempted return home.   Many, finding their homes destroyed or unable to make it home, continued to wander (Hoch 1987; Ropers 1988).   Some of these tramps or vagabonds were able to find work in a country experiencing rapid economic expansion (Hoch 1987).   The kinds of work that many of these soldiers were able to find consisted of migratory labor.   These men became the miners, railroad workers, and cowboys of the West (Axelson and Dail 1988; Miller 1991).   Those unsuccessful in job searches were left to wander aimlessly (Ropers 1988) or to become vagabond gangs of outlaws.

Sparked by the Civil War with its uprooted homeless men and women, the flood of European immigrants, and the economic panic of 1873 known as Black September, skid rows[2] emerged in the 1870s in various cities (Cohen and Sokolovsky 1989; Erickson and Wilhelm 1986; Hoch 1987; Lang 1989).   As a result of Black September, unemployment rates rose to an estimated 30-40 percent of the population (Wallace 1965).   In efforts to provide for growing numbers of people thrust into destitution by Black September, the number of bread lines, soup kitchens, and emergency shelters increased (Erickson and Wilhelm 1986).   With this development of skid rows the term homeless became a generic term given to single, unattached workers who lived on skid rows while they were between jobs (Cohen and Sokolovsky 1989).

The Hobo

The age during which hobos could be found in camps along railroads or in skid rows began in 1900 and continued until about 1930 (Cohen and Sokolovsky 1989).   At the beginning of the twentieth century, the American labor force began to be divided between two groups: (a) workers who were skilled and settled and (b) workers who formed a reserve of untrained, unskilled, and unsettled laborers who often lived on the edge of the law and who became known as "hobos" (Miller 1991). Hobos migrated to various locations in search of work. They provided a cheap labor force for temporary, seasonal jobs found around the country (Axelson and Dail 1988; Cohen and Sokolovsky 1989). When seasonal work was difficult to find, hobos migrated to cities such as Chicago to find odd jobs through the winter months. As a result, traditional institutions arose within skid rows[3] to meet the needs of hobos. These institutions included cheap restaurants, lodging (ranging from boarding houses to cheap hotel rooms), saloons, and employment offices (providing day labor) (Cohen and Sokolovsky 1989; Erickson and Wilhelm 1986; Rossi 1989a; Schneider 1986).

Hobos' lives were a precarious balance between local police who did not want them in their towns, railroads who wanted hobos off their trains, and townsfolk who fluctuated between tolerance and violent intolerance. Hobos congregated close to railroads in "jungles." These "jungles" provided a location for socialization and exchange of information regarding jobs and transportation hazards. These areas also represented places of danger to young boys who were adopting the life of the hobo and women and girls who were traveling the rails (Anderson 1923; Miller 1991).

Hobos were recruited as members of the Industrial Workers of the World; more commonly known as the Wobblies (Anderson 1923; Erickson and Wilhelm 1986; Miller 1991). Refusal to join the Wobblies often was met with violent physical attacks with men being thrown from trains. Industrial Workers of the World led marches (Coxey's Army) to Washington to petition for governmental aid during the economic downturn of the 1890s and led strikes along the West Coast which resulted in riots (Cohen and Sokolovsky 1989; Hoch 1987; Miller 1991). Hobos, then, were quite different from "the bums" who were to follow, in that they were organized, politically conscious, and worked (Miller 1991).

Anderson's Study of the Hobo

Nels Anderson (1923, 89-99) studied hobos in and around Chicago in 1922 using a combination of participant-observation and case study.[4] Anderson found that homeless men in Chicago fell into five distinct groups: (a) seasonal laborers who had definite occupations during varying seasons, (b) migratory casual laborers (hobos) who worked at whatever was available or resorted to begging between jobs, (c) migratory non-workers (tramps) who were able-bodied individuals who lived by getting by, (d) non-migratory casual laborers (home guard) who were relatively stationary, and (e) bums, who, unwilling to work, lived by begging or stealing.

Anderson (1923, 61-85) reported the causes for men leaving their homes as (a) economic, many of their occupations were seasonal causing periods of unemployment; (b) men were unable to work due to physical handicaps, alcoholism or drug addiction, and/or old age; (c) personality defects such as mental illness or feeblemindedness; (d) personal crises such as family conflict or fleeing disgrace or embarrassment; (e) discrimination against blacks and foreign-born individuals; and (f) longing for new experiences on the road.

Additionally, Anderson (1923, 265-66) found that Chicago became a hub for hobos because the city provided work, it was a center of transportation, it operated as a clearinghouse for employment for the Mississippi Valley states, and it provided many services in the skid-row area, such as employment agencies, restaurants, lodging-houses, pawnshops, missions, and burlesque theaters. Through Anderson's study of the hobo, we gain a better understanding of the daily lives of these men, the role traditional institutions play in their lives, and the role of national economics in increasing or reducing the numbers of homeless men.

The Great Depression

In 1929 the country experienced the devastating effects of the stock market crash. Extensive unemployment created by the Depression helped transform main stems into skid rows (Cohen and Sokolovsky 1989; Miller 1991). Many institutions (e.g., saloons, lodging-houses and flophouses, and free lunch counters) were still present in the 1930s. However, Anderson (1940) felt "Skid Roads," "Bowerys," and similar homeless quarters had lost much of their liveliness. In Anderson's (1940) eyes, the Depression, in conjunction with decreased demand for unskilled and semi-skilled migrant labor, marked the end of the hobo (see also, Axelson and Dail 1988; Erickson and Wilhelm 1986; Hoch 1987; Schneider 1986). A new form of transient took the hobos' place, a transient created by the Depression.

Unlike hobos, transients of the Depression were present in larger numbers and had no possibility of work in the future (Axelson and Dail 1988; Cohen and Sokolovsky 1989; Miller 1991; Rossi 1989a, 1989b). In the early years of the Depression, those who lost their jobs could not expect aid from the federal government. Only when social workers, faced with large numbers of unemployed, led a campaign calling for federal government intervention, was aid provided (Meltzer 1986; Miller 1991).

Public and private shelters increased in number to the extent they became the focus and symbol of skid rows (Cohen and Sokolovsky 1989). The unemployed began to hustle for their daily living. This hustling included peddling small items on street corners, shining shoes, peddling fruits and vegetables, and begging. Even though begging was widespread, beggars experienced shame. Beggars saw this activity as a symbol of personal defeat. The employed and unemployed suffered psychological costs such as anxiety and grave uncertainty during the Depression (Meltzer 1991; Miller 1991).

By 1932 the number of people out of work was estimated at 25 percent of the labor force, or thirteen to sixteen million people (Miller 1991). In January 1933 a study conducted by the National Committee on the Care of the Transient and Homeless estimated that the national total of homeless or migrant people was 1.5 million (Miller 1991). Grace Abbott testified before a Senate Committee that, based on data collected from railroads, the number of people ejected from freight train box cars had more than doubled between 1929 and 1930 and had doubled again between 1930 and 1931 (Miller 1991, 167).

Unlike hobos, the unemployed of Depression moved between communities more randomly based on rumors and misinformation provided concerning availability of employment in other areas (Anderson 1940; Miller 1991). People followed rumors only to discover jobs were not available or had been taken by those arriving before them.

Large numbers of people needing aid placed a burden on community aid or private charities which could not be met. Since the idea of unemployment was still emerging as a concept in 1933, transients were labeled vagrants, and available aid was limited to local residents. Many communities adopted a method of "greyhound relief" (Rossi 1989a, 18) in which the transient was placed on a bus bound for a bordering state. Other methods included stopping vagrants at city limits and turning them away or driving them out-of-town (Miller 1991; Rossi 1989a). These methods are reminiscent of the "warning out" system utilized in the Colonies in the 1600s. Settlement laws were once again used to determine treatment of vagrants and to make vagrants a responsibility of local governments (Miller 1991).

As the Depression deepened and the numbers of unemployed grew, small settlements of shacks made of discarded materials sprang up in vacant lots, city parks, and under bridges. These communities were called Hoovervilles. Residents of Hoovervilles were more permanent than the residents of hobo jungles. Unlike the hobo jungle, residents of Hoovervilles did not see them as a type of way station between employment but rather saw them as their ultimate destination. Additionally, Hoovervilles sprang up in order to provide transients with a place to live and not to provide a place to pressure for political reform (Meltzer 1991; Miller 1991).[5]

Government relief came in 1932 in the form of the Federal Emergency Relief Act. This act organized the Federal Transients Bureau in order to help people without shelter (Erickson and Wilhelm 1986; Miller 1991). It was with this bureau that transiency was recognized as a condition of victimization rather than a criminal act.

The Federal Transients Bureau attempted to meet the needs of local homeless by developing a transient camp similar to the Civilian Conservation Corps which was to follow. Other programs included development of shelters and hostels and information referral centers. However, the bureau was plagued by the belief that transients represented a danger. Residents of local communities believed that the Bureau actually encouraged transiency by making transients' lives too easy (Hoch 1987; Lynd and Lynd 1965; Miller 1991). Therefore, in September 1935 the Federal Transients Bureau had its activities curtailed and the new Social Security Act and the program of public works took its place. These programs, like the Poor Law of Elizabeth, distinguished between worthy and unworthy poor by putting those with residences to work and ignoring those without residences (Hoch 1987; Miller 1991).

Originally, this bureau attempted to make the distinction between migrants and transients, but this was soon perceived as futile. Therefore, a typology was developed and consisted of four categories: (a) migratory-casual people who were reminiscent of hobos; (b) unattached transients who were on the road in search of employment and permanent domiciles; (c) local homeless who were too sick, old, timid, or weary to travel in search of employment; and (d) migratory families who were intact families traveling in efforts to find employment (Miller 1991).

Sutherland and Locke Study

Sutherland and Locke (1936, 34-35) conducted intensive interviews of four hundred men housed in a shelter for homeless men in Chicago. They found these men to be poorly educated, unskilled, unmarried, and largely isolated from normal social contacts. Additionally, they developed few close personal friendships.

Sutherland and Locke (1936) identified two roads to dependency, one long-term and the other short-term. The long-term road was marked by an economic transition in which the men had been working at marginal low-wage jobs prior to the Depression which were eventually lost. The long-term road also involved marital and sexual problems where they experienced the disorganization brought about by loss of the family, alcoholism, physical injuries or illnesses which made it difficult for them to continue working, cultural conflict in which their rural values came in conflict with the urban setting, and detachment from their family. The short-term road involved a radical decline in income, an inability to find employment, depletion of limited savings, and an accumulation of debts. (For studies of family life during the Depression, see Angell 1965; Cavan and Ranck 1969; Elder 1974; Stouffer and Lazarsfeld 1972.)

In conducting the interviews, Sutherland and Locke (1936, 144) noticed the men in the shelter went through a process wherein they adapted to life in the shelter and to the situation of status reduction brought about by unemployment and a dependency on public relief. They called this process "shelterization." The first step toward shelterization occurs when a man goes to the shelter seeking a place to sleep and something to eat, only to undergo questioning he finds irritating and depressing. The individual enters the shelter expecting to remain there for a short time until he can find employment. As time passes an industrious nature begins to change to listlessness and indifference. A man eventually becomes absorbed into the shelter group and acquires the shelter group's customs and traditions. At this point he has lost ambition, is not sensitive to the passage of time, has lost his sense of pride, self-respect, and confidence, and has begun to avoid former friends. Sutherland and Locke (1936) found the degree of shelterization to vary with the type of neighborhood a man had as a more permanent residence, the economic class to which he belonged, and the type and location of the shelter.

World War II

The country did not completely recover from the Depression until World War II when most of the migrants were absorbed into the military or into war industries (Cohen and Sokolovsky 1989; Miller 1991). At the end of the war the government attempted to prevent returning soldiers from swelling the ranks of skid-row residents by providing aid and reintegration support through (a) the G.I. Bill of Rights, (b) the Veteran's Administration, (c) disability benefits, (d) Social Security, (e) pension plans, and (f) welfare benefits (Cohen and Sokolovsky 1989). Additionally, the country entered a period of prosperity when most Americans were employed thus reducing the numbers of unemployed inhabiting skid rows (Rossi 1989a, 1989b).

The Depression and World War II brought about changes in the types of individuals who could be found residing in skid-row areas of cities. Skid-row residents were mostly men who had never been married. Additionally, their kinship ties were tenuous since few had maintained any contacts with family and kin. Most of the men on skid row had no one they would consider a good friend (Bogue 1986; Erickson and Wilhelm 1986). This new group was less likely to be politically active and exhibited a sense of hopelessness (Cohen and Sokolovsky 1989).

1950-1970

After World War II skid row became home to alcoholics who experienced frequent arrest, social isolation, extreme poverty, disability, and social disaffiliation (Bahr 1973; Bahr and Caplow 1973; Rossi 1989b; Schneider 1986). Six types of men were identified amongst those living on the Bowery in 1972: (a) old pensioners; (b) resident workers who held jobs as kitchen helpers, truck loaders, bartenders, and cooks; (c) alcoholics; (d) transient workers, even though their numbers were on the decline; (e) young black men; and (f) drug addicts (Levinson 1974).

During this time skid-row populations began to decrease. Reasons for the decline included (a) advances in technology created a need for skilled labor thus causing a decline in the numbers of transient workers, (b) availability of welfare and other entitlements allowed individuals to live outside the skid rows, (c) arrival of young, generally minority, men who, upon victimization from older residents, did not remain in the skid row long but rather moved to the periphery, and (d) urban renewal projects adopted by many cities eliminated many skid-row areas (Rossi 1989a, 1989b).

Summary

Previous sections presented the history of homelessness in England during the 1300s up through the United States in 1970. This historical description illustrates fluctuations in the numbers of homeless individuals that were concurrent with oscillations in unemployment, economic conditions, and periodic disruptions brought about by war, rebellion, famine, and plagues. Throughout European and American history the characteristics of homeless individuals have remained fairly constant. Homeless individuals tended to be white, young, and male. Females were present in the populations throughout history but in much smaller numbers in comparison with men, and they may or may not have been accompanied by children.

One of the first references to the presence of intact families amongst the homeless is found in the literature of the Great Depression. Miller (1991) mentions that the unemployed veteran encampment on the Anacostia River included families. Additionally, the Federal Transients Bureau included intact migratory families as one of the categories in the typology developed to distinguish between migrants and transients (Miller 1991). Kinship ties of skid-row residents were tenuous with few of the men maintaining any contacts with friends and families (Bogue 1986; Erickson and Wilhelm 1986). Consequently, homeless individuals from early history until after World War II were mostly single men leading a solitary life with few (if any) contacts with friends and family.

In the 1970s skid rows experienced an increase in population primarily due to deinstitutionalization of the mentally ill and the mildly retarded, economic decline of the lower classes, and a decline of low cost housing due to gentrification (Cohen and Sokolovsky 1989; Rossi 1989a). At the same time individuals were becoming younger, more females were present among the inhabitants, and more intact families were present (Ropers 1988; Rossi 1989a).

Many residents of skid-row areas were forced by economic decline and gentrification into moving in with relatives and friends prior to the final move to skid-row areas (Cohen and Sokolovsky 1989; Rossi 1989a). This residential pattern prior to skid-row life often left ties with families and friends strained with few skid-row dwellers feeling they could turn to these individuals for further aid.

The next section discusses changes that have occurred in the homeless population as the United States experienced economic downturns in the 1980s. Characteristics of the current population and theories concerning causes of the increase in the population is presented along with attempts to resolve the problem.

The 1980s to the Present

This section continues the history of homelessness with a discussion of the 1980s and the beginning of the 1990s. This discussion focuses on three topics: (a) characteristics of the contemporaneous population of homeless individuals and families in the United States, (b) causes cited in literature for the increase in the homeless population in the U. S., and (c) reactions of American charitable organizations, local and federal governments, and homeless people themselves to the phenomenon of homelessness.

Characteristics of the Current Homeless Population

The 1980s was a decade of rising numbers of homeless individuals in the United States. As numbers increased, characteristics of people asking for assistance at shelters and soup kitchens began changing from the descriptions provided by earlier Depression-era studies of hobos and skid-row residents. In the 1950s homeless persons were typically described as elderly, white, male, and often alcoholic (Appelbaum 1988). However, since the 1980s, characteristics of "new" homeless individuals, when compared to homeless individuals of the past, have changed with regard to age, gender, ethnicity, and the number of families living on the streets.

Gender

Males are still predominant in the homeless population in the cities as reported in Table 2-1.[6] Memphis, Tennessee, and Austin, Texas, reported the largest differences in gender representation with 90 percent of the population being male and only 10 percent female. However, gender distribution in two northeastern cities of Manhattan

TABLE 2-1

A Comparison of Homeless Population Samples and General Census Population Characteristics from Select Cities (in percentages)

	Northeast					
	Boston		**Manhattan**		**Washington, DC**	
Characteristics	Homeless	Census	Homeless	Census[a]	Homeless	Census
Sample Size	501[b]	562994	158	7071639	215[b]	63833
Gender						
Male	80	47	59	46	53	46
Female	20	53	41	54	47	54
Ethnicity/Race						
White	61	68	30	52	64[k]	26
African American	39[d]	22	55	24	18	70
Hispanic	-	6	14[i]	20	2	3
Native American	-	0.2	1	0.2	-	0.2
Asian	-	3	-	3	-	1
Other	-	1	-	0.8	1	0.5
Age						
< 40 Years	59	52	63	53	75	53
40-59 Years	28	29	28	27	18	29
60 Years Plus	13	20	7	20	8	20
Mean Age	38	-	37	-	30	-
Median Age	34	29	-	33	-	31
Marital Status[e]						
Never Married	57	-	59	-	-	-
Married	10	-	15	-	-	-
Divorced/ Separated	29	-	23	-	-	-
Widowed	4	-	3	-	-	-
Education						
< High School Graduation	54	-	44	-	-	-
High School Graduate	43	68[f]	27	60	-	67
> High School Graduation	3	20[g]	20[j]	17	-	28

TABLE 2-1
(continued)

| | South | | | |
| | Birmingham | | Memphis | |
Characteristics	Homeless	Census	Homeless	Census
Sample Size	495	284413	543	646356
Gender				
Male	76	46	90	47
Female	24	54	10	53
Ethnicity/Race				
White	65	44	-	51
African American	35[d]	55	48[m]	47
Hispanic	-	0.8	-	0.8
Native American	-	0.1	-	0.1
Asian	-	0.3	-	0.4
Other	-	0.1	-	0.2
Age				
< 40 Years	62	54	-	57
40-59 Years	32	26	-	26
60 Years Plus	6	20	4[n]	17
Mean Age	35	-	-	-
Median Age	-	30	34	28
Marital Status[e]				
Never Married	-	-	57	-
Married	-	-	9	-
Divorced/ Separated	-	-	30	-
Widowed	-	-	4	-
Education				
< High School Graduation	-	-	34	-
High School Graduate	-	60	44	63
> High School Graduation	-	13	22	15

TABLE 2-1
(continued)

| Characteristics | Midwest | | | | | |
| | Austin | | Chicago | | Dallas | |
	Homeless	Census	Homeless	Census	Homeless	Census
Sample Size	767	345496	722	3005072	104	904078
Gender						
Male	90	49	76	47	88	48
Female	10	51	24	53	12	52
Ethnicity/Race						
White	75	67	31	43	53	57
African American	12	12	53	40	37	29
Hispanic	12	19	7	14	7	12
Native American	-	0.3	5	0.2	3	0.4
Asian	-	1	1	2	-	0.8
Other	1	0.6	3	0.7	-	0.4
Age						
< 40 Years	73	55	51	56	-	56
40-59 Years	26	30	38	26	-	28
60 Years Plus	1	15	11	18	-	16
Mean Age	35	-	40	-	-	-
Median Age	-	26	39	29	33	29
Marital Status[e]						
Never Married	63	-	57	-	44	-
Married	8	-	7	-	12	-
Divorced/ Separated	28	-	32	-	40	-
Widowed	1	-	4	-	4	-
Education						
< High School Graduation	-	-	45	-	48	-
High School Graduate	-	75	32	56	34	69
> High School Graduation	-	31	24	14	18	22

TABLE 2-1
(continued)

	West					
	Denver		Los Angeles		Portland	
Characteristics	Homeless	Census	Homeless	Census	Homeless	Census
Sample Size	249[b]	492365	107	2966850	131	366383
Gender						
Male	68	48	78	49	85	48
Female	32	52	22	51	15	52
Ethnicity/Race						
White	56	66	47	48	77	85
African American	12	12	34	17	6	8
Hispanic	29	19	12	27	4	2
Native American	2	0.8	4	0.6	10	1
Asian	0	1	1	7	-	3
Other	1	0.8	2	0.8	1	1
Age						
< 40 Years	57	52	52	54	60	51
40-59 Years	34	28	36	28	33	27
60 Years Plus	9	20	12	18	7	22
Mean Age	37	-	38	-	38	-
Median Age	-	30	-	30	-	31
Marital Status[e]						
Never Married	-	-	57	-	40	-
Married	-	-	6	-	12	-
Divorced/ Separated	-	-	35	-	36	-
Widowed	-	-	2	-	5[q]	-
Education						
< High School Graduation	-	-	40	-	29	-
High School Graduate	-	75	29	69	47	76
> High School Graduation	-	25	31[p]	20	24[p]	22

TABLE 2-1
(continued)

Sources for TABLE 2-1:

Census data for cities, from U. S. Bureau of the Census: Gender, Ethnicity/Race, Age from Tables 68, 69, and 70 *General population characteristics*, 1982; Education, Employment Status from Table C *County and city data book*; Marital Status from Table A *State and metropolitan area data book*, 1988.

City of Boston, from G. R. Garrett and R. K. Schutt (1989, 85). Sample size 501 for Gender, 44 for Ethnicity/Race, 487 for Age, 371 for Marital Status, 299 for Education; sample taken from shelter clients.

City of Manhattan, from B. E. Jones, B. A. Gray, and D. B. Goldstein (1986, 52). Sample size 158; sample taken from shelter clients and individuals living on the street.

City of Washington, DC, from J. L. Hagen (1987a, 453). Sample size 215 for Gender, 188 for Ethnicity/Race, 250 for Age; sample taken from individuals seen by a centralized intake agency.

City of Birmingham, from M. La Gory et al. (1989, 8). Sample size 495; sample taken from shelter clients.

City of Memphis, from B. A. Lee (1989, 198). Sample size 543; sample taken from service clients.

City of Austin, from S. G. Baker and D. A. Snow (1989, 211). Sample size 767; sample taken from service clients.

City of Chicago, from P. H. Rossi (1989, 118, 121, 123, 127, 129, and 135). Sample size 722; sample taken from shelter clients and nonsheltered individuals.

City of Dallas, from R. Ropers (1988, 36-37). Sample size 104; sample taken from shelter clients.

City of Denver, from H. A. Morrow-Jones and W. van Vliet (1989, 27). Sample size 249 for Gender and Age, 255 for Ethnicity/Race; sample taken from clients seen in the Health Care for the Homeless Project.

City of Los Angeles, from R. Ropers and M. Robertson (1984, 22-24). Sample size 107; sample taken from mission clients.

City of Portland, from R. Ropers (1988, 36-37). Sample size 131; source of sample unknown.

Notes

[a] Census data reported is for New York City.
[b] See source list above for variations in sample size.
[c] Reported full-time employment, part-time employment, or day labor.
[d] Reported category as "minority" rather than any specific ethnic\racial group.
[e] Census data for marital status does not include the categories of separated or widowed therefore the total percentages do not equal 100 percent.
[f] Census data reported the percent completing 12 years of education or more.

TABLE 2-1
(continued)

---

g Census data reported the percent completing 16 years of education or more.

h Employment data for Census data is the percent of the civilian labor force population employed in 1980.

i Reported category as "Hispanic or other."

j A category of No Response accounted for 8 percent of the sample.

k A category labeled "unknown" accounted for 15 percent of the sample.

l Reported source of income as "job."

m African American was the only group reported.

n Sixty Years and older the only age group reported.

o This figure from United States Conference of Mayors (December 1991, 64). Sample size unknown; sample taken from agency clients.

p Reported category as "some postsecondary education."

q The marital status category had 7 percent of the sample unaccounted for in the table.

and Washington, DC, approached equality in the 1980s. Manhattan reports that 41 percent of its homeless population is female (Jones, Gray, and Goldstein 1986, 52) and Washington, DC, reports 47 percent is female (Hagen 1987a, 453). None of the reporting cities from southern, midwestern, or western regions of the United States come this close to equality. Therefore, with the exceptions of the nation's capital and Manhattan, females are either less likely to (a) become members of the homeless population or to (b) become part of the statistics collected for the many studies conducted regarding the characteristics of the homeless population. When compared to the Census figures for each city, males are over-represented and females are under-represented in all cities. The homeless population comes closest to the city's gender distribution in Manhattan and Washington, DC.

When characteristics by state are compared, males are still predominant in the homeless population (see Table 2-2). Texas has the greatest difference in gender reporting 91 percent of its homeless population as male and only 9 percent female (Baker and Snow 1989, 211). New Jersey, however, approaches equality by reporting 56 percent of the homeless population as male and 41 percent female (Gioglio 1989, 119). New Jersey is the only state where the distribution of males and females approaches that of the general population.

Regional pattern of cities is only partially reflected in the reports of states. One state that approaches equity in gender representation is in the northeast while no state from the south, midwest, or west demonstrates equity. Conversely, Census reports demonstrate how

TABLE 2-2

A Comparison of Homeless Population Samples and General Census Population Characteristics from Select States (in percentages)

	Northeast				South	
	New Jersey		**New York**[g]		**Alabama**	
Characteristics	Homeless	Census	Homeless	Census	Homeless	Census
Sample Size	2047	7364823	7884	17558072	1164	3893888
Gender						
Male	56	48	78	47	75	48
Female	41[c]	52	22	53	25	52
Ethnicity/Race						
White	40	79	14	75	70.	73
African American	47	12	64	13	30[i]	25
Hispanic	13	7	18	9	-	0.9
Native American	-	0.1	-	0.2	-	0.2
Asian	-	1	-	2	-	0.2
Other	-	0.4	4	0.5	-	0.1
Age						
<40 Years	80	61	66	61	61[j]	64
40 -59 Years	14	22	29	22	32	20
60 Years Plus	3[d]	17	5	17	6	16
Mean Age	25	36	36	36	36	35
Median Age	-	-	-	-	-	-
Marital Status[a]						
Never Married	-	28	-	31	-	23
Married	-	56	-	52	-	59
Divorced/ Separated	-	8	-	8	-	8
Widowed	-	8	-	9	-	9
Education						
< High School Graduation	-	-	34	-	-	-
High School Graduate	-	79[e]	47	77	-	63
> High School Graduation	-	26[f]	19[h]	23	-	12

TABLE 2-2
(continued)

| | | Midwest | | | West | |
| | Ohio | | Texas | | Utah | |
Characteristics	Homeless	Census	Homeless	Census	Homeless	Census
Sample Size	979	10797630	1103[h]	14229191	243	1461037
Gender						
Male	81	48	91	49	79	50
Female	19	52	9	51	21	50
Ethnicity/Race						
White	65	88	73	66	84	92
African American	30	10	12	12	3	0.6
Hispanic	4	1	14	21	3	4
Native American	-	0.1	-	0.3	6	1
Asian	-	0.4	-	0.8	-	1
Other	1	0.2	1	0.3	4	0.5
Age						
<40 Years	62[k]	64	73	67	-	74
40 -59 Years	30	21	25	19	-	16
60 Years Plus	6	15	2	13	-	10
Mean Age	37	35	34	33	34	29
Median Age	-	-	-	-	-	-
Marital Status[a]						
Never Married	45	25	65	24	-	25
Married	11	59	8	60	-	63
Divorced/	43[l]	8	27	9	-	7
Separated						
Widowed	-	8	1	7	-	5
Education						
< High School Graduation	54[m]	-	-	-	-	-
High School Graduate	30	78	-	74	12[o]	88
> High School Graduation	14	18	-	22	-	24

TABLE 2-2
(continued)

Characteristics	National Studies	
	Urban Institute	HUD Survey
Sample Size	600000	192000
Gender		
Male	78	65
Female	8	13[p]
Ethnicity/Race		
White	46	-
African American	41	-
Hispanic	10	-
Native American	-	-
Asian	-	-
Other	3	44[q]
Age		
<40 Years	61	-
40 -59 Years	32	-
60 Years Plus	8	-
Mean Age	35	-
Median Age	-	34[r]
Marital Status[a]		
Never Married	-	-
Married	-	21[s]
Divorced/ Separated	-	-
Widowed	-	-
Education		
< High School Graduation	-	-
High School Graduate	-	-
> High School Graduation	-	-

TABLE 2-2
(continued)

	National Studies				
	1980 Census Homeless			National Sample Homeless	
Characteristics	Male	Female	Total	Male	Female
Sample Size	40468	8483	48951	1163	537
Gender					
Male	83			68	
Female		17			32
Ethnicity/Race					
White	-	-	-	49	30
African American	-	-	-	39	50
Hispanic	-	-	-	9	14
Native American	-	-	-	-	-
Asian	-	-	-	-	-
Other	-	-	-	2	5
Age					
<40 Years	50	60	52	58	75
40 -59 Years	34	21	32	35	22
60 Years Plus	16	19	16	6	3
Mean Age	41	38	41	36	33
Median Age	-	-	-	-	-
Marital Status[a]					
Never Married	47	43	47	57	49
Married	14	25	16	9	17
Divorced/ Separated	32	18	30	29	30
Widowed	6	14	8	5	5
Education					
< High School Graduation			-	49	46
High School Graduate	-	-	-	31	38
> High School Graduation	-	-	-	21	15

TABLE 2-2
(continued)

Characteristics	Male	National Studies 1980 General Census Female	Total
Sample Size	110053161	116492644	226545805
Gender			
Male			49
Female			51
Ethnicity/Race			
White	80	79	80
African American	11	12	11
Hispanic	7	6	7
Native American	0.6	0.6	0.6
Asian	1	2	1
Other	0.3	0.3	0.3
Age			
<40 Years	66	62	64
40 -59 Years	20	20	20
60 Years Plus	14	18	16
Mean Age	-	-	35
Median Age	29	31	30
Marital Status[a]			
Never Married	30[t]	23[u]	26
Married	60	55	57
Divorced/ Separated	7	10	9
Widowed	3	12	8
Education			
< High School Graduation			23[v]
High School Graduate			39
> High School Graduation			38

TABLE 2-2
(continued)

Sources for TABLE 2-2:

Census data for states, from U. S. Bureau of the Census; Ethnicity/Race, Age, Education from *Statistical abstract of the United States: 1991b* (xviii, 22, 23, 140, 348); Gender, Marital Status from Tables 62 and 65, *General Population Characteristics*.

State of New Jersey, from G. R. Gioglio (1989, 119). Sample size 2047; sample taken from clients served by agencies and shelters.

State of New York, from R. Ropers (1988, 36-37). Sample size 7884; sample taken from shelter clients.

State of Alabama, from M. La Gory et al. (1989, 8). Sample size 1164; sample taken from shelter clients.

State of Ohio, from D. Roth (1989, 153). Sample size 979; sample taken from service clients.

State of Texas, from S. G. Baker and D. A. Snow (1989, 211). Sample size 1103 for Gender and Marital Status, 906 for Ethnicity/Race, 964 for Age; sample taken from service clients.

State of Utah, from R. Ropers (1988, 36-37). Sample size 243; source of sample unknown.

Urban Institute, from Interagency Council on the Homeless (1991, 24-25, 31-32). Sample size 600,000; sample taken from shelter and soup kitchen clients.

HUD Survey, from K. Proch and M. A. Taber (1987, 6). Sample size 192,000; sample taken from shelter and agency clients.

1980 Census, from U. S. Bureau of the Census (1984, 815-16). Sample size 40468 males, 8483 females, 48951 total sample; sample of individuals 15 years and older taken from low cost transient quarters (sampling procedures suggest that the sample may include individuals who are not homeless).

National Sample, from M. R. Burt (1992, 14-15, 20). Sample size 1163 males, 537 females; sample taken from shelter and soup kitchen clients.

Notes:

[a] Population sizes for census data for marital status include people 15 years and older: Sample size for New Jersey 5787246, New York 13831208, Alabama 2955230, Ohio 8302375, Texas 10710253, Utah 999207, Total Male sample 83835851, Total Female sample 91419615, Total National sample 175260000.

[b] Reported full-time employment, part-time employment, or day labor.

[c] The gender of 3 percent of the sample is unknown.

[d] The age of 3 percent of the sample is unknown.

[e] Census data reported individuals who had completed high school.

[f] Census data reported individuals who had graduated from college.

[g] These statistics are for New York City. Hirschl and Momeni (1989, 135) report that New York City contains about 85 percent of the state's homeless population.

TABLE 2-2
(continued)

h Reported category as "some postsecondary education."
i Ethnicity/Race were reported as "White" and "Nonwhite."
j The ages of 6 individuals (0.5 percent) were not reported.
k The ages of 12 individuals (2 percent) are unknown.
l Widowed individuals included in this percentage.
m The educational attainment of 7 individuals (1 percent) is unknown.
n See the source list above for variations which occur in the sample size.
o Reported as average years of high school completed.
p The gender category was divided into categories of male, female, and individuals with members of their immediate families who accounted for 22 percent of the sample.
q Reported category as "minority" rather than any specific ethnic\racial group.
r Ages of the children in the sample were excluded before calculating the median age.
s Represent individuals with members of immediate family present.
t Reported for males over the age of 15 years.
u Reported for females over the age of 15 years.
v These statistics are from *Statistical abstract of the United States: 1991b* (38).

the distribution of domiciled males to domiciled females are similar for all regions.

Ethnicity/Race

In data on cities whites tend to represent a larger percentage of the homeless populations than any of the minority groups (see Table 2-1), with the exceptions of Manhattan and Chicago where African Americans represent the largest category; 55 percent and 53 percent, respectively (Jones, Gray, and Goldstein 1986, 52; Rossi 1989a, 123).

According to Table 2-1, in cities where whites are the majority in the homeless population, the second largest group consists of African Americans with two exceptions. Denver reports that the second largest category is Hispanic (29 percent) (Morrow-Jones and van Vliet 1989, 27), while in Portland Native Americans comprise the second largest group (10 percent) (Ropers 1988, 36-37). In Manhattan and Chicago where African Americans represent the majority of homeless individuals, whites are the second largest classification, contributing 30 percent in Manhattan (Jones, Gray, and Goldstein 1986, 52) and 31 percent in Chicago (Rossi 1989a, 123).

Except in Denver, Hispanics, Native Americans, and Asians generally contribute less than ten percent to homeless populations of almost all cities (Morrow-Jones and van Vliet 1989, 27). Native Americans and Asians each provide less than five percent to the homeless populations of most cities in the west (Baker and Snow 1989; Hagen 1987a; Jones, Gray, and Goldstein 1986; Morrow-Jones and van Vliet 1989; Ropers 1988; Ropers and Robertson 1984; Rossi 1989a).

When homeless populations of cities are compared to Census figures for domiciled populations (see Table 2-1), whites are over-represented in three cities; Washington, DC, Birmingham, and Austin. African Americans, as a group, are over-represented in homeless populations of Boston, Manhattan, Chicago, Dallas, and Los Angeles. Where data is reported, Hispanics are over-represented in Denver and Portland; Native Americans are over-represented in Chicago, Dallas, Denver, Los Angeles, and Portland. Comparisons of homeless samples with Census figures for the general population suggest the over-representation of minorities amongst homeless populations.

Again, as Table 2-2 indicates, reporting states follow the same pattern as cities, wherein whites are predominant in the homeless population. Exceptions to this pattern are the two Northeastern states of New Jersey and New York, where whites represent 40 percent and 14 percent of the population respectively. In these two states the largest representation is the African-American group, which provides 47 percent of the homeless population of New Jersey and 64 percent of the homeless population of New York (Gioglio 1989, 119; Ropers 1988, 36-37).

In New York state Hispanics constitute the second largest group (18 percent), while whites in New York are only 14 percent of the homeless population (Ropers 1988, 36-37). Hispanics are also the second largest ethnic group in Texas (14 percent) (Baker and Snow 1989, 211). In Alabama and Ohio, African Americans constitute the second largest group (La Gory et al. 1989, 8; Roth 1989, 153). Native Americans are the second largest group in the state of Utah (6 percent) (Ropers 1988, 36-37).

Therefore, homeless populations of reporting cities and states are similar in that whites tend to be the predominant group. The second largest group in the cities tends to be African American. The second largest ethnic group in homeless populations for the states tends to be African American with the exceptions of Texas and Utah (Baker and Snow 1989; Ropers 1988).

In comparison to the Census statistics for the general domiciled population (see Table 2-2), whites are more likely to become homeless in Texas. African Americans, however, are over-represented in all states (except Texas) and in national studies.[7] Hispanics are over-represented in New Jersey, New York, Ohio, and

in the Urban Institute's study. er are over-represented
represent the majority group in hoew York, and Texas.
represented when compared to Cen are under-represented i
one state. Minorities are more like and the male samples fo
except Texas as well as in the tional Sample. However
National Sample. percentage of homeless fe

As for the findings of national d population present in t
(see Table 2-2) follows the same viduals aged 60 years and
states, with the largest racial grou e general Census populati
and the second African American ne exception, the 1980
on the Homeless 1991, 24-25). males and females aged
percentages of individuals who a nsus population are simila
minority groups provide only 44 ulation.
the assumption that the rest of
Taber 1987, 6). The Nationa
gender, indicates whites are in
(49 percent), while African An rital status[8] present a h
male homeless population. Ho been married; ranging fi
different ethnic composition fr ortland (Baker and Snow
that African-American females cond largest category ir
homeless population and whit or separated. The sr
(Burt 1992, 14-15). iduals. Homeless people
a small portion to the
t in Los Angeles to 15 pe

Age

ldstein 1986, 52; Ropers

The age group with people tus of homeless populati
largest representation in the ci 2-2). As in cities, the la
group is the 40 to 59 year of reported never having l
more has the smallest represen p as divorced or separa
The homeless population of eing married range fron
general population (see Table (Baker and Snow 1989, 2
largest percentage of domici ed populations for Ohio a
younger age group. The sma he second largest group
Even though trends are simi s is antithetical to the patte
younger tend to be over- ates.
homeless populations in Ch reports that 57 percent
numbers of homeless peopl ever married. The secon
aged 60 years or older are ntly divorced or separated
in all cities. sample reported ever bein

States reveal the same ag men (Burt 1992, 14-15).
old or younger contribute t dividuals are compared to
(see Table 2-2). Additional pulation (see Table 2-2), it
those individuals aged 4 more likely to have never
individuals aged 60 years rated than the domiciled
populations. iciled population is more

Age distribution of h les.
figures is more varied tha

of the homeless population were natives of Alabama and nearly 51 percent were natives of Birmingham. Gioglio (1989) found that 72 percent of the shelter population and 82 percent of the homeless using agencies in New Jersey were from the county or the immediate locale where the shelter or agency was located. In Colorado, only 36 percent of homeless individuals interviewed considered themselves transient (Morrow-Jones and van Vliet 1989). Roth (1989) found that 64 percent of the homeless population of her study in Ohio were either long-term or permanent residents of the area. Askagrant (1990a) found slightly over half of shelter residents interviewed had resided in Arid Acropolis six months or longer. Bassuk (1992) reported that most of the homeless mothers in her study had grown up in the area where they had asked for shelter assistance. In addition, other recent studies have found that homeless populations in several areas are relatively stable with many homeless individuals seeking aid in the city where they had resided for six months or longer (Breakey 1992; Burt and Cohen 1990; Rossi 1989a; Roth, Toomey, and First 1992; White 1992). These studies suggest that homelessness is a local problem in that homeless people are residents of the area where they ask for help, therefore, they exhibit geographic stability.

Conversely, studies conducted by Blake and Abbott (1989), Maurin and Russell (1989), and Miller (1991) offered examples of exceptions to the geographic stability of homeless populations. Blake and Abbott (1989) found mixed results in their study of homelessness in Oregon. While Portland shelters reported only 23 percent of homeless individuals seeking help at local shelters were natives of Portland or Oregon, Seattle reported 70 percent of homeless individuals seeking help at Seattle shelters were residents. Similarly, Maurin and Russell (1989) reported the homeless population of Utah demonstrated considerable mobility that varied with the seasons. A larger percentage of homeless individuals living in shelters during winter months had resided in Utah for six months or more than individuals living in the shelters during summer months. Miller (1991, 128) found slightly over 68 percent of street people in Berkeley were Chronics, a term he applied to individuals "who had never spent an appreciable length of time in any one place, but who moved about." Therefore, even though most of the studies found that homeless people tended to be residents of cities where they asked for assistance, there seems to be some regional variations in the residential stability of homeless people.

Summary

In summary, males still predominate among homeless populations. However, females are nearly equal to the size of the male population in the cities of Manhattan and Washington, DC, and New Jersey. Whites are the predominant group within homeless populations.

However, when homeless populations are compared to general Census figures, minorities are seen to be over-represented amongst homeless populations. Homeless populations tend to be 39 years or younger. Individuals aged 60 years and older are under-represented in homeless populations when compared to domiciled Census figures. Additionally, homeless individuals are most likely to have never married or, if they had been married, to be divorced or separated. Homeless populations are undereducated, although 27 to 47 percent report having graduated from high school. Finally, homeless people ask for assistance in the same locale where they had resided for six months or longer. Therefore, demographic characteristics of current homeless population is similar to earlier homeless groups by being predominantly male, not married, and undereducated. However, differences are noticeable in that more women are present in some cities and states and the number of minority homeless individuals has increased.

Ties to Families and Friends

In earlier studies of skid-row residents, homeless individuals were characterized as disaffiliated, estranged from families and friends (Bahr and Caplow 1973; Bogue 1986; Wallace 1965). Lack of ties to community and, more specifically, to social networks was given as a reason for skid-row occupants' homelessness. More recent studies have also emphasized the disaffiliation of homeless individuals. In past studies, homeless individuals reported either (a) not having any friends or relatives on which they feel they can depend (Committee 1988; Roth 1989; Wright 1989) or (b) having contacts with friends and relatives but feeling unable to ask them for help (Cohen and Sokolovsky 1989; Rossi and Wright 1987; Shinn, Knickman, and Weitzman 1991). Conversely, other studies showed that ties do exist between homeless individuals and their families and friends. These ties are described as (a) having only fragmented or minimal social support networks to turn to for aid (Bassuk 1992; Committee 1988; Dornbusch et al. 1991; Rossi 1989a), (b) having social networks that tend to be smaller than comparison groups of domiciled individuals (Hoch and Slayton 1989; Molnar et al. 1991), (c) having contact with families but reported having trouble getting along with relatives (Jones, Gray, and Goldstein 1986), (d) having periods of sporadic contact with families and friends alternating with periods of close contact (Miller 1991), or (e) having substantial contact with families or friends (Lee 1989; Liebow 1993; Piliavin, Sosin, and Westerfelt 1988). Hence, there is disagreement within literature as to the extent and usefulness of contacts with families and friends as well as the strength and extent of social support networks in preventing homelessness.

There is also some disagreement as to the importance of lack of social support networks as a factor in producing homelessness. On the one hand, Calsyn and Morse (1991) found that homeless populations lack strong social support networks to turn to for aid and concluded that this deficiency related to prolonged homelessness. Wright (1989), too, suggested the destruction of family support systems is a critical element in becoming homeless. On the other hand, Kunz (1989) questioned whether lack of social support network is the cause of homelessness or created by the homeless condition.

Disagreement between researchers, such as Calsyn and Morse and Kunz, may result from differences in populations studied. Men may have different relationships with families and friends than do women and families (Jencks 1994). Additionally, the presence of children may affect strength of families' ties. Molnar and her associates (1991) found that children played a major role in providing emotional support for mothers. Their conclusion was supported by Hagen (1987b), who suggested that children provide a vital link in maintaining supportive relationships within families. Migration of homeless people may serve to sever ties with families and friends or limit the effectiveness of the support system. However, homeless people tend to be non-transients who live in the same locale where they have friends and/or families. Additionally, transient homeless individuals reported to researchers they moved in order to be closer to family and friends (Lee 1989; Roth 1989). Walsh (1992), in her study of homeless families accompanied by children, concluded that the physical distance between homeless families and extended families is not critical to the determination of the strength of family ties. The most profound change of family ties is precipitated by homeless families' moves into homelessness. Therefore, regional variation in transiency (Blake and Abbott 1989; Maurin and Russell 1989) may explain some of the variation in the presence of support networks. However, it does not explain all the variation since, for some, migration means moving closer to family support systems. Another possible variation in study results may originate from diverse methodologies utilized. Studies using participant observation may have limited samples in which the nature of affiliation remains hidden from the researcher. Surveys with close-ended questions may not uncover existing social support networks because of the complexity of the relationships (Cohen and Sokolovsky 1989).

Thus, the relationship between the lack of ties to families and friends and homelessness remains clouded. Literature provides conflicting views on the extent of a homeless individual's social network and its role in becoming homeless. However, literature does suggest differences in ties to the social network depending on the concurrent homelessness of additional family members. Thus, homeless families, especially those accompanied by their children, are more likely to maintain ties to their social network than single homeless individuals.

Summary

Characteristics of homeless individuals have undergone changes in the past decade. By comparing descriptions of homeless populations of various cities and states to the general population, a description of "new" homeless individuals can be developed. Homeless individuals are predominantly male, are less than 40 years old with a mean age of 33.5 to 34.5, have never been married, and are residents of the locale where they became homeless and asked for assistance. In most cities and states surveyed, most homeless individuals are not high school graduates. When compared to the domiciled population, fewer homeless individuals have graduated from high school.

Ethnicity and race show regional variations. Homeless persons in the south, midwest, or west are most likely to be white, while homeless individuals in the northeast are predominantly African American. However, in the cities of Boston and Washington, DC, members of the homeless population are predominantly white. When comparing homeless populations of Washington, DC, and Boston with the general populations of these cities, African Americans are less likely to be homeless while whites are more likely to become homeless, thus explaining the predominance of whites in homeless populations. Despite the fact that 52 percent of the domiciled population of New York state are white, the homeless population is most likely to be African American. Chicago varies from the other midwestern cities in that homeless people there are most likely to be African American despite the fact that the size of its domiciled white and African-American populations are nearly equal.

Social connectedness of homeless people with family and friends is unclear from literature with the strength of the relationships varying from no contact to close relationships with family and friends. Nevertheless, homeless individuals accompanied by children tend to have more contact with families and friends than single homeless individuals without children. Additionally, many homeless individuals who have moved to the area where they asked for help report to the researcher they moved to be closer to family and friends.

The statistics reported above include all homeless individuals regardless of marital or family status. The next section describes characteristics of homeless families.

Characteristics of Homeless Families

The number of families found living on the streets and in shelters increased during the 1980s. It is now estimated that members of families represent between 20 and 25 percent of all homeless individuals (Phillips et al. 1986). In 1994 the U. S. Conference of Mayors estimated that families constituted 39 percent of homeless populations in thirty cities surveyed (U. S. Conference of Mayors 1994). Other estimates of the numbers of people who are members of families range from 16 percent reported in sixteen of the cities in Wright's study (1988) to 75 percent in Massachusetts (Merves 1992). Two-parent families are present among homeless peoples but do not represent the majority of families (Committee 1988; U. S. Conference of Mayors 1994). An exception to this pattern is Utah where 61 percent of all homeless families were intact families (Maurin and Russell 1989).

Single females accompanied by their children are the largest category of all family types (Burt 1992; Committee 1988; Dornbusch et al. 1991; Merves 1992; Phillips et al. 1986; Solarz 1992; Wright 1988). Mothers of these families are 27 to 29 years of age on average (Bassuk and Rosenberg 1988; Bassuk, Rubin, and Lauriat 1986; Committee 1988; Kozol 1988a; Maza and Hall 1988; Phillips et al. 1986). Bassuk and her collaborators (1986) reported that 43 percent of these mothers have never been married, while 45 percent reported being separated, divorced, or widowed.[9] These mothers, regardless of marital status, are accompanied by two to three children (Bassuk and Rosenberg 1988; Bassuk, Rubin, and Lauriat 1986; Dail 1990; Kozol 1988b). However, not all of their children may be with them on the streets or in the shelters. Some mothers and fathers (if present) arrange for one or more of their children to live with a relative (normally the children's grandparents), thereby protecting them from the hardships of a homeless existence.

Often entire families lived with relatives prior to street existence or shelter living. This particular form of housing is commonly known as "doubling up." It represents an attempt on the part of near-homeless families to delay (if not avoid) becoming homeless. Doubling up is limited by the length of time homeless families may remain with guest families. Families involved in this form of living situation are generally crowded into living space designed for one family. As a result they begin to suffer from overcrowding and resulting tensions (Committee 1988; Dornbusch et al. 1991; Kunz 1989). Additionally, host families begin to see its economic resources dwindle from the burden of providing for two families (Kunz 1989). Near-homeless families experience the shame of having to depend upon others for subsistence. Guest families may be asked to leave host families' residences when (a) host families cannot financially bear the burden any longer, (b) tensions have grown unbearable, or (c) host families may face eviction if homeless families do not leave (Bassuk, Rubin, and Lauriat 1986; Rosenthal 1994).

Homeless families may have few alternatives other than living in shelters or on the streets. In efforts to protect their children from street life, homeless parents may ask host families or other relatives or friends to care for their children while they search for a place to live (Solarz 1992). Another option taken by few parents is to place children with Child Protective Services until they are able to find a place to live (Committee 1988; Hope and Young 1986; Solarz 1992). Consequently, some parents may approach shelters or other agencies without their children.

Summary

The number of homeless families have increased in the last decade. The majority of homeless families are headed by single females. Intact families are also found living in shelters and on the streets but are fewer in number than single female headed families. Adults have an average of two to three children who may have accompanied them into homelessness. However, some parents have children who are living elsewhere in efforts to protect them from the stresses of the homeless lifestyle.

The next section discusses reasons individuals have given to researchers in efforts to explain their homelessness.

Antecedents to Homelessness

Eviction from a relative's home is only one of the variety of reasons given by families or individuals to explain their homeless condition. The main proximate reasons for homelessness can be grouped into four categories: (1) economic reasons--such as loss of job or a cut in welfare payments being received; (2) lack of affordable housing--loss of a home through eviction, fire, or gentrification and then being unable to locate new, affordable housing; (3) deinstitutionalization--release of individuals from mental hospitals and reluctance to commit people to these institutions; and (4) personal--includes varied reasons such as spouse abuse, addictions, mental illness, and/or disability. Many individuals who are homeless were economically marginal prior to catastrophes which spelled homelessness for them. However, many domiciled people are faced with the same challenges as homeless individuals but do not become homeless. They have the ability to call upon resources such as savings, borrowing power, marketable skills, friends, and family. Without these resources individuals are more prone to becoming homeless and more likely to remain homeless for longer periods of time.

Economic Reasons

Unemployment or underemployment was reported by homeless individuals as one of the primary reasons for becoming homeless in several studies (Blake and Abbott 1989; Committee 1988; U. S.

Conference of Mayors 1994; Hagen 1987a, 1987b; Kunz 1989; Rosenthal 1994). Many individuals recounted stories that described a series of steps into homelessness that included doubling up with family and friends or living in a series of hotels and motel rooms. For many these steps began with the loss of employment (Committee 1988; Maza and Hall 1988; Redburn and Buss 1986; Timmer, Eitzen, and Talley 1994).

Hagen (1987a) reported in a study of Albany, New York, that fifty-three percent of a sample of individuals asking for aid from the Capital District Travelers' Aid Society reported having some form of income. Thirteen percent of the individuals having income said it was received from jobs. The Committee on Health Care for Homeless People (1988) reported in its study many homeless families lived at the socioeconomic margins prior to homeless episodes. This precarious situation made any reduction or loss of families' incomes crises in which housing was lost and new affordable housing could not be located.[10] Sullivan and Damrosch (1987) identified the 1982 recession as an underlying cause in dropping to destitution for many families.

Families whose income placed them in poverty or in precarious positions at the socioeconomic margins often depended upon governmental assistance (Committee 1988). This assistance spells the difference between remaining housed and losing domiciles. Policy changes initiated during the Reagan administration served to reduce amounts of assistance families might expect to receive, or sometimes to eliminate completely assistance to families (Redburn and Buss 1986; Timmer, Eitzen, and Talley 1994). For example, reductions occurred in General Assistance, Welfare assistance, Supplemental Security Income, and various Social Security benefits. These reductions provided devastating blows to families who were economically marginal and had little hope for aid from other sources, such as private charities, families, and friends (Hagen 1987a; Redburn and Buss 1986). Therefore, as a result of the reductions, families found themselves slipping into homelessness (Hope and Young 1986; Kunz 1989).

Lack of Affordable Housing

Homes can be lost through fire, flood, and other natural disasters, as well as repossession and eviction. The most common self-reported reason given for homelessness by individuals and families is eviction from homes by landlords or primary tenants (Gioglio 1989; Hirschl and Momeni 1989; Kozol 1988a; Maza and Hall 1988). Due to pressures of overcrowding created by families doubling up, primary tenants ask homeless individuals or families to leave (Hope and Young 1986). Families are evicted by landlords due to inability to pay rent (Maza and Hall 1988). In searching for replacement housing many families find they are unable to locate affordable housing (Blake and Abbott 1989; U. S. Conference of Mayors 1994; Elliot and Krivo 1991; Hagen 1987b; Hope and Young 1986; Sullivan and Damrosch 1987; Timmer, Eitzen, and Talley 1994).

The search for replacement homes is made even more difficult by the current high cost of housing. Families may not be able to afford the rents for units that are available (Hope and Young 1986; Kozol 1988a). Kunz (1989) reported low-income families were paying large percentages of family income for rent. Families spending disproportionately large amounts of income for rent are at risk of becoming homeless (Committee 1988; Dornbusch et al. 1991). Reductions in amounts of income caused by illness of wage earners or loss of income through job loss may spell disaster for families (Hope and Young 1986). When families experience reduction of income, there are few alternatives except to vacate residences in which they live and search for new homes in housing markets in which most rents are beyond their ability to pay.

Furthermore, there is a shortage of low-cost housing with large numbers of families competing for the few vacant low-cost units. The 1980s saw a reduction in the number of low-cost housing units available for rent. This reduction resulted from federal cutbacks which removed some low-cost housing units from the market, gentrification of low-cost housing into more profitable higher rent apartments or condominium complexes, and deterioration of existing low-cost housing (Blake and Abbott 1989; Committee 1988; Hope and Young 1986; Kozol 1988a; Kunz 1989; Leavitt 1992; Redburn and Buss 1986). The result is that families at the socioeconomic margins are faced with the task of finding affordable housing in an ever-shrinking market.

For some families the domicile problem is compounded by the reality that even the cheapest of low-cost housing is beyond their ability to pay. This problem is of special concern to families who are dependent upon federal financial assistance for rent payments. Unfortunately for these families the federal government has made reductions in amounts of rent payments allowed to the needy. Combined with increase in rents, reductions have served to require families who can least afford to commit limited income to rent to pay an increasing share of the rent burden (Blake and Abbott 1989; Gioglio 1989; Hirschl and Momeni 1989; Kozol 1988a; Sullivan and Damrosch 1987; Wilson 1987).

Together a range of interconnected factors contributes to the failure to find affordable housing; i.e., rent increases, shortage of affordable housing itself, cuts in federal housing subsidies, gentrification, deterioration of existing units, conversion, demolition, and fire (Kunz 1989; Phillips et al. 1986).

Deinstitutionalization

The 1950s were marked by reports of harsh and/or overcrowded conditions of mental hospitals, high costs of institutional care, development of psychoactive drugs, and a growing belief in the desirability of returning institutionalized mental patients to their communities for continuation of treatments (Curtis 1986; Sullivan and Damrosch 1987). This resulted in a major shift in treatment away from long-term institutionalization in mental hospitals toward community-based treatment (Redburn and Buss 1986). As a result, in the 1960s the Community Mental Health and the Mental Retardation Facilities and Community Mental Health Centers Construction Acts were passed. These Acts allowed for the release of large numbers of patients and shifted the focus of mental healthcare from institutions to communities (Curtis 1986; Sullivan and Damrosch 1987). "Between 1955 and 1980 populations of state mental institutions decreased by 75 percent" (Sullivan and Damrosch 1987, 86). Closely aligned with the desire to release hospitalized mental patients was the belief that others should not be hospitalized for long periods of time. Additionally, it was believed that individuals could be treated more effectively within their community resulting in reluctance to hospitalize individuals except in cases where individuals posed threats to themselves or others (Committee 1988). Therefore, mental patients were released from institutions and returned the communities for continuation of treatments.

Unfortunately, the policy providing for release of mental patients did not adequately plan for the community lives of ex-patients (Sullivan and Damrosch 1987). The Acts did not require development of provisions for financial assistance or shelter for released individuals (Goldman and Morrissey 1985). As a result many deinstitutionalized individuals were unable to live in sheltered environments and to provide for their own needs. When financial assistance was provided it came in forms of fixed stipends. With increases in rents and other living costs, released patients often found themselves unable to maintain residences. As a result many of these same individuals found themselves living on the streets or in homeless shelters (Hirschl and Momeni 1989). The process of deinstitutionalization (linked with non-institutionalization) was seen as a contributing factor to the significant increase in the numbers of homeless individuals in the 1980s (Committee 1988). Nevertheless, not all agree with the extent of the role deinstitutionalization played in the increase in numbers of homeless individuals.

Arguing contrarily, Gioglio (1989) compared homeless individuals who reported having a history of institutionalization in mental hospitals with homeless individuals who had not been hospitalized. He found the two groups were similar in demographic characteristics and experiences. Furthermore, reports revealed no significant differences in reasons given for the current state of homelessness. Miller (1991), in his study of street people, found that 22 percent had at some time been institutionalized in mental hospitals. However, he notes most of these hospitalizations occurred after individuals became homeless.

Hope and Young (1986), Hirschl and Momeni (1989), and Dornbusch and his associates (1991) reported mental illness was not a major factor for families becoming homeless. In studying single-parent mothers residing in homeless shelters, Dail (1990) found mothers were coping relatively well with stresses associated with lives of homeless individuals. Solarz (1992) reported heads of homeless families had high levels of depression and demoralization but were less likely than other homeless adults to have histories of mental illness. Additionally, Bassuk, Rubin, and Lauriat (1986) reported over 70 percent of homeless mothers in their study were diagnosed with personality disorders while very few were diagnosed with psychoses. However, since the diagnoses of personality disorders did not factor in the effects of such environmental influences as poverty, racism, and gender-bias, this condition may be the result of poverty and homelessness rather than the cause.

Mental illness of family members may serve to strain family ties thereby limiting effectiveness of social support network provided by extended families. The process of deinstitutionalization often made families of mentally ill persons responsible for their welfare. These families frequently faced behaviors that disrupted their daily lives. In coping with behaviors of mentally ill members, other family members experienced exhaustion, stress, frustration, and a sense of loss of freedom (Isaac and Armat 1990). In efforts to acquire treatment for ill members, families might resort to fabricating stories thereby making ill members seem dangerous, hence, meeting eligibility requirements for institutionalization (Isaac and Armat 1990).

Faced with the continuing strains of caring for untreated mentally ill members, some families disintegrate (Isaac and Armat 1990; Shore and Cohen 1992). Other families confronting disintegration evict mentally ill members with some going so far as to obtain court orders barring mentally ill members from trespassing on their properties (Isaac and Armat 1990; Lamb 1986; Shore and Cohen 1992; Wright 1989). Results of evictions and hostile feelings due to families' efforts to institutionalize and eventual evictions, are disintegration of family ties leaving mentally ill persons without support networks which could most help.

Gioglio (1989), in his study of New Jersey homelessness, reported 10 percent of shelter residents and 5 percent utilizing agencies stated they or accompanying family members had been institutionalized during the year prior to the study. Results of his study disclosed significantly larger numbers of unaccompanied adults were found to have mental health related problems than adults accompanied by family members. Thus, mentally ill homeless people may more closely resemble the solitary disaffiliated skid-row bums than do homeless people who do not suffer from mental illness.

Thus, disagreement exists between numbers and characteristics of mentally ill individuals living homeless lives. Redburn and Buss (1986) provided insight into how reported numbers of mentally ill homeless individuals may be inflated. First, homeless individuals may exhibit behaviors that appear abnormal on the surface but taken in the context of homelessness they are quite functional. Such behaviors as talking loudly to oneself or passing auto traffic serves to frighten people and keep them at a distance. In this way homeless individuals are able to insulate themselves from people who may be a threat to their physical well-being. Likewise, behaviors such as acting paranoid reflect the reality of street life rather than being a psychopathological symptom (Redburn and Buss 1986).

Redburn and Buss (1986, 80) warned of the hazards of imposing "norms or values of the mental health profession on the homeless, who represent a different subculture." These two researchers further argued that homeless individuals who are unable to locate shelters at services designed for homeless populations may accept temporary placement at mental institutions in efforts to obtain food and shelter. Therefore, individuals who are desperate for shelter and food but are not mentally ill may appear in the reports on homeless mentally ill. Thus, by ignoring problems highlighted by Redburn and Buss (1986), overestimates of numbers of homeless people suffering from mental illness may result.

The role mental illness plays in forcing people into homelessness is open to debate. Some researchers (Committee 1988; Hirschl and Momeni 1989) suggested that deinstitutionalization and restrictions placed on institutionalization served to increase the numbers of people who are currently homeless. Others (Blau 1992; Gioglio 1989, Miller 1991) suggested deinstitutionalization does not explain increases in homeless populations in the 1980s. Further, some researchers (Isaac and Armat 1990; Lamb 1986; Shore and Cohen 1992; Wright 1989) suggested deinstitutionalization or non-institutionalization are not causes of homelessness. Rather, homelessness is caused by disintegration of families' ties and support networks culminating in eviction of mentally ill members from family homes. Additionally, research evidence (Bassuk, Rubin, and Lauriat 1986; Hirschl and Momeni 1989; Hope and Young 1986; Solarz 1992) suggested mental illness plays only a small role in the occurrences of family homelessness.

Personal Reasons

Personal problems of homeless individuals or families can create situations which lead to homelessness. There is some uncertainty in the literature whether personal problems represent a primary cause or a contributing factor. Personal reasons given for homelessness include (a) alcohol or substance abuse on the part of reporting persons, (b) domestic violence, and c) unstable relationships and domestic disruption.

Hagen (1987a), in a study of sheltered people in Albany, New York, reported substance abuse was a contributing factor in the development of homelessness for 15 percent of the sample, and alcohol abuse was a contributing factor for 12 percent of the sample. Contrarily, Hope and Young (1986) reported homeless episodes for families were rarely the result of addiction. Rather, families become homeless because they are unable to pay rent and unable to find cheaper housing. Additionally, Dornbusch and his associates (1991) found homeless parents were less likely than homeless individuals to have histories of drug abuse and alcoholism.

Domestic violence is a second personal reason given by homeless individuals for homelessness. Gioglio (1989) related that in New Jersey, domestic violence was one of the major reasons given by homeless people for homelessness.[11] Sullivan and Damrosch (1987) found a larger percentage of their sample of mothers were homeless primarily in attempts to escape domestic violence. However, Hagen (1987a) reported domestic violence was the cause of family homelessness in seven percent of her sample. Regardless of the varying numbers of individuals reporting domestic violence as the reason for their homelessness, seeking escape from abusive homes does move some individuals (and possibly their children) into homelessness.

Bassuk (1992), in her study of homeless shelters in Massachusetts, discovered that forty percent of women reported having lived in abusive relationships but frequently did not report domestic violence as the primary cause for their homelessness. Women in Bassuk's study related histories of unstable family relationships. Major disruptions in families of origin caused by mental illness, death, or divorce of parents, had often occurred while women were still adolescents or youngsters. A third of the women reported moving from homes of parents into homes of men who battered them. These men tended to be substance or alcohol abusers. Women related that battering was frequently related to intake of alcohol. Additionally, Sullivan and Damrosch (1987) reported two-thirds of families in their study stated the cause of homelessness as a major family disruption. Therefore, as the studies of Bassuk (1992) and Sullivan and Damrosch (1987) related, homelessness can be caused by unstable family relationships or disruptions in the family. Unstable or disrupted families are unable to provide assistance or are unavailable to homeless individuals and families for assistance. The result is that women in unstable relationships or who have suffered family disruptions do not have the necessary resources available to avoid homelessness and must instead turn to shelters.

Personal problems may be a primary factor in homelessness or may become a contributing factor in becoming homeless when families or individuals lack resources which could be called upon to avoid homelessness. Therefore, it may be the isolation of homeless individuals or families from relatives and friends, economic marginality, or housing shortages taken together with personal problems that causes homelessness.

Summary

Reasons given by homeless people for loss of homes include: economics, lack of affordable housing, deinstitutionalization, and personal grounds. Economic reasons, unemployment or underemployment, are closely linked to lack of affordable housing. When people lose their homes they are placed into competition with others for available housing. People who live in poverty or near the poverty level find a market with limited available housing, i.e., housing they are able to afford. At this level, competition for housing becomes fierce with many losing and becoming homeless.

The impact of deinstitutionalization is a source of debate in the literature. One side emphasizes that the policy of deinstitutionalization and restrictions placed on institutionalizing individuals have contributed heavily to the homeless problem. They posit the numbers of homeless people increased as mentally ill individuals were thrust onto the street because of lack of resources or from eviction by frustrated families. The other side suggests that the recent increase of homeless people cannot be attributed to the emptying of mental institutions. They propose that the mental health problems of many homeless individuals are the result of stresses of homelessness and occurred after individuals became homeless.

Mental illness is not a major factor for families becoming homeless. Adult members of homeless families may experience depression and demoralization due to the homeless condition but appear to cope reasonably well with these stresses.

Personal reasons for homelessness include alcohol and drug abuse, domestic violence, and unstable relationships. It is argued that families rarely become homeless due to addiction problems but may suffer from the others. Personal problems such as these may leave individuals or families without close ties to families or friends who could provide social support networks. Consequently, when confronted with loss of homes, individuals or families, possessing at best weak social support systems, have few alternatives to homelessness.

Thus, reasons for homelessness may vary given circumstances of individuals or families. Rather than being caused by a single problem, it appears that several problems acting in unison place families at risk for homelessness.

The next section discusses the reaction various segments of society have had to homelessness.

Reactions To Homelessness

In the 1980s as homeless individuals became more visible on the streets of cities, a variety of reactions developed to address the plight of homeless people. These reactions are structured by beliefs and attitudes of the past as discussed in the first sections of this chapter. Therefore, in some reactions, divisions between worthy and unworthy poor can be seen. Additionally, determination of the responsibility of providing assistance to the homeless population can be seen to rest with local agencies and governments rather than being a national problem. These reactions are discussed from the vantage point of many fronts: charitable organizations responding to needs, homeless people acting on their own behalf, efforts of the federal government, and rulings of the courts.

Private Charitable Organizations

Private charitable organizations responding to growing numbers of people who were requesting help from them, expanded many of their operations, adapted others to special needs of homeless people, and developed new operations in efforts to meet the unique needs of the homeless population (Blau 1992; Ringheim 1990; Robertson and Greenblatt 1992). Soup kitchens which had been in existence in skid-row areas were expanded as numbers of people being served swelled (Kozol 1988a). Arrangements were made to take food to various sites around cities in efforts to provide meals to homeless people who were unable to get to soup kitchens. Organizations continued to distribute clothing to individuals living on the streets or in shelters. Food banks already serving the poor of communities, modified food boxes distributed to homeless people to accommodate their inability to store perishable foods (Wiclad 1990). Additionally, in attempts to provide sleeping quarters and other services, many private charitable organizations began developing temporary shelters for homeless individuals or families (Kozol 1988a; Rossi 1989b).

Daily needs of homeless people for food and shelter are met by private charities (with the aid of monetary grants from state and federal governments) through soup kitchens, food banks, and shelters (Cohen and Burt 1990; Cooper 1987; Hoch and Slayton 1989). Public assistance offered by various levels of government tends to be limited to existing welfare structures (such as Aid to Families with Dependent Children and food stamps) and housing vouchers (Blau 1992; Koch 1987). One exception is the provision of vouchers for rooms in private hotels (Blau 1992; Kozol 1988b). This program provides homeless families and individuals with housing vouchers for pre-selected hotels. The voucher when presented at the hotel serves as cash in paying for lodging for a night, a week, or longer. Jonathan Kozol (1988b) and Joel Blau (1992) reported on welfare hotels in New York City where families may live for months using vouchers supplied by the city. (A more complete discussion of governmental assistance can be found in a later section.)

Nonetheless, private organizations, better able to respond quickly, provide emergency relief in forms of meals and emergency housing (Cohen and Burt 1990; Cooper 1987; Hoch and Slayton 1989). Private responses, however, often are not coordinated so efforts are frequently duplicated between agencies (Askagrant 1990b; Findaroom 1989; Question 1991). Thus, in some areas of assistance, there may be an abundance of support (such as soup kitchens) while in others support may be difficult to locate (such as shelters designed for homeless families).

Activism

Homeless individuals became active in efforts to force local, state, and federal governments to provide for their needs (Blau 1992; Ropers 1988; Wagner and Cohen 1991; White 1992). Activists in major cities across the United States have led homeless people on marches in front of government buildings and have set up tent cities (Blau 1992). These represent attempts to draw attention to the plight of homeless people and to force lawmakers to recognize that people are desperately in need of housing and food.

One activist, Mitch Snyder, successfully led a series of demonstrations involving homeless men and women in Washington, DC, compelling the government to provide a location for a shelter (Blau 1992; Hoch and Slayton 1989; White 1992). Justiceville, a tent city organized by Ted Hayes, became a symbol of hope and dignity for homeless people in Los Angeles (Blau 1992; Hoch and Slayton 1989; Ropers 1988). In Phoenix, Arizona, the homeless population petitioned the government to provide assistance to homeless people living at a site along railroad tracks (Blau 1992). More recently, in the summer of 1992, by camping out in front of various State and Local Government agencies, homeless individuals of Phoenix moved the state government to provide shelter during the hot summer months (Ferraro 1994; Field Notes 1992).

Work of activists is not easy and not always successful. Homeless individuals are difficult to organize, and once organized, the momentum of the movement is difficult to maintain. Problems of political activism revolve around the fact that homeless populations are transient and homeless. Being homeless brings a stigma that interferes with needed self-confidence and self-image to bring about change. Homeless people begin to accept the worldview of them as inconsequential. Therefore, activists must first convince homeless people their needs are important and their voices can be heard. Additionally, because organizations representing homeless populations are unable to contribute to campaigns and homeless individuals are less likely to vote, politicians are likely to ignore requests of homeless people and their organizations (Hoch and Slayton 1989). As a result organized efforts by homeless individuals are relatively uncommon (Blau 1992).

Governmental Reactions

The Federal Government has reacted to the problem of homelessness by viewing it as a local problem and therefore not a priority for Federal governmental response (Ropers 1988). As a result many programs have been limited in efforts at addressing the problems of homelessness (Blau 1992). Money provided to programs aimed at helping homeless populations has been inadequate, and funds that are available are limited in areas of allocation. Hence, programs do not allow for concerted efforts to address problems (Blau 1992; Ropers 1988).

The Federal Emergency Management Agency (FEMA) was enacted by public law in 1983. The purpose of this agency is to administer emergency food and shelter programs designed to provide relief to people suffering from natural disasters and to homeless populations (Blau 1992; Ropers 1988; Solarz 1992). Unfortunately, this program constrains administrators to view the problem of homelessness as a natural disaster, much like a hurricane, requiring emergency short-term funding rather than as a problem requiring continuing, long-term funding (Blau 1992; Solarz 1992).

The Stewart B. McKinney Act of 1987 was developed to combine twenty different provisions into one act.[12] This Act set up a group to oversee dispersion of funds to various local agencies. Money is disbursed among agencies and programs designed to meet the needs of homeless people through competitive grants, block grants, and formula allocations (Blau 1992; Rossi 1989b; Solarz 1992; Walker 1988). However, the McKinney Act has been consistently underfunded, leaving many local programs without the necessary federal funds to continue service (Blau 1992; Walker 1988).

In addition to the belief that homelessness is a local problem, the federal government has made cuts in aid such as Supplemental Security Insurance (SSI), Women, Infants, and Children (WIC) payments, Aid to Families with Dependent Children (AFDC) and welfare benefits (Koch 1987; Ropers 1988; White 1992; Wright 1989; Yeich 1994). These cuts have forced people into homelessness and have frustrated the efforts of many individuals in extricating themselves from homelessness (Koch 1987; Merves 1992; Sullivan and Damrosch 1987).

At least until now the national administration has contended the problems of homeless people arc being addressed effectively at local levels (Ropers 1988). President Reagan, in commenting on the problem of homelessness, expressed a viewpoint that guided his administration's approach to providing federal aid for the homeless population (Ropers 1988; Snow and Anderson 1993). "'They make it their own choice for staying out there,' . . . 'There are shelters in virtually every city, and shelters here, and those people still prefer out there on the grates or the lawn to going into one of those shelters'" (Miller 1991, 161).

President Bush, upon taking office in 1989, called for a kinder and gentler society that needed to care and guide the poor and homeless members of society (Bush 1989). One program he developed to aid the poor was called Homeownership Opportunities for People Everywhere (HOPE). This program, through allocation of funds, was designed to enable tenants in public housing to purchase their own apartments. However, failure to provide low-interest loans prevented many poor people from purchasing their own home. Additionally, this program did not add any new housing to the limited supply of existing low-income housing (Blau 1992). This meant that the program had limited success in its ability to help provide homeownership to the poor.

Furthermore, the budget proposed by Bush for 1991 called for a reduction of 359 million dollars from the budget of all subsidized housing programs (Blau 1992, 73). In addition it proposed drastic cuts in several programs designed to assist people with low incomes. Increases in taxes during the Bush Administration raised tax rates for the poorest 20 percent of the American population by 16 percent while reducing taxes for the wealthy (Ropers 1991, 193). The budget proposed by the Bush Administration had the appearance of a restructured Reagan-era type federal budget that favored the rich and did nothing to assist the poor or near-poor (Ropers 1991, 193). Thus, even though Bush had a different personal style than Reagan, under the surface it appeared to be business as usual.

However, one major variation from the views of the Reagan Administration was the Bush Administration's willingness to recognize the magnitude of homelessness and the attempt, albeit limited, made to confront the issue (Ropers 1991).

Legal Cases

Distinction between worthy and unworthy poor, having been transported from England with the colonists, provided the basis for decisions concerning the legality of treatment of hobos, tramps, and homeless individuals. As a result of being deemed unworthy, vagrants could be placed in the stocks, vagrants could be arrested and jailed for vagrancy or public intoxication, individuals could be jailed for sleeping in public, and homeless individuals did not have a recognized right to assistance such as shelter. Cases brought before local, state, and federal courts brought about limited changes in the view of homeless individuals as unworthy poor.

The offense of public drunkenness was reaffirmed in 1967, when in *Seattle v. Hill*, the Supreme Court of the State of Washington upheld laws making public drunkenness an offense (Spradley 1970). One year later, in 1968, the Supreme Court of the United States upheld laws which made public drunkenness an offense in every state of the Union in the case of *Powell v. Texas* (Spradley 1970). These laws, according to the writing of the justices were an attempt to protect individuals from injury due to their intoxicated state. However, this law could be used to make life on skid row uncomfortable thereby encouraging residents to move on, preferably to another city.

It was not until the 1970s that the Supreme Court ruled in *Papchristu v. United States*, that vagrancy was not a crime (Cohen and Sokolovsky 1989; White 1992). This ruling served to make the arrest of a person on the basis of their status unconstitutional. However, in 1985, in *Davenport v. People of the State of California*, the Supreme Court of California reversed a lower court's decision making a county statute banning sleeping in public at night unconstitutional. The National Coalition for the Homeless petitioned the Supreme Court of the United States to review the convictions of homeless individuals arrested under this ban. The Court refused to consider the cases (Hombs 1990; Stoner 1995). Results of these cases served to criminalize some of the activities which are an integral part of a homeless existence. Homeless individuals who are not in shelters are committing a crime by attempting to sleep at night in any public area.

Individuals' rights to shelter have been contested frequently in the courts. In a 1972 case, *Lindsey v. Normet*, the United States Supreme Court refused to recognize an individual's right to shelter. However, eleven years later in 1981 the New York State Court recognized a right to shelter by mandating that the City of New York had to provide shelter for homeless men who occupied its streets in the 1979 case of *Callahan v. Carey* (Blau 1992; Cohen and Sokolovsky 1989; Hombs 1990; Hopper and Cox 1986). Later in *Eldredge v. Koch* (1983), the New York Supreme Court extended the standards for shelters set by *Callahan v. Carey* to women's shelters (Blau 1992; Hombs 1990). Additionally, in 1983 the court of Nassau County, New York recognized the rights of homeless families to shelter in *Koster v. Webb* (Hombs 1990). Three years later in 1986 the New York Supreme Court extended *Koster v. Webb* by guaranteeing homeless families a right to emergency shelter in *McCain v. Koch* (Blau 1992; Hombs 1990).

Homeless people have been making some inroads into court recognition of issues concerning the receipt of welfare assistance. In 1984, the statutes of Milwaukee County, Wisconsin, and New Orleans, Louisiana, required a fixed address as a prerequisite to receiving welfare aid. In 1985 the eligibility requirement was ruled illegal in *Martin v. Milwaukee County* (Blau 1992). Legal efforts in New Orleans were less successful. In 1989 requirement for a fixed address was set aside by the courts in *Turner v. City of New Orleans*. However, the court allowed the provision of aid to be determined by availability of funds (Blau 1992).

Homeless men, women, and families frequently have lost all their belongings, including their identification documents. The latter yields special hardships on people when documents are required to show eligibility for aid. In 1984, in *Eisenheim v. Board of Supervisors*, a group of Los Angeles advocates won a case that challenged the need for documentation before receiving aid and reduced the length of time before that aid could be received (Blau 1992; Ropers 1988). *Eisenheim* required agencies to issue vouchers for hotel rooms the same day as homeless individuals applied for them. Unfortunately, hotel rooms were often below health standards set by Los Angeles Board of Health. Additionally, hotels accepting vouchers tended to fill quickly in spite of living conditions (Blau 1992; Ropers 1988). *Ross v. Board of Supervisors*, in 1984, required increasing the allotment allowed for hotel rooms from the original eight dollars to sixteen dollars (Blau 1992; Ropers 1988). This increase served to make more rooms available. However, people were still living in substandard rooms, which often had been closed by the Board of Health for building code violations (Blau 1992). In order to address substandard living conditions, advocates brought suit in *Paris v. Board of Supervisors* in 1984. The *Paris* decision prohibited the county from issuing housing vouchers for hotels which could not meet the Board of Health's minimum standards (Blau 1992).

Another issue pertains to the requirement of attendance at a work project in exchange for general assistance. In Los Angeles recipients who were late for work or failed to follow any of the program's other regulations, could have their benefits withheld (Blau 1992; Ropers 1988). In 1984 *Bannister v. Board of Supervisors of Los Angeles County* challenged these restrictions. The county could no longer arbitrarily withhold a person's assistance, and benefits could not be withheld if the individual could show just cause for not fulfilling an obligation (Blau 1992; Ropers 1988).

Particularly in California, legal cases relating to homeless families addressed policies in providing aid to families. Prior to *Hansen v. McMahon* in 1987, children of homeless families would have to be removed from their families before parents could receive any assistance. *Hansen* ruled that acceptance of assistance was not contingent upon the breakup of families through the removal of children (Blau 1992). Other states have similar provisions. Courts in Delaware, Illinois, Pennsylvania, and New York do not allow removal of children from homes where the primary reason for removal is the families' homelessness (Blau 1992). These court decisions have instituted new law: Being homeless is no longer seen as a primary reason for the state to take charge of a family's children.

Changes in the legal status of homeless people have occurred in the last two decades. Vagrancy is no longer considered a crime. Homeless people have achieved legal success in state and local courts wherein the courts recognized an individual's right to shelter. State courts have eliminated the requirement of a fixed address for receipt of welfare aid while local courts have challenged the need for documentation for the receipt of aid. Additionally, courts have eliminated homelessness as a primary reason for taking charge of a family's children. Consequently, state and local courts have removed some of the encumbrances to the receipt of welfare aid and shelter and protected the sanctity of homeless families. Nevertheless, some rulings, such as allowing arrest for sleeping in public and allowing provision of aid to be dependent on availability of funds, still provide pitfalls for homeless individuals whereby they may be arrested or refused aid. Thus, in some respects homeless individuals are still considered unworthy of societal acceptance or undeniable assistance.

Summary

Private charities, being able to react more quickly than local governments, developed or expanded existing soup kitchens, food and clothing banks, and shelters to meet the immediate needs of homeless populations. Homeless individuals have assisted themselves through activism in isolated instances where they were able to have their needs heard by various local and state governments. Through their own efforts homeless populations have been able to move the governments to take action, albeit limited, to provide shelter and assistance. The federal government generally views the homeless problem as a local problem and, as a result, out of its jurisdiction. However, some changes in that view occurred during the Bush Administration with the recognition of the problem and limited efforts to help.

Finally, homeless populations have met with some success in winning court cases. These victories have removed vagrancy from criminal status, affirmed rights to shelter, have eliminated or reduced required documents needed to receive assistance, and removed homelessness as a primary reason for the state to take charge of a family's children.

Therefore, there seems to be a movement away from ignoring the plight of homeless people and toward a recognition of the worthiness of homeless people and the seriousness of their needs.

Summary

The history of homelessness is also a history of the economic prosperity and decline within nations. As a country experiences prosperity, the numbers of homeless people tends to decline as individuals secure employment. Economic decline generally means an increase in the numbers of homeless individuals as the population experiences increased unemployment. Throughout history, in conjunction with the ebb and flow of vagrants, transients, or homeless people, governments (United States being no different) have taken steps in attempting to deal with problems of the idle worker. These solutions take various forms depending upon the view of unemployed and homeless workers. Until the Black Plague in England, charity was given to transients. Beggars were tolerated, and those unable to work were cared for by families in their towns. However, after the Black Plague, laws such as the Statute of Laborers made vagrancy a crime. When these laws proved unsuccessful at eliminating vagrancy attempts were made to force vagrants to work by enacting the Poor Laws. The Poor Laws of 1602 and the Settlement Acts of 1662, in requiring that vagrants work, distinguished between those worthy (individuals unable to work such as the impotent poor) and those unworthy (able-bodied individuals) of assistance.

This trend has been continued in the United States with the differentiation between worthy and unworthy poor. Those deemed unworthy of assistance were warned out of communities in the colonies. Later, these individuals were given bus tickets which would take them as far as the next state. In colonial United States vagrants could be put in the stocks. This treatment continued into the United States of the twentieth century when vagrants could be arrested for the crime of vagrancy and placed in jail or on county prison farms.

The final section focuses on studies of homeless individuals and families which have been conducted in the last decade. By comparing characteristics of hobos and tramps of the past with current homeless populations, changes in demographic characteristics of homeless populations can be traced over time to demonstrate how the current population differs from homeless populations in earlier decades. Homeless individuals in the 1980s tend to be younger than tramps, hobos, or skid-row inhabitants of earlier times. More females are represented in demographic statistics of the current population, and the number of families experiencing homelessness have been increasing steadily. Minorities experiencing homelessness have increased in numbers; however, whites still retain a narrow margin in many areas of the country. Nevertheless, some characteristics have remained stable over time. Accordingly, most homeless people have never been married and lack a high school education.

Ties homeless individuals have with families and friends represent a controversial issue with researchers reporting variations in types of ties maintained. Those individuals accompanied by children seem to fare better at preserving familial and friendship ties. Homeless families are most likely to be headed by single women who are in their late 20s and report having never been married. These women are accompanied by two to three children. However, not all children will necessarily accompany adults into homelessness. Rather, some children may be placed with relatives, most likely grandparents, for some or all of the time parents spend homeless. Second, the presence of families among homeless populations has produced a new series of social concerns: (a) maintaining ties with families and friends and (b) the treatment of children.

Third, antecedents of homelessness, as reported by homeless individuals, include reasons of economics, lack of affordable housing, deinstitutionalization, and personal grounds. Loss of employment, linked with shortages of low-cost housing, can spell homelessness for individuals or families. There is some controversy concerning the impact of release of mental patients from hospitals in the 1950s and 1960s on the numbers of people who became and remained homeless. However, research results suggest that very few families become homeless because of deinstitutionalization or non-institutionalization. Personal reasons for homelessness include alcohol or drug abuse, escaping from an abusive relationship, and disability.

Fourth, the recent increase in the visibility of homeless people has created an environment in which charitable organizations have developed new methods of providing aid, expanded existing programs, and altered programs to serve the new homeless population more effectively. As charities have been increasing their efforts, homeless populations have become more actively involved in pressuring governments for aid. However, homeless activists encounter problems in organizing and maintaining movements due to homeless peoples' sense of powerlessness, as well as the mobility of the group. The Federal government has generally viewed homelessness as a local problem which is best served by aid coming from charities or local governments. Therefore, little unified support has come from the Federal government. However, cases brought before the courts on the part of homeless people have met with some success. Vagrancy no longer constitutes a crime. It was not until the 1980s that the right to shelter was universally recognized and legal bans on sleeping in public places at night were considered unconstitutional (Blau 1992; Cohen and Sokolovsky 1989; Hombs 1990). The right to shelter with adequate living condition standards has been recognized by the courts. Restrictions to receipt of aid have been removed or reduced. Families are no longer required to place children with Child Protective Services in return for aid. Changes brought about by these court cases help to demarcate changes in attitudes toward homeless people. For some, homelessness is no longer seen as precipitated by personal defects, rather, the effects of economic recessions and housing shortages are recognized as creating insurmountable pressures. Yet, some of the normal, daily activities of homeless populations are still defined legally as criminal, i.e., sleeping in public. Despite this, however, homeless people are coming to be viewed as being among the deserving poor, as victims of a series of social problems rather than creators of their own dilemmas.

Notes

1. Distinction between worthy and unworthy poor was used by governmental agencies and the populace to determine who was deserving of aid. Worthy poor was considered to be deserving of aid because their poverty was due to uncontrollable circumstances or personal defects, such as a loss of a limb, being aged, or being mentally retarded.

2. Skid rows received their name from the practice of loggers in Seattle of skidding logs down icy roads to the river for transportation to mills. Along this route a conglomeration of cheap hotels, saloons, and cheap restaurants sprang up to meet the needs of the loggers. This row of establishments acquired the name "skid road" which eventually got transformed to "skid row" (Cohen and Sokolovsky 1989; Miller 1991; Ropers 1988; Schneider 1986).

3. The term skid row was not used by hobos until the 1930s. Rather, inhabitants referred to the area as the main stem (Schneider 1986).

4. In a later book, *The American hobo*, Nels Anderson related he relied considerably upon his own experiences in the research and writing of *The hobo* (Anderson 1975). *The American hobo* was an autobiography in which Anderson related how his family lived the life of migrant workers.

5. The one exception was an encampment on the Anacostia River in Washington, DC. Unemployed veterans and their families gathered in the Anacostia during the summer of 1932, in order to plead with the government to provide them with their soldiers' bonus. On July 28, 1932, the real army was called on to protect the President from this group. They attacked the group killing two and injuring several others. The remainder of the Anacostia families left the city (Miller 1991, 59-60).

6. Statistics reported in Tables 2-1 and 2-2 were taken from a variety of studies. Characteristics have been gathered from different locations and assorted service providers. These variations in methodology have been noted on the tables. However, care should be taken when comparing these statistics since an individual's propensity to seek aid from various agencies may serve as a selection factor which could affect the characteristics of the samples.

7. William J. Wilson (1987) argued that historic discrimination and migration timing and trends kept minority populations living in metropolitan areas young and created a problem of weak labor-force participation. This served to create vulnerability to economic changes, especially for minorities. The shift from a goods-producing economy to a service-centered economy exacerbated the problem of weak labor-force attachment thus resulting in increased rates of joblessness, particularly in industrial centers of the

Northeast and Midwest regions of the United States (1991). This provides one explanation for over-representation of African Americans in homeless populations of these areas.

8. It can be very difficult to determine marital status of homeless individuals. Instances where individuals consider themselves married when there is no legal bond or because of abandonment they may not know if they are divorced or widowed can mislead researchers who are not cognizant of these difficulties.

9. Phillips and his collaborators (1986) placed the number of mothers who have never been married at 45 percent of all homeless mothers with children.

10. Maza and Hall (1988) reported that male job losses are more critical than female job losses as factors leading to family homelessness. Males generally have higher paying jobs, therefore, losses of male jobs would reduce families' incomes more than losses of female jobs.

11. Area domestic violence shelters are all too often full, leaving battered women with decisions to take their families to homeless shelters or continue living with the batterers (Pinstripe 1990).

12. President Reagan signed the McKinney Act late at night to dramatize his indifference (Blau 1992).

CHAPTER 3

Arrangements for Assistance

Families tend to function in ways that ensure survival of its members. One way is in the distribution of resources. Family members share resources with one another with the understanding of reciprocation at some time in the future (Levi-Strauss 1969). Thereby, through reciprocal giving members are assured their future needs will be met. Kin as a source of needed resources has been described in ideal terms; one of which assures survival of all family members. Ideally this description suggests there is no cost for assistance to the recipient. In the event the exchange incurs some cost, the favor can be repaid through reciprocal gift giving either immediately or at some future date. Therefore, this chapter focuses on how needs of family members are met through reciprocity, characteristics of reciprocal arrangements, forms of assistance, and what happens when arrangements for assistance within families fail to supply the needs of members.

Reciprocity

Meyer Fortes (1969) suggested that kinsfolk have an irresistible claim on one another for assistance and support simply because they are kinsmen. Ideally, kinsmen are bound to one another through kinship which creates unavoidable moral obligations. According to Fortes (1969, 246), kinsmen cannot "contract debts with one another, for ideally they are bound to share freely." What kinsmen give to another is ideally done without placing a price on the item given or received. Reciprocal giving is done freely and not in response to coercive sanctions or in response to contractual agreements. When aid is received from kinsmen, recipients assume positions of dependence in relationship to the provider. Reciprocal giving provides a method of exchange in which dependence is less likely to result (Litwak 1965). Reciprocal giving may or may not be in kind and the process of exchange may occur over a period of time (Litwak 1965). "These gifts are either exchanged immediately for equivalent gifts or are received by beneficiaries on condition that at a later date they will give counter-gifts often exceeding the original goods in value, but which in turn bring about a subsequent right to receive new gifts surpassing the original ones in sumptuousness" (Levi-Strauss 1969, 52). Reciprocal gifts may not necessarily be given until much later when aid is needed by the original provider. An example of this situation is where parents in their elderly years become dependent upon their adult children. Parents have provided for their children during their childhood and children reciprocate the gift when their parents are elderly and in need of aid.

The reciprocators may, in fact, give gifts of greater worth in an effort to make the original providers dependent upon the reciprocal givers thus continuing the exchange relationship. As a result series of exchanges are established whereby participants can assure themselves of future aid in the event it is needed. Pressure to continue exchanges develop from desire to avoid both a sense of dependence and a possibility of being judged harshly by kinsmen who feel they have not received gifts of equal or greater value. Ideally, then, reciprocity assures the original providers' assistance will be available in times of need, thereby providing members with a sense of security.

Levi-Strauss (1969) reported that gifts as a form of exchange in tribal societies was so common that lending and borrowing occurred without much concern for restitution. Sharing of property, food, or other necessities was performed so automatically that being denied was not a consideration. Therefore, Levi-Strauss (1969) viewed aid given by kin as ideally without obligation, indebtedness, or fear of rejection.

Exchange Relationships with Friends and Neighbors

Exchange relationships can be formed with friends and neighbors. Exchange with friends and neighbors, however, can become far more complex than exchange with kinsmen. Individuals can accrue debts with friends and neighbors, but unlike kinsmen, friends and neighbors expect exchanges to be of equal value and to occur within a reasonable amount of time of the original transaction (Fortes 1969). Additionally, when entering into exchanges with non-kin, participants are unable to trust one another in the same way they trust their kin. Therefore, exchanges with non-kin may be marked with contractual agreements, legal paperwork, and legal redress if debts are not paid (Fortes 1969). Non-kin may provide reciprocal assistance when active kinship ties are not available but this assistance may lack variety and quantity of support that parents would provide if available (Wellman 1990). The exchange process with non-kin often ends when the friends cannot or will not be helpful. These limitations were considered by the Torontonians studied by Wellman (1990) when they made claims on friends and some kin. "It is not that friends are unsupportive when asked, but that people often do not feel confident that they can *ask* their friends for aid" (Wellman 1990, 216). It is often assumed these people feel they can ask relatives, especially parents, for aid.

Exchanges Help Meet the Needs of Family Members

Resources exchanged in the process of reciprocation are not limited to money. Families have many goods and services to offer their members. Gifts of clothing, food, or furniture may be provided based on the need. Families also provide such services as childcare, care for the elderly, employment information, and lodging in their homes. The following studies illustrate methods by which family members help one another in times of need.

The Great Depression resulted in family members having to rely on one another to survive. Cavan and Ranck (1969) studied one hundred families living in Chicago during the Great Depression to determine the effect of loss of employment and financial instability on the structure of the family. They found families demonstrated several adaptive procedures in meeting needs of individual members. Family members began to depend upon one another to help supply the necessities of life. They reported parents and their younger children would move in with married children in order to share the expense of rent. A variation on this method was for the young married son or daughter to continually move between the homes of the wife's parents and the husband's parents or the husband would move in with his parents and the wife with her parents. In instances where a son or daughter were fortunate enough to have employment, they would assume financial responsibility for their family. According to Cavan and Ranck (1969), only rarely did children rebel against providing financially for the family. When this occurred it usually involved the desire to be able to have some small sum of money for personal use. This provision of aid demonstrated a strengthening of family unity in an effort to meet the desperate needs of families in the Depression. Frequency of aid and rarity of rebellion seems to suggest that providing members accepted provisions of aid as legitimate requests from the family.

In a study of middle-class families, Farmer (1970) reported that parents often provided financial help to their married children often with little more than the broadest of hints from the children. When parents provided assistance, the gift was imparted in a manner that allowed the young couple to save face and not feel obligated to the parents. Farmer (1970) stated people feel free to ask kinsmen for aid and relief is expected. Furthermore, people prefer asking kinsmen over friends or neighbors even if they do not especially like their kinsmen. The only factors which limit kin aid noted by Farmer (1970) were proximity and closeness of the group.

In the 1960s Carol Stack (1970) conducted an ethnographic study of poor black families living in an urban area she called The Flats. Her investigation revealed a complex network of reciprocal giving involving friends and relatives. These networks allowed families to survive on wages and/or welfare which were inadequate to meet the various daily needs or to meet any special or emergency needs. Stack (1970) found families shared whatever they had freely. Furniture or articles of clothing readily changed hands. Care of children was also shared as the need presented itself. When members of the network discovered parents having difficulty with childrearing, a statement that the child was going to live with them for a while was all that was required for the child to move from the parental home. Likelihood of denial was minimal. In fact, denial or failure to reciprocate would result in being judged harshly or being eliminated from the network. Thus, reciprocal relationships of The Flats were obligatory and expected. Stack (1970, 28) remarked, "People would tell me, 'You have to have help from everybody and anybody,' and 'the poorer you are, the more likely you are to pay back.'" The financial desperation of these families made reciprocal relationships of the network of prime importance to their existence and to the survival of their family (see, also, Bott 1971). Separation from the network would mean the inability of families to survive--loss of home, inability to handle emergencies, and inability to care for their children.

Contemporary studies also reveal expectations of receiving aid from relatives without fear of denial or indebtedness. For his study of kith and kin networks, Barry Wellman (1990, 197) used a baseline of "networks of white, northern-European ethnicity, employed, once-married, North American, forty year old (sub)urban women and men with a child in primary school." He reports that parents and adult children are prominent sources for financial assistance even though they may not enjoy each other. Unlike friendship ties which must continually be renewed and reinforced, kinship ties are readily available and, so long as the individual has remained in good standing, direct reciprocity is not necessary.

In summary families assure survival of their members through sharing of a variety of resources. Family members secure future assistance by participating in a network of exchange. Provision of aid through this network is viewed as incontrovertible, without binding obligation or indebtedness, procured without fear of rejection, and opportune in that it will be received when needed. Continuation of reciprocal giving is maintained through fear of ostracism from the exchange network, desire to avoid harsh judgment of relatives, and desire to avoid a sense of dependency on the giver.

Contrary to the ideal, aid expected from kin is not absolute or without limitations. In a study of sixty women in London, O'Connor and Brown (1984) found the respondents (a) felt they had close relationships, (b) felt they could call upon these kin for help, and (c) felt availability of these kin was important. However, the researchers reported that very few respondents actually had such close relationships and practical help from existing relationships was quite small. Thus, even though individuals may feel assistance from kin is available, this may not reflect the reality of existence of such aid. Therefore, people may respond to a questionnaire that they feel they can ask family members for aid, however, if such aid was requested it may not be provided.

Limitations

The studies of Farmer (1970) and Wellman (1990) suggested there are limitations on the amount of aid that can be expected. These limitations were related to proximity of the family members (Farmer 1970) and past behavior of individuals regarding timely reciprocation (Wellman 1990). Families in these studies were middle class with resources to commit to exchanges. Unlike these families, poor families have limited resources with which to provide security.

Under conditions of poverty or unemployment, individuals lack the incontrovertible aid of their families. Family members unable to provide assistance to all members may be resigned to selecting individuals they are able to aid or types of assistance they are able to provide. Therefore, provision of aid is not certain and may be based upon criteria involving prior experience with the needy member, amount of resources available, level of hardship the provision of aid will work on the family providing it, and type of aid requested. These limitations are presented in the following studies which selected poor families as respondents.

In studying forty families living in one ward of a city in the North-East of England, Allatt and Yeandle (1986) found that the families with unemployed youth aged 18-20 years expressed an acceptance of limits to kin assistance. Some families who had drawn on kin for help in locating employment found them unable to help. There was acceptance of this limitation and kin ties continued on a social level with members being invited to functions such as graduation parties, engagement parties, and weddings. Also, some families had not drawn upon kin for help but felt confident they could if needed.

Acceptance of limits to kin assistance does not necessarily suggest non-monetary forms of aid are not available. Pearce and McAdoo (1984), in their study of single mothers living in poverty, found extended families could provide only limited financial help. In spite of this limitation, families would often continue providing emotional support in an effort to help the mother survive the stress of poverty. There seemed to be recognition that families could only provide limited amounts of assistance and were not responsible for lifting the families out of poverty.

In addition to limitations of available assistance, types of response to the sense of kin obligation may affect the exchange. Firth, Hubert, and Forge (1970) studied kinship in a middle-class sector of London. They identified three types of response to kin obligation: (a) prior conduct of kinsmen is used as justification for fulfillment or non-fulfillment even at times for parents, (b) a sense of guilt developed over inadequate fulfillment (real or felt) of obligations may be used to embarrass kinsmen into providing assistance, and (c) placement of responsibility and duty. The last type of response involves the recognition of obligations to provide assistance but unwillingness to perform the obligation (or to grudgingly fulfill the obligation) because it is determined that another family member is in a better position to provide assistance.[1] Therefore, even though assistance of kin is seen as an obligation, it is not necessarily interpreted as absolute.

Level or type of assistance may be affected by such factors as personal likes or dislikes and perceptions of past help. Qureshi (1986) interviewed 299 elderly people along with 58 carers of these elderly people in an effort to determine responses to dependency. She found people gave assistance to elderly relatives without regard to perception of past help. However, she recognizes this does not eliminate the fact that the perception of past help may affect current assistance since non-carers were not interviewed. Even though carers provided assistance despite attitudes toward the elderly person or perceptions of past help, these two factors affected willingness to form a joint household.

Level of assistance may further be affected by ability and willingness to provide aid. In their study of young welfare mothers, Parish, Hao, and Hogan (1991) used the National Longitudinal Survey of Labor Force Behavior, Youth Survey. This survey interviewed individuals who were 14-21 years of age in 1979 and then re-interviewed these individuals annually thereafter. They found that kin networks can improve the quality of life for young mothers but this network does have limitations as to amounts and types of assistance it is able to provide. Movement from a parent's home may inhibit such assistance as in-kind aid and cash flow. Parent's ability to provide aid also has important effects on amount of assistance received. Parish, Hao, and Hogan (1991) found the amount of childcare a young mother could expect to receive from her kin was dependent upon the amount of effort it involved for the provider. As the number of hours of childcare needed increased, willingness of relatives to provide assistance decreased. Data suggested kin were willing to provide childcare only for limited times each day. Again, kin provided some assistance but amount was determined by factors such as ability of kin to provide aid, geographic distance between provider and recipient, and amount of effort required.

Finch (1989), in her discussion of family obligation literature, found that presence of assistance from kin was not certain but dependent upon many factors. First, Finch (1989) suggested that personal liking and preference were important in the decision to render aid. Prime consideration in determination of whether to give assistance was the relationship between provider and recipient. Parents most often overcame dislike of a child or the child's spouse to render aid and children were expected to overcome dislike to render aid to parents, but this was not certain. Additionally, siblings had greater obligation to assist each other in spite of their personal feelings. Beyond these relationships, personal preference can undermine the possibility of any assistance. Quality of the relationship was important in determining the possibility of receiving aid from in-laws, especially parents-in-law. Second, assistance not requiring reciprocation was expected in the grandparent to grandchild relationship. This assistance tended to be impulsive or provided for special events such as birthdays or graduations. Therefore, gift giving, because of the impulsive nature, cannot be relied on to meet periodic needs of the family. Third, it was proper for a provider to take their own family's need into account when determining whether to provide assistance to kin. Fourth, ensuring independence of the person assisted was important in the determination.

In summary it is not necessarily automatic for one relative to offer support and it may be problematic for another to accept it; in general, there is pressure to reciprocate any aid received. Provision of financial assistance or practical support is not automatically given nor do needs for such assistance demand an automatic response. In fact, recipients, even those unemployed, do worry about their ability to reciprocate and providers can determine whether to provide assistance based on past behavior of the recipient. Additionally, amounts and forms of aid may vary depending on limitations placed on exchange relationship by economic conditions of the provider, personal feelings toward the recipient, or geographic proximity of giver and recipient.

Forms of Assistance

Families provide members many types of resources, such as housing, food, clothing, furniture, money, childcare, care for the elderly, care for ailing members, and a sense of community (Allatt and Yeandle 1986; Cavan and Ranck 1969; Farmer 1970; Pearce and McAdoo 1984; Stack 1970; Wellman 1990). Types of assistance provided, whether from friends or relatives, takes various forms and have been categorized a variety of ways.

Pearce and McAdoo (1984), in their study of single mothers in poverty, identified two forms of assistance: material and non-material. Material assistance included forms of aid as financial help, provision of food, or provision of items such as clothing and furniture. Non-material support included activities as childcare, emotional support, and providing the recipient with feelings of being loved.

Three forms of assistance were delineated by Finch (1989) from social support literature: (a) economic support, (b) practical support, (c) emotional and moral support. Economic support encompassed financial support, food, and various household items. Practical support involved short-term childcare, doing each other's shopping and laundry, and other non-material service-oriented activities. Relatives who provided information which relieved personal anxieties and fears, gave advice, listened, and helped individuals put their lives in perspective, provided emotional and moral support.

Five forms of assistance were identified by Fiore, Becker, and Coppel (1983): (a) cognitive guidance, (b) emotional support, (c) socializing, (d) tangible assistance, and (e) availability of someone for self-disclosure. Cognitive guidance included provision of advice, guidance, and information. Emotional support was the feeling of being loved and cared for; it was the assurance that the individual was worthy. Socializing provided the individual with a sense of commonly shared interests; of being a part of a neighborhood or family, in other words, provided a sense of social integration. These three categories combined were the emotional support category in Finch's (1989) scheme. Tangible assistance included concrete assistance as money, clothing, food, or furniture. This category was the material category of Pearce and McAdoo (1984) and a combination of economic and practical support of Finch (1989). Being available to someone for self-disclosure meant being the individual's confidante or confessor. This classification was unlike any category found in categorizations of either Finch (1989) or Pearce and McAdoo (1984).

Families living in poverty may not have all forms of assistance available in times of need. As a commodity cash is generally unavailable. Families living in poverty often receive non-monetary forms of governmental assistance, such as food stamps, housing vouchers, and commodity coupons like those given by federal programs. What cash families may have is generally required to pay portions of rent not paid by housing vouchers, pay utilities, provide transportation, and purchase clothing or food not covered by food stamps. Providing cash to relatives generally works hardships on providing families because this limits amounts of cash available for rent or utilities payments (Stack 1970). This suggests cash, being in short supply, is generally not available for assistance to relatives. Therefore, families in poverty more frequently involve themselves in assistance processes whereby material objects, i.e., food, clothing, or furniture, are exchanged rather than cash. Additionally, families may be involved in forms of barter in which these same material goods are exchanged for labor around the house, i.e., repairing kitchen cabinets in exchange for childcare (Hardey 1989).

The need for adaptation of the kin assistance arrangements to poverty conditions have led families to adopt rather intricate patterns of assistance. In developing descriptive categories of assistance which retain intricate patterns suggested by families in poverty, schemes discussed above are used as frameworks. However, each classification scheme has some important limitations which must be recognized. Broad categories of assistance recognized by Pearce and McAdoo (1984) lose the flavor of arrangements of assistance which exist within families living in poverty. Fiore and her collaborators (1983) provided a rich description of various emotional forms of assistance but were weak in their description of material forms of assistance. Finch (1989) provided a method by which to investigate the richness of material support systems. However, in discussing emotional forms of support, Finch (1989) did not differentiate emotional assistance from socializing assistance whereby individuals get a sense of belonging.

Families in poverty may provide assistance to their members but forms of assistance may vary depending upon what is available. This diversity needs to be reflected in the categories developed. To understand the complexity of assistance arrangements for families in poverty, four forms of assistance have been identified:

1. Financial assistance in the form of money;
2. Provision of goods and services. This form can be divided into two areas: (a) material assistance, representing provision of food, loan of a car, providing needed furniture (such as a crib for a new born), feeding children of the needy relative, and other services in which actual exchange of money does not occur; and (b) non-material assistance representing provision of childcare, caring for family members during illnesses, sharing information concerning job availabilities, providing references to potential employers, and sharing provider's home with families in need of assistance;

3. Emotional assistance, i.e., advice giving, operating as a confidante, and providing encouragement; and
4. Socializing which provide individuals with sense of belonging, sense of community, and sense of social integration.

Financial assistance allows recipient families to purchase needed goods or services. Money may be given in cash so families are able to pay bills, visit the doctor, make down payments on large purchases such as homes, or meet emergency needs. However, not all forms of financial assistance involve provision of cash by one individual to another. In attempting to meet needs of entire families during recessions or depressions, family members pool cash incomes so families can pay rent, utilities, or purchase food (Angell 1965; Cavan and Ranck 1969; Modell 1979). Additionally, family members with employment become primary providers for their families. Cavan and Ranck (1969), in their study of families during the Great Depression, found evidence of employed sons and/or daughters who assumed financial responsibility for the entire family. Consequently, financial assistance may involve a variety of activities, i.e., providing monetary gifts, providing loans, pooling family financial resources, or reversing roles so that sons or daughters become primary providers for the family.

Provision of goods and services is the form of assistance whereby daily needs of recipient families are met. This form of assistance is divided into two separate but not necessarily distinct categories. Material assistance involves exchange of goods other than money. In this situation recipient families benefit from receipt of goods such as furniture, clothing, household items, or use of a car. This form of assistance involves provision of items families would normally find a need to purchase. Consequently, provision of these items aids recipient families by supplying needed articles and by freeing the monetary resources of the recipient families. In this way the cash saved by not having to purchase these items may be used on other necessary expenditures, such as renting and maintaining residences.

The non-material category includes provision of housing for recipient families. Some or all family members will move into the household depending on space available and agreement between provider and recipient. During the Great Depression families shared living quarters thereby allowing the members to maintain a residence (Burgess, Locke, and Thomes 1963; Cavan and Ranck 1969). Variations on this method of assistance include providing housing for children of families while parents live elsewhere, having married children living in homes of parents part of the year while the rest of the year is spent in homes of the child's in-laws (Cavan and Ranck 1969). Another alternative was for each married child to move into the home of their own parents (Cavan and Ranck 1969). During the recession of the last decade, researchers reported it was not uncommon for homeless families to share living quarters with relatives prior to seeking assistance at homeless shelters (Solarz 1992).

Other types of non-material assistance include supplying family members with information concerning employment opportunities, introducing family members to potential employers, caring for the children of needy members (Burton and Dilworth-Anderson 1991), and caring for ailing members of families. This category overlaps the material support category where material needs are met while families are residing in the homes of the provider. While living in the provider's home, recipients are fed and other resources such as clothing and transportation are provided. However, providing non-material support does not necessarily entail the provision of material support. Some forms of non-material support, such as introducing unemployed family members to prospective employers, does not necessitate the additional provision of material support. Thus, categories of material and non-material assistance, while delineating differences in types of assistance provided, are not distinct categories. Instead, the two categories are concurrent.

Emotional assistance entails providing family members with encouragement and advice. As family members face obstacles, families provide advice concerning alternative actions that can be taken to resolve the problem. Burton and Dilworth-Anderson (1991) reported elderly blacks gave advice and economic support to their adult children while receiving support and care from their children. Furthermore, under conditions of stress, encouragement received from family can help relieve feelings of helplessness (Angell 1965; Cavan and Ranck 1969) and provide family members with the tenacity to continue. Family members because of the inherent emotional attachments also serve as trustworthy confidantes.

The importance of socializing assistance is demonstrated by families in the study of Cavan and Ranck (1969) who reported excessive worry and depression led many to consider, attempt, or commit suicide. Families who were able to provide a sense of belonging and community amongst their members were less likely to experience this trauma or were able to prevent their members from attempting suicide. Thus, socializing assistance provided needed stability in some families.

Types of assistance families provide their members in times of need are not limited to provision of money. Instead, much richer networks of assistance are available to members of families. Therefore, poor families, unable to provide cash to needy members, have others types of assistance with which to meet needs and obligations. The next section discusses what happens when even these varied forms of assistance are not available to members or members fail to meet obligations to kin networks.

When Kin Assistance Fails

Failure of members to meet obligatory exchange agreements may result in the breakdown of the exchange network, or at least that portion of the network which is directly effected.   Members requesting aid are left to meet current needs through some other avenue, either from other family members or friends who are obligated to these persons or through more formal networks such as governmental assistance programs.   Members who refuse to honor obligations run the risk of being eliminated not only from exchange relationships with this one member but from entire familial exchange networks.   Additionally, by refusing to provide assistance, noncomplying parties are at risk of harsh judgment or sanction from the family.   Moreover, when some future need presents itself, noncomplying members may find themselves being denied assistance.

Stack (1970) related the experiences of a woman who had received assistance from her family but was unwilling to reciprocate. She was judged harshly and had been eliminated from the exchange network even though she was the provider's cousin. Friends and relatives who had not upheld their part of the reciprocal agreement often were severely criticized by the individual members of the network. It was recognized that the family was able to survive only because of the reciprocal relationship with kin. Failure of this relationship meant failure of the family as measured by eviction, hunger, and other unmet needs.

Coward and Jackson (1983), in their study of rural families facing financial crises, found that rural families may not have informal support available to them and the prospects of formal support may be limited. Rural families because of weak exchange networks were at a disadvantage in meeting crisis situations.   Resources normally accessible through exchange networks were not available. This served to put rural families at disadvantages in their efforts at coping with the stress of financial loss. This inability spelled the likely disruption of the family.

Disaffiliation of skid-row dwellers and homeless individuals from friends and family is viewed by some as a cause of homelessness (Bahr and Caplow 1973; Bogue 1986; Roth 1989; Wright 1989). Homeless individuals reported feeling they cannot elicit help from family or friends (Roth 1989; Wright 1989). In not having a network of friends and relatives for exchange, homeless individuals are unable to amass resources necessary to extricate themselves from the homeless condition.[2] Therefore, breakdown of exchange relationships places homeless individuals at disadvantages in competition for shelter.

These studies illustrate how loss of family assistance places families in positions of being unable to meet their needs. Maintenance of exchange relationships is an important factor in families' survival of crises. Absence of exchange networks does not necessarily spell disaster for families. However, the ability of families to cope with crises is obstructed causing families to suffer losses more intensely.

The next chapter discusses how women in Baghdad and Starlight Inns met the challenges of being homeless and living in shelters through alternative assistance arrangements.

Notes

1. In his study of families during the Great Depression, Angell (1965, 234) reported that a respondent's mother resented the presence of her mother-in-law in her household but felt it was "her cross to bear." In this family obligation to care for a parent was grudgingly being fulfilled.

2. The ties homeless individuals have with family and friends is discussed in more detail in Chapter 4.

CHAPTER 4

Meeting the Needs of Homeless Families

Arrangements for Meeting Needs Revisited

The family is the first line of defense in times of distress in meeting the needs of its members. Through sharing of resources families can assure survival of all its members. However, families are not the only group that may be used in times of need. Litwak (1985) and Litwak and Szelenyi (1969) described four primary group structures, each with tasks to perform which are expressly suited to it and which are not easily performed by any of the other groups. These four groups are the nuclear family, extended kin, friends, and neighbors.

The nuclear family group may routinely perform tasks which are best handled by one or two adults. However, Litwak and Szelenyi (1969) argued that because of limited resources from which nuclear families can draw, the other groups are needed to provide supplemental resources during times of need.

According to Litwak and Szelenyi (1969), precisely because of kinship obligations, extended kin are best suited to provide needs to nuclear families: (a) in situations where there are few face-to-face contacts, such as where the nuclear family is geographically isolated; and (b) where needs require long-term or permanent commitments. These needs encompass provisions for the elderly and others who are unable to care for themselves, adoption of orphaned children, and tasks which involve oversight of the nuclear family's funds.

Friends, because the ties are affective, are also useful in situations which do not demand constant face-to-face relationships. Therefore, they are well suited for functions requiring considerable time. However, since institutional pressures encouraging the continuation of friend-ties are absent, they are more vulnerable to breakdown than extended kin ties. Hence, the long-term commitment cannot be of a permanent nature as it can with extended kin (Litwak and Szelenyi 1969). For example, friends may consider baby sitting for a child after school or on weekends or during an extended period of illness of a parent but would not consider permanently taking the child. Conversely, extended kin may consider taking the child on a more permanent basis, such as adoption of an orphaned child.

The final primary group, neighbors, (Litwak and Szelenyi 1969) function in performing tasks which require frequent face-to-face contact and short-term commitments. Neighbors are good at meeting the emergencies which occur in the life of the nuclear family, such as taking care of a child while the mother makes an unplanned trip to the doctor with a second child.

The family provides for needs other than the more material needs discussed by Litwak (1985) and Litwak and Szelenyi (1969). Families often provide members with a sense of identity, a sense of community, a sense of social integration, and serves to place the individual within the social hierarchy (Farber 1974; Rosser and Harris 1983). The member's location in the familial hierarchy is defined through interactions with other members thereby providing an identity based on their relationship to others (i.e., son, daughter, parent, grandparent) (Rosser and Harris 1983). Recognition of placement within the family and the resulting identity provides the individual with a feeling of belonging. Thus, strong sentiments toward the family group result. Additionally, the individual is provided a sense of security through the knowledge that they belong to a group which may be petitioned for aid and support in emergency situations (Levi-Strauss 1969; Litwak 1965).

A question arises as to what happens when the extended family is unable or unwilling to shoulder its responsibilities? What alternatives, if any, does the individual or the nuclear family have at their disposal if the extended family does not perform its functions?

Relevant studies have attempted to describe institutions or individuals utilized by the nuclear family to meet its needs in times of crisis, most specifically, the development and utilization of fictive- or quasi-kin. Additionally, studies have attempted to describe the impact of isolation of the nuclear family due to geographic or occupational mobility, and the consequences of poverty and/or unemployment of wage-earners on the nuclear family's available sources of assistance. In determining who outside the periphery of extended family may be called upon in times of need, these studies have tended to focus on middle- or working-class families.

A study by Blumberg and Bell (1959, 332) illustrated an instance in which outsiders to the kinship network are brought into a relationship so they may perform tasks of extended family thereby creating fictive- or quasi-kin. In their study of migration of Southerners to the Detroit area, Blumberg and Bell noticed that when relatives were not available the individual turned to people who had come from the same original geographic area for assistance. These people, often contacted in "hillbilly taverns," would supply information about jobs, housing, and emotional support for the newly immigrated. Through contacts with the people from their home area the immigrant developed what Blumberg and Bell call "pseudo-kin relationships."

Parents may provide financial help to their married children often after little more than a hint from the child (Farmer 1970). In Farmer's study the gift was imparted in a manner that allowed the young couple to save face and not feel obligated to the parents. According to Farmer (1970), people feel free to ask their kinsmen for aid and expect to receive relief. In fact, people prefer asking kinsmen over friends or neighbors even if they do not especially like their kinsmen. The only factors which limit kin aid noted by Farmer (1970) are proximity and the closeness of the group.[1]

Studies which focused on the isolating effects of geographic mobility of the nuclear family sought to ascertain the impact of infrequent contact on kinship ties. A primary purpose of the studies was to determine changes in the extent of nuclear family isolation during the period of industrialization. As a result of his findings, Parsons (1968) argued that the nuclear family was more isolated as a unit and therefore was unable to function in the same way as it had prior to industrialization. Similarly, Taietz (1970) concluded in his study of elderly in the Netherlands that occupational mobility was leading to a breakdown in extended family relations. With the advance of industrialization and concurrent occupational mobility, families were no longer engaged in the same type of relationship as previously. They were, instead, making fewer visits to their parents and siblings and were less willing to take elderly parents who were unable to care for themselves into their homes.

However, Sussman and Burchinal (1962, 237-38) concluded the nuclear family has not become isolated during occupational or geographic mobility but rather patterns of help offered by extended kin have undergone changes. Since relationships outside the kin network are more difficult to develop due to lack of permanence in residence, extended family has become even more important as a source of support during times of crisis. Services which are performed by extended family include care of children, advice giving, physical care of elderly, providing shelter, attendance at family rituals such as weddings or funerals, and support in maintenance of family status.

A final group of studies investigated the effect of poverty on the ability of extended families to fulfill their functions. Cavan and Ranck (1969) studied one hundred families living in Chicago during the Great Depression to determine the effect of loss of employment and financial instability on family structure. They found families demonstrated several adaptive procedures in meeting needs of individual members; such as parents and married children living together in one household sharing rental costs. In instances where a son or daughter was fortunate enough to have employment, they would assume financial responsibility of their family. Frequency of aid and rarity of rebellion seems to suggest that the providing member accepted the provision of aid as a legitimate request from the family.

Sussman (1959), in a study of families in Detroit, found that the family's social class was more significant in determination of services which were exchanged between extended family members than willingness of members to participate in the network. This study found that middle-class families were more likely to provide financial assistance than working-class families. Further, middle-class grandmothers were more likely than their working-class counterparts to provide baby-sitting services. Sussman suggested differences were due more to the ability of middle-class families to provide services than a disparity in willingness.

Newman (1988) discussed the effect of downward mobility on the ability of middle-class American families to utilize extended family ties as resources. For families who had exhausted conventional sources, the turn to kin for help produced conflict and embarrassment. Families, in receiving aid, were faced with the necessity of reciprocating the gift or losing independence to the gift-giver. However, in attempting to recompense the gift and thereby retain independence, recipients were confronted with the likelihood of insulting the gift-giver and/or labeling the gift-giver as an outsider to the family. Therefore, the families in Newman's study felt it preferable to turn to impersonal institutions thereby avoiding the embarrassment of requesting help from relatives.

In a study of households during periods of unemployment, McKee (1987) determined the resourcefulness of the household in meeting the nuclear family's needs. The sample was comprised of families who were either recently unemployed or had experienced long-term unemployment. McKee reported that while many families felt regular interaction with extended family was supportive, many more found continuous interaction to be problematic. This was especially true when the unemployed family felt pressure to reciprocate. Many were concerned that they would not be able to repay the debt.

In addition, McKee (1987) reported the acceptance of assistance contributed to an increase of tensions within the husband/wife relationship. When recipients made comparisons regarding the amount and kinds of help given by respective parents, conflicts would arise. Parents, because of their role as provider, felt open to criticize daughters- or sons-in-law. Thus, provision of aid carried a price for the receiving family. In efforts to avoid problems, many families living in neighborhoods with several unemployed families found support and aid amongst their neighbors while other families tended to isolate themselves.

In the 1960s Elliot Liebow (1967, 162) conducted an ethnographic study of low-income African-American adult males (streetcorner men). The men of Liebow's study developed a personal community composed of a "web-like arrangement" of kin and friends. The central members of this personal community could be relied on for assistance in times of need. Liebow recounts how members would exchange goods and services in effort to provide for members in need.[2]

Michael Hardey (1989) conducted a study of single female parents with dependent children. The parents of this study reported utilizing charities, governmental agencies, part-time jobs, or a barter system to procure needed household items rather than depending on extended family. These parents entered into trade deals with non-kin in which they supplied a service (i.e., baby-sitting) in exchange for needed assistance (i.e., household repairs). In spite of these interactions, most parents reported feeling isolated from the adult world. In Hardey's (1989, 127) study nearly a quarter of the single parents reported sharing a home with other single parents. This arrangement provided parents with more power in the housing market and reduced their sense of isolation.

The studies discussed attempt to answer the question of who provides for a family in times of need. Each study, with one exception, has approached the question with the assumption that extended family was present and able to be of assistance. These studies have suggested: (a) that differences exist in an extended family's ability to provide assistance and the types of assistance available, (b) the need to reciprocate has the potential of creating conflicts within the family network, and (c) pressures to reciprocate may lead needy families to approach other more impersonal sources of aid. Finally, the poor single parents in Hardey's (1989) study did not report using extended family to meet their immediate needs. These parents met their needs through cooperation with each other, charitable organizations, governmental organizations, and a system of barter.

Under conditions of poverty or unemployment, individuals lack the incontrovertible aid of their families (Allatt and Yeandle 1986; Farmer 1970; Wellman 1990). Family members unable to provide assistance to all members may be resigned to selecting individuals they are able to aid or types of assistance they are able to provide. Therefore, provision of aid is not certain and may be based upon criteria involving prior experience with the needy member (Qureshi

1986), amount of resources available (Pearce and McAdoo 1984), level of hardship the provision of aid will work on the family providing it (Finch 1989; Parish, Hao, and Hogan 1991), and type of aid requested (Finch 1989). Additionally, families who are unable to provide material support on a consistent basis may provide emotional support to needy members (Liebow 1993).

Homeless families tend to be in desperate need of aid from extended family and friends but often find themselves in situations where they are isolated from these groups (Bahr and Caplow 1973). Disaffiliation of skid-row dwellers and homeless individuals from friends and family is viewed by some as a cause of homelessness (Bahr and Caplow 1973; Bogue 1986; Roth 1989; Wright 1989). Homeless individuals report feeling they cannot elicit help from family or friends (Roth 1989; Wright 1989). In not having a network of friends and relatives for exchange, homeless individuals are unable to amass resources necessary to extricate themselves from the homeless condition. Homeless families who are in contact with at least one relative may be unable or unwilling to ask for help for reasons which include the extreme poverty of the relative, a contentious relationship with the relative, or the overextension of the limits of aid the relative considers reasonable (Alter et al. 1986; Jencks 1994; Rosenthal 1994; Rossi 1989a,b). For these reasons homeless families often find themselves in situations where they must depend on non-kin and agencies to meet their needs. This chapter explains what steps homeless families in Arid Acropolis took to meet their needs in the event they were unable or unwilling to utilize their extended families.

Mothers and Assistance they Received

A majority of mothers who had partners in the shelters with them were married while a majority of the single mothers reported they had never been married. The marital status served to increase the number of relatives available for assistance since relatives of husband and wife could be called on for aid. Contrarily, Jencks (1994) reported that families of skidders were more likely to support women than to support men. Therefore, even though married mothers had more relatives to ask for assistance, single women may receive more assistance because of the propensity for families to provide more aid to females. However, in this study both groups, despite receiving assistance from relatives, frequently found themselves using non-kin networks of assistance for many of their needs.

Sixty-one percent (17) of the mothers with partners with them in the shelter reported having contact with extended family (see Table 4-1). The majority of these families had received some assistance from extended family members. The most common forms of assistance

TABLE 4-1

Assistance Patterns Experienced by Mothers Attending
Parenting Classes at Baghdad Inn

	Couples[a] (n=28)		Single[b] (n=33)	
	Number	Percent	Number	Percent
Contact With Relatives				
Yes	17	61	16	48
No	4	14	3	9
Undetermined	7	25	14	42
Assistance Received From Relatives[c]				
Yes	10	59	9	56
No	7	41	7	44
Types Of Assistance Received[d]				
Childcare	5	33	6	46
Money/Goods	2	13	2	15
Lodging	4	27	2	15
Transportation	-	-	1	8
Holiday/Weekend/Overnight Visits	3	20	2	15
Unclear	1	7	-	-

Notes:

[a] Families in which mothers entered the shelter with male partners.
[b] Families in which mothers entered the shelter without male partners.
[c] Includes only families who had contact with relatives; Couples n=17, Singles n=16.
[d] Includes only families who reported receiving assistance. Families could receive assistance in more than one category; Couples n=15, Singles n=13.

received was childcare (33 percent) and lodging (27 percent). Childcare represented having a child live with a relative for a period of time. The five mothers reporting childcare had children living with relatives at the time of the study.[3] The category lodging referred to situations in which the mother and her children had lived in the house of a relative for a period of time longer than a weekend.[4] All of these mothers commented that this alternative to the shelter simply had not worked out, that tensions had become too great leading to departure from the relative's home.

Sixteen single mothers (48 percent) reported they did have contact with relatives (see Table 4-1). Over fifty percent of the single mothers had received assistance from relatives. The most frequent form of assistance was in terms of childcare with the relative keeping one or more children for an unspecified period of time. Six single mothers who reported receiving childcare related they had left children in the care of relatives. Three other forms of assistance were equally used by single mothers; lodging (living with a relative), the receipt of money or goods, and staying with a relative during a holiday, for a weekend, or overnight.

Fewer mothers in couples than single mothers (33 percent compared to 46 percent) had children living elsewhere while they lived in the shelter. Therefore, women who had male assistance were more likely to keep their children with them while living at a shelter. Additionally, mothers in couples tended to maintain contact with relatives with slightly over half receiving some form of assistance from these relatives. The form of assistance most frequently utilized by mothers in couples was childcare with only slightly fewer accepting lodging with relatives.

Not quite fifty percent of the single mothers had some contact with their relatives. Of these, just over half had received assistance from these relatives. The assistance received by single mothers was most likely to take the form of childcare. However, they were also likely to accept offers of money or goods, transportation, and to stay for holidays, weekends, or overnight in the homes of relatives.

The majority of mothers in this study were not totally isolated from relatives and received some benefit from this contact in the form of assistance. However, many mothers were concerned that they were taking too much assistance from relatives. They worried that relatives may be giving more assistance than they could afford. Sharon was living in the shelter with her husband and one child. In addition to the child with her in the shelter, she had a daughter who was soon to be married, a son who had run away at the age of 14, and two younger children (she would not speak of the younger children). The oldest daughter was employed but receiving minimum wage and so was able to help her mother but only at a cost to herself. Therefore, Sharon would not ask this daughter for aid fearing any assistance her daughter provided would jeopardize her future. In addition to her older children, Sharon had an aunt living in a neighboring community. When the aunt became extremely ill from cancer and was not expected to live, Sharon spent a weekend with her. This family had only limited resources which had been severely depleted by the aunt's prolonged illness. Consequently, they were unable to offer any help beyond providing meals when Sharon visited.

Jane lived in the shelter with her two children. Jane had family living in Arid Acropolis but did not feel she could ask them for help because of the family's own extreme poverty. Jane's parents were barely able to live on their income and had no other resources with which to help any of their children. Additionally, Jane was reluctant to ask for aid from her parents because of fear stemming from a childhood marked by physical abuse. Jane's only other source of potential assistance was her ex-spouse who lived in Arid Acropolis. However, she adamantly refused to have any interaction with him even if contact with him meant she and her children could move out of the shelter.

Some mothers complained about what they felt was meddling from relatives who did provide assistance. This was a frequent reason given for having moved out of a relative's home. Marjie, a young unmarried mother with a two year old son and a newborn daughter prior to coming to the shelter, had lived in Denver with her mother. She had left her mother's home because of a disagreement over her educational and occupational goals. Marjie felt her mother was attempting to impose her dreams for Marjie's future in return for help. In an effort to end what she felt was meddling, Marjie moved from her mother's home in Denver and into the Baghdad Inn. When she left Denver, her 15 year old daughter remained with her mother. Marjie felt it was important for her daughter to have a stable environment during her teen years, something Marjie's mother could offer and she could not. Toward the end of the study Marjie and her mother began to open lines of communication. However, Marjie made it clear she would not return to her mother's home unless her mother accepted the fact that she was going to follow her own goals for her future. Since Marjie and her mother continued to disagree on what Marjie should do in the future, it was unlikely that Marjie would return to her mother's home.[5]

Some mothers found maintaining stable relationships with family difficult. Hurt feelings caused by past arguments made some mothers reluctant or unwilling to ask for assistance from relatives. Sally, a mother of three girls, reported the lack of a stable relationship with her mother. She informed me that both she and her mother had undergone counseling in an effort to develop better lines of communication but that the effort had failed. In spite of this, Sally's mother is caring for her two older children both from a previous marriage. Sally has maintained only limited contact with her mother in order to maintain contact with her children. Her husband, Joe, upon their youngest girl's first birthday, called his mother for the first time informing her of their homelessness. At that time Joe's mother apparently agreed to send money to the family but had not followed through on her promise. Subsequently, Sally and Joe, after several angry arguments concerning a choice not to accept assistance from their families, filed for legal separation. Upon separation Sally returned to the shelter with her 14 month old daughter to live for an additional four months before finding housing.[6]

Michelle, like Sally, felt unable to ask for help from her mother because of what she characterized as a stormy relationship. She was reluctant to have long conversations with her mother because she feared they would argue as they had in the past. She expressed her unwillingness to accept aid from her mother even if it were offered. Michelle reported she had contacted her sister in an effort to arrange for the adoption of her unborn child. I do not know if legal arrangements for adoption were completed since Michelle left the shelter prior to her child's birth.

As the examples of Sharon and Jane illustrated, many mothers were concerned about continuing what they characterized as an unequal exchange with relatives fearing they would be unable to reciprocate. In addition, some mothers, as illustrated by Marjie, worried that family members who were supplying assistance would continue to meddle in their lives thereby creating tension between themselves and these relatives. Other mothers, such as Sally and Michelle, felt they could not ask for assistance because they regarded the relationship they had with their relatives as unstable or non-supportive. As a result many of the mothers were reluctant to ask for further assistance thereby effectively limiting the amount of assistance they could reasonably expect to receive. In addition to these mothers, seven mothers in couples and seven single mothers had not received any assistance from their relatives nor did they expect to receive any future assistance. This raises the question as to how mothers living in Baghdad Inn met needs commonly fulfilled by family; needs such as short-term childcare, emotional support, and information concerning meeting daily needs (obtaining welfare assistance, birth control procedures, and problem solving).

Mothers and Their Alternative Support Network

Homeless families living in shelters in Arid Acropolis tended not to be isolated from extended family in the sense that they lacked contact with family members. Rather, families were generally receiving the limit of aid they could expect from family or the amount they were willing to accept. Therefore, the majority of parents in the study were isolated from extended families to the extent that they were unwilling to ask for help or were unwilling to accept aid from family members beyond caring for dependent children. Following the argument of Litwak and Szelenyi (1969), functions of extended family must then be performed by others.

Since the normal stay is only two months, homeless parents rarely get to know other parents in the shelter beyond superficial relationships living in such close proximity produces. In addition, homeless parents tend to be distrustful of people they do not know and are fearful that because of some overheard criticism of the shelter or its staff the family will be asked to leave. These roadblocks to the development of meaningful relationships create an environment in which alternate provider relationships are difficult to develop. However, in spite of difficulties, parents and families living in Baghdad and Starlight Inns developed an alternative structure which provided many of the supportive functions of extended kin; childrearing, baby-sitting, emotional support, support during pregnancy, and general childcare needs.

Childcare and much of the child's early socialization is provided by the shelter system. The shelter provides a daycare and a one-room school system for children residing at the shelters. Parents enroll their children in the appropriate center upon entry into the shelters; except for instances when an older child is still enrolled and attending local public schools. Children spend the entire day for the school (8:00 A.M. until 3:30 P.M.) and for daycare (8:00 A.M. until 6:00 P.M.) within the confines of the shelter. Mothers, unless they are ill and have permission of the doctor to remain inside, must leave the shelter at 8:30 A.M. and cannot return to the dormitory until 3:30 P.M. This system leaves children in the care of teachers for most of their waking hours. It becomes the teachers' duty to help socialize the child, attending to such activities as toilet training, discipline, social etiquette, and proper group behavior. Therefore, teachers in the daycare or school become alternate socializing agents for children.

Another source of childhood socialization may be provided by mothers living in the shelter. Many of the mothers correct a child's behavior if the child's mother is out of the dormitory, is not aware of the child's behavior, or is not taking steps to correct disruptive behavior. The ability of another mother to correct the behavior of a child who is not her own is limited. There were mothers within the shelter who were viewed by others as being "poor" mothers. These mothers would be verbally accosted if they attempted to correct any child other than their own. Cathy, a mother of two children, was not allowed to correct any child's behavior other than her own even by scolding the child. The other mothers told me on several occasions that they had seen Cathy abusing her own children. They also complained that she did not watch her children closely. Behaviors exhibited by Cathy earned her the label of an abusive mother and therefore unqualified to discipline any other child. Several mothers reported threatening Cathy if she even raised her voice to any other child. Threats ranged from physical attacks to reporting her to Child Protective Services for child abuse. Additionally, mothers frequently baby sat another mother's children while she ran errands, had time alone with her spouse, or took an ill child to the clinic. With the rare exceptions of mothers such as Cathy, mothers individually at various times became alternate socializing agents for children in the shelter.

Mothers frequently provided emotional support for one another in a number of areas. An example of emotional support is provided by the relationship between Judy, a mother of two girls, and Marjie, who was expecting her second child. Judy was participating in a program in which an individual would guarantee that rent, utilities, and insurance on a home would be paid. This individual would select the family to be helped, assist the homeless family in locating an acceptable home, and help the family move into the home. The sponsor could request certain requirements concerning the home (such as location, presence of major appliances, proximity to a school, and so forth) be met before giving approval for the family to move into the home. Judy experienced frustration when the sponsor placed requirements on her selection of a home she felt were unrealistic (such as requiring the home to be located in a upper-middle class neighborhood). Judy experienced a particularly stressful period of time while she was waiting to hear about her home. She became extremely frustrated with the process, expressing several times that she just wanted to give up and remain in the shelter. During these distressful times, Marjie would frequently talk with Judy, reminding her of the desire to get out of the shelter and her children's needs to live in a home. The quiet talks between Judy and Marjie gave Judy the strength to meet the next challenge eventually paying off when she moved into her home. In reciprocation, when Marjie entered the hospital to give birth to her daughter, Judy provided "coaching" services during delivery. Additionally, Judy cared for Marjie's son during her stay in the hospital. Once Marjie was released from the hospital, she spent several days with Judy in her home recuperating. Thus, these two women provided the kinds of assistance one might expect to receive from family.

Another example of the emotional support homeless mothers provide one another occurred one night about six weeks after Charlene and her husband had come to the shelter. The Baghdad Inn required that adult men and male children age seven and over be housed in a separate shelter from women, female children, and male children under age seven. As a result of this separation, Charlene lamented she and her husband had been experiencing some difficulties within their marriage. Charlene complained her husband had become withdrawn, not seeming to want to participate in family discussions or in decisions regarding their two children. She expressed concern that their marriage could not withstand much more strain. The stress of the shelter and the effect it was having on her marriage became more than Charlene could tolerate and she began to cry uncontrollably. Only through the kindness and concern of other mothers was Charlene able to regain control and deal with her problems. The women sat throughout the night with Charlene discussing her problems and offering possible solutions and their strength. After several hours of discussion and consoling, Charlene was able to cope again with the stresses until she and her family became domiciled two weeks later.

Mothers frequently provided information to one another concerning meeting daily needs. Janice, a mother who had been in several other shelters, frequently provided information concerning welfare services to other mothers. She provided assistance in filling out the myriad of forms required by the state while explaining that the way they answered questions was as important to receiving aid as information provided. When a new arrival was faced with completing welfare applications, mothers frequently suggested that she sit down with Janice to fill out the forms. Additionally, mothers who had been in the shelter the longest would provide information concerning local clothing, food, and furniture banks. They informed new arrivals of the best places for the nicest clothes or furniture, which banks were most likely to have infant or toddler's clothing, and where it was easiest to get a food box.

Mothers also provided companionship to each other, especially prevalent among the mothers who did not have a male companion in the shelter. Mothers frequently related day trips to local swimming pools, window-shopping at the malls, or to picnics sponsored by religious organizations. Peg and Alice frequently spent time with one another shopping or attending a variety of activities. Peg confided she was too self conscious about her homeless status to face these groups alone. Therefore it was very important to have someone go with her into a new environment or into a situation where she would be interacting with the domiciled population. Alice filled this need. They provided support for one another in those uncomfortable situations where they interacted with domiciled people as well as in circumstances where they felt uncomfortable being by themselves.

It is interesting to note that much of the alternative support activity was centered within the group of mothers who attended parenting class at the same time. These mothers seem to genuinely care for one another and expressed concern in their willingness to give whatever assistance was needed. This group interacted to the exclusion of other mothers who were in the dormitory at the same time but were not attending parenting classes. It is possible that parenting classes helped facilitate cohesion and camaraderie among the mothers thereby enhancing their willingness to assist each other.

In areas where mothers are unable to provide needed services, respondents turned to particular people who worked in agencies which serviced the homeless population. Women who taught parenting classes were used as sources of information regarding such diverse subjects as educational institutions, dietary concerns, and birth control procedures. These women were also used as a conduit for complaints mothers had about shelter conditions, concerns over how some mothers treated their children, and theft of food primarily by single women living on the same floor of the shelter. Mothers shared these concerns and complaints with parenting class leaders with full knowledge the concerns would be shared with shelter administration in a way which protected mothers from any perceived reparations from administration or shelter staff. Other sources that provide needed services: (a) Nurses from the Homeless Outreach were used for information concerning health problems, health concerns, and birth control; (b) a worker with W.I.C. (Women Infants and Children--a federal food program) provided mothers with help in filling out the multitudinous forms required to obtain assistance from state and federal government; (c) the family counselor at the shelter was used as referral for jobs, tokens for bus trips, and possible housing; and (d) the director of Homeless Outreach was used to help solve problems mothers had in the shelter, with the free clinic, or with paperwork they must complete.

In summary even though these mother's and their families are isolated from aid of extended families they were not without support. They appeared to have developed alternative networks among other families in the shelter, service workers, and each other. Through these networks their needs for emotional support, companionship, childrearing aid, and help in securing homes were met. By use of alternative networks they developed, mothers were able to overcome obstacles and isolation of homelessness thereby meeting more of their needs than if alternative support networks were not present.

The networks developed were a patchwork of associations reminiscent of the networks of assistance presented by Stack (1970) and Liebow (1967). Members of the network may include family but only marginally. The more central figures to this network included facilitators of parenting classes, agency workers and administrators, nurses, shelter staff, and each other.

Notes

1. For a more complete discussion of the limits of kin assistance, see Chapter 3.

2. Carol Stack (1970) found a similar network of friends and family that could be relied on for assistance in times of desperation.

3. In Chapter 5 living arrangements of children are discussed. Not all children are placed with relatives. Generally, older children were placed in homes of relatives, while younger children, primarily infants, remained with mothers in the shelter.

4. Jencks (1994, 72-73) reported some of the skidders in his study lived in the homes of relatives and friends in efforts to afford their children a "normal" life.

5. While conducting research on another project, I learned that Marjie had moved into a house and had brought her daughter from Denver to live with her. Unfortunately, Marjie and her daughter argued a great deal and the daughter eventually requested that she be returned to Marjie's mother's home to live. Marjie reluctantly agreed and the daughter returned to her grandmother's home.

6. I was unable to learn what happened to Joe after the separation. I only know he did not return to the shelter where I was conducting my study.

CHAPTER 5

Shelter Guests

Several studies (e.g., Appelbaum 1990; Blau 1992; Ropers 1988; Rossi 1989a,b) have described characteristics of homeless populations in the United States. (For a complete description of homeless populations, see Chapter 2.) There are similarities in homeless populations nationwide in that homeless people are in their late twenties to mid-thirties, women are under-represented, and African Americans, Hispanics, and Native Americans are over-represented in homeless populations. However, there are regional variations in demographic makeups of homeless populations (Ropers 1988). Therefore, the present chapter presents a demographic profile of homeless populations of Arid Acropolis and Baghdad Inn. Demographic characteristics of homeless populations of Baghdad Inn and Arid Acropolis were compared to Census information for the State.

Two sources provide census-type information on guests of Baghdad Inn. In 1990 the shelter services administrator for Baghdad Inn, Ron Askagrant (1990a), issued a report of characteristics of homeless people who had been guests of the Inn for at least one night in the late 1980s. These data were compiled from intake forms, which are completed upon entry into the shelter. Additionally, intake forms were supplemented by a survey of 132 respondents. Data also found in the Askagrant (1990a) report provided information peculiar to homeless populations; i.e., information concerning length of current homeless episodes, individuals' residences prior to entry into the shelter, and number of nights individuals had resided in the shelter at the time of the survey.

The second part of the chapter presents demographic descriptions of mothers and/or fathers who participated in parenting classes at Baghdad Inn and/or Starlight Inn and whose stories are the basis of this study. Information relating numbers of children present in the shelter, numbers of children placed elsewhere, and ages of children are presented.

Four-Year Account: 1987-1990

When homeless individuals or families first enter Baghdad Inn, intake forms are completed. This form asks for information concerning (a) individuals' most recent residences, (b) any financial assistance individuals are receiving, (c) length of time individuals or families have spent in the State, (d) length of time individuals have spent homeless, (e) veteran status, (f) highest level of education individuals have achieved, (g) unemployment status, and (h) reasons given for individuals' or families' homelessness. Information acquired from intake forms became the four-year demographic profile report presented by Ron Askagrant (1990a).

During the four years from 1987 to 1990, 8,617 people lived at Baghdad Inn for at least one night. Baghdad Inn is designed to accommodate more men than women. Of the 406 beds available, 332 beds (82 percent) accommodate men as compared to 44 beds (11 percent) for single women, and 30 beds (7 percent) for women with children. A large majority of residents of Baghdad Inn were single men (Table 5-1) (Askagrant 1990a). However, despite design allocation of 11 percent of beds, single women comprised nearly one quarter of Baghdad Inn's population, while accounting for only eight percent of the estimated homeless population of Arid Acropolis. Single women may be over-represented in the shelter for three reasons:

1. Women may use shelters more than men because they feel safer in the shelter than on the streets.
2. Unsheltered women may find it easier than unsheltered men to find temporary housing in homes of friends, relatives, or boyfriend. This would prevent these women from being counted as homeless thereby reducing estimated numbers of women in total homeless populations.
3. Unsheltered women may conceal themselves more effectively than unsheltered men while on the streets, thereby eluding enumerators and reducing estimated numbers of women in total homeless populations.

TABLE 5-1

Demographic Characteristics of Three Populations: Residents of Baghdad Inn, Homeless Population of Arid Acropolis, and Census Population of the State (in percentages)

	Residents of Baghdad Inn[a]	Homeless Population of Arid Acropolis[b]	Census Population of the state
Living Arrangements			
Single Men	62.0	64.0	
Single Women	23.0	8.0	
Families	12.0	25.0	
Unaccompanied Youth	3.0	3.0	
Age			
0 to 4 Years	2.0		8.0[c]
5 to 14 Years	2.0		14.7[c]
15 to 34 Years	50.0		32.1[c]
35 to 44 Years	27.0		14.4[c]
45 to 64 Years	17.0		17.7[c]
65 Plus Years	1.0		13.0[c]
Race/Ethnicity			
White	60.0	47.0	80.8[d]
African American	18.0	14.0	3.0[d]
Hispanic	15.0	20.0	18.8[d]
Native American	6.0	-	5.6[d]
Other	1.0	19.0	1.5[d]
Labor Force Status			
Unemployed	88.0	45.0	5.4[e]
Employed	7.0	-	61.8[e]
Full-Time	3.0	-	-
Part-Time	4.0	-	-
Not in the Labor Force	5.0	-	32.8[e]
Educational Level			
11th Grade or Less	37.9[f]		-
High School Graduate	46.4[f]		80.6[d]
Some College	7.4[f]		-
Currently a Student	1.0[f]		-
College Graduate	6.3[f]		22.2[d]

[a] Based on a total of 8,617 guests in residence at Baghdad Inn from 1987-1990 (Askagrant 1990a).

[b] Source of data is United States Conference of Mayors (1991, table following page 62) *Status reports of hunger and homelessness in America's cities: 1991.*

[c] Source of data is *County and city extra* (Slater and Hall 1992, 50-51) .

TABLE 5-1

(Continued)

---

d Source of data is *Statistical abstract of the United States 1991* (U. S.
   Bureau of the Census 1991b, 22, 140).
e Source of data is *State and metropolitan area data book 1991* (U. S.
   Bureau of the Census 1991a, 242-43).
f Based on a total of 8,014 guests aged 20 years or older who resided at
   Baghdad Inn from 1987-1990 (Askagrant 1990a).

Hence, in terms of use, the shelter design creates an over-crowding of
space allocated to women. Homeless families residing at the shelter
under-represented the percentage of families in the homeless
population of Arid Acropolis. The fact that families comprise only
twelve percent of the shelter's resident population while constituting a
quarter of the homeless population of Arid Acropolis is partially
explained by the limited number of families that can be
accommodated. Despite the limited number of families who were
accommodated, over-crowded living conditions are created by the
shelter's design.

Residents at Baghdad Inn are generally young (Table 5-1), half
being 15 to 34 years of age. When compared to populations of the
State, the most striking differences were smaller numbers of children,
larger numbers of people aged 15 to 44, and smaller numbers of
individuals who were 65 or older residing in the shelter.

Ages of individuals residing at Baghdad Inn, when viewed in
smaller age groups (Table 5-2), showed similar trends. The largest
age group was composed of individuals 20 to 34 years of age at the
time they entered the shelter. The next largest group was the 35 to 44
age group. Children and teenagers (ages 0 to 19) accounted for seven
percent of the shelter population (Askagrant 1990a). It was not
possible to determine how many children and teenagers were members
of families and how many were living in the shelter unattended by
parents.

Of 603 children and teenagers who resided at Baghdad Inn from
1987 to 1990 (Table 5-2), forty-three percent were in the 15 to 19
years age group. Twenty-nine percent of children were infants aged 0
to 4 years; twenty-eight percent were children aged 5 to 14 years.
Table 5-1 highlights the relatively small number of children aged 0 to
14 present in the shelter; four percent of the 8,617 individuals who
resided at the Inn between 1987 and 1990, as compared to the State's
Census population, nearly twenty-three percent. This difference may
result from parents placing children with relatives or in foster homes
to prevent them from being homeless. Percentage of children aged 0
to 4 years is equal to the percent of children 5 to 14 in the shelter.

TABLE 5-2

Age Distribution of Residents of Baghdad Inn

Age	Number of Individuals	Percent
0 to 4 Years	172	2
5 to 9 Years	86	1
10 to 14 Years	86	1
15 to 19 Years	259	3
20 to 34 Years	4050	47
35 to 44 Years	2327	27
45 to 64 Years	1465	17
65 Plus Years	86	1

Based on a total of 8,617 guests in residence at Baghdad Inn from 1987-1990 (Askagrant 1990a).

However, when age groups are divided into four-year groupings; 0 to 4 years, 5 to 9 years, and 10 to 14 years, differences between groups appear. The number of children aged 0 to 4 (172) is twice the size of the 5 to 9 age group (86) and twice the size of the 10 to 14 age group (86). This variation in size of age groups may be the result of parents keeping infants with them while placing older children.

Small numbers of individuals 65 and older present in the shelter, when compared to Census data (Table 5-1), may be due to the fact that Arid Acropolis has a second shelter, the Manazo, designed specifically for elderly men and women. Therefore, if someone over 65 were to come to Baghdad Inn, attempts would be made to transfer them to Manazo, where their needs could be better met. Additionally, elderly individuals often have "safety nets" in forms of Social Security and pensions. This "net" may keep elderly from becoming homeless, or once they have become homeless, helps to get them off the streets and sheltered in permanent housing in a timely fashion.

Whites were the largest racial/ethnic group in the shelter (Table 5-1), while African Americans were almost equal to Hispanics in representation. Slightly more whites were located in shelter populations than were found in homeless populations of Arid Acropolis. However, they were under-represented when compared to Census data for the State. Conversely, African Americans were over-represented among both homeless populations for Arid Acropolis and Baghdad Inn when compared to populations of the State. The percentage of Hispanics present in Baghdad Inn were similar to representative percentages in homeless populations of Arid Acropolis as well as the population of the State. Native Americans contributed a percentage of residents to the shelter comparable to the percent of Native Americans living in the State.

Of the 8,617 residents of Baghdad Inn, the vast majority (88 percent) reported being unemployed at the time they entered the shelter (Table 5-1), as compared to 45 percent of the homeless population of Arid Acropolis. Unemployment rates for homeless populations of Arid Acropolis and Baghdad Inn were vastly greater than unemployment rates for domiciled populations of the State. Unfortunately, no data on jobs were available for employed individuals in the shelter.

Of the residents[1] aged 20 years or older, 3,533 individuals (37.9 percent) had not graduated from high school (Table 5-1). When compared with Census data, residents of Baghdad Inn tended to be under-educated with only forty-six percent having graduated from high school compared with over eighty percent of the State's population (Table 5-1).

1990 Survey Sample

Questions concerning marital status of individuals, length of time persons spent living in the State prior to coming to the shelter, length of time individuals had been homeless, and persons' residences prior to coming to the Inn were not asked during intake procedures. Therefore, in efforts to gain better understanding of shelter populations, Mr. Askagrant conducted a survey of 132 individuals who resided at Baghdad Inn in 1990 in which he asked these questions.[2]

Seventy-seven percent (102 respondents) of individuals from the 1990 Baghdad Inn sample (Askagrant 1990a) were not in marital relationships (Table 5-3). Half of those not in marital relationships (51 respondents) had never been married while forty-three percent (44 respondents) had been divorced (Table 5-3). Of the remaining 26 respondents only a small percent (6 percent) were currently married and living together, while 18 (69 percent) were separated when they entered the shelter.

Over fifty percent of the sample lived in the State less than one year (Table 5-3). Of the individuals who lived in the State less than one year, forty-seven percent lived in the State less than six months. Twenty-nine percent of the 132 individuals surveyed lived in the State one to nine years.

Respondents of the 1990 survey were asked how long they had been homeless before seeking shelter at Baghdad Inn. Most respondents were recent arrivals on the street (Table 5-3). Fifty-nine percent had been homeless less than six months. Twenty percent were homeless from one to four years, while seven percent were homeless more than five years.

Survey respondents were queried as to residences prior to entering the shelter. If they had not been living in a house before coming to the shelter they were asked where they had slept the night preceding shelter entry. Twenty-five individuals (19 percent) lived in their own house prior to entering the Inn (Table 5-3). One quarter of the individuals surveyed by Askagrant (1990a) lived in campgrounds prior to entering the shelter. Sixty-two individuals (47 percent)

TABLE 5-3

Characteristics of Homeless Individuals Residing at Baghdad Inn in 1990[a]

	Number of Individuals	Percent
Marital Status		
Never Married	51	39
Married	8	6
Separated	18	14
Divorced	44	33
Widowed	7	5
Not Ascertained	3	2
Time Spent in the State Prior to Shelter Stay		
Less than 1 Month	22	17
1 to 5 Months	40	30
6 to 11 Months	5	4
1 to 4 Years	24	18
5 to 9 Years	15	11
10 to 14 Years	5	4
15 to 19 Years	3	2
20 Years or More	16	12
Not Ascertained	3	2
Time Spent Homeless Prior to Shelter Stay		
Less than 1 Month	21	16
1 to 5 Months	57	43
6 to 11 Months	12	9
1 to 4 Years	26	20
5 to 9 Years	4	3
10 to 14 Years	1	1
15 to 19 Years	1	1
20 Years or More	3	2
Not Ascertained	7	5

Table 5-3
(Continued)

	Number of Individuals	Percent
Residence Prior to Shelter Stay		
Not Homeless	25	19
Campground	33	25
Riverbed/Desert	3	2
Car/Truck	18	14
Friend/Relative	5	4
Elsewhere in State	8	6
Another State	12	9
Other Shelter	8	6
Doorways/Streets	8	6
Do not Know/Not Ascertained	13	10
Nights Spent in the Shelter		
One Night	7	5
2 to 7 Nights	18	14
8 to 21 Nights	33	25
22 to 35 Nights	57	43
36 to 49 Nights	3	2
50 Nights or More	9	7
Not Ascertained	7	5

[a] Based on a survey sample of 132 of the estimated 8,805 men, women, and children who were in residence at Baghdad Inn during 1990 (Askagrant 1990a).

reported being unsheltered prior to entering the shelter; they lived in campgrounds, on the river bed, in the desert, in a car or truck, in doorways or on the streets. Living with friends or relatives (4 percent) was used only slightly less often than living in doorways or on the streets (6 percent).

Surveyed individuals were asked the number of nights they had been at the shelter. The modal stay in the shelter was from 22 to 35 nights (43 percent) (Table 5-3). Another quarter of respondents remained in the shelter from eight to twenty-one nights. Few surveyed individuals had remained at the shelter for more than 35 nights.

Summary

As demographic variables show, the majority of Baghdad Inn residents were single males. Families were slightly under-represented in the Inn's population as compared to the estimated number of families in homeless populations of Arid Acropolis. Residents were most likely to be young, aged 20 to 34 years old. Those who have completed high school are only slightly greater than residents who completed through the eleventh grade. Whites were the largest racial/ethnic group in the shelter; however, African Americans and Hispanics were over-represented when the shelter population was compared to Census data for the State.

Most residents of Baghdad Inn were unemployed. They were more likely to never have been married than to have been in marital relationships. Residents were recent arrivals to the State, with the largest percentage having been in the State for less than six months. Similarly, residents became homeless within one to five months prior to their arrival at the shelter. Before coming to the shelter, one quarter of residents had spent time living in campgrounds and 47 percent of residents had spent some time unsheltered. Upon arrival at the shelter, nearly half of the residents remained in the shelter from 22 to 35 nights.

Therefore, the picture became predominantly one of single, white, never-married, unemployed males who were recent arrivals to the State and to the condition of homelessness. These individuals were not domiciled prior to entering the shelter and spent at least 35 days in the shelter.

Characteristics of Parents in Parenting Classes

Askagrant's (1990a) survey included data on single men and single women living in the shelter. In order to describe families living in the shelter, characteristics of parents who participated in parenting class meetings are presented. This study's participant-observation of parenting classes at Baghdad Inn took place from 1988 to 1990. During that time I met 35 women who had male partners with them in the shelter, 64 single mothers, (women who did not have male partners with them in the shelter), and four single fathers.[3] The number of contacts with these parents ranged from single meetings to friendships which extended over a year and involved 40 to 50 encounters.

Mothers in Parenting Classes

Mothers who had male partners in the shelter with them were most likely to be white (46 percent) (Table 5-4).   African-American mothers in couples were over a third of the sample. Correspondingly, single mothers were most likely to be white (33 percent) while twenty-eight percent of single mothers were African American. This was not unlike the racial/ethnic makeup of the total shelter population as seen in Table 5-1. However, African-American mothers, single and in couples, constituted larger portions of the sample than did African-American residents of the total shelter population. Additionally, whites are under-represented in the sample when compared to the total shelter population

Smaller percentages classified as Hispanic mothers, compared to Hispanics in the shelter population generally, may be the result of self-selection process involving language.   Since neither the class facilitator nor myself could speak Spanish, mothers speaking Spanish only were not required to come to classes. During the two years of data gathering, twelve mothers spoke Spanish only.[4]

Women in couples overwhelmingly reported being married[5] to men they were with in the shelter (Table 5-4). Nine mothers living with partners but not married reported having relationships in which male partners participated in rearing of the children. One couple in which the male partner took an active role in educating and rearing two daughters had been living together for over eleven years (the age of their oldest daughter). Two women shortly after entering the shelter became engaged to male partners and, in another case, a couple had been engaged prior to entering the shelter.   Again, these mothers reported their partners participated fully in the education and rearing of the children.

Most single women indicated they had never been married (Table 5-4).   Three single women who reported being currently married had left abusive husbands and had been unable to gain admittance to domestic violence shelters. Rather than return home, they came to Baghdad Inn. Some single women reported a series of partners while at the shelter. Due to the brevity of these relationships, these women were considered single rather than in partnerships. Joan who had been living with a man entered the shelter as a single woman with children. In the five weeks she was at Baghdad Inn, she established a series of relationships with different male occupants of the shelter. In each instance Joan insisted that they were in long-term relationships and would assuredly be getting married soon. Another woman, Sara, who reported being in a relationship with a man in the shelter changed partners frequently in the time I knew her. However, Sara differed from Joan in that she did not see her relationships as long-term or involving any serious commitment from the men.

Table 5-4

**Characteristics of Mothers Attending Parenting Classes at
Baghdad Inn and Starlight Inn in the Late 1980s**

	Couples[a] (n=35)		Single[b] (n=64)	
	Number	Percent	Number	Percent
Race/Ethnicity of Mother				
White	16	46	21	33
African American	13	37	18	28
Hispanic	4	11	8	12
Native American	1	3	4	6
Other	1	3	5	8
Undetermined	-	-	8	12
Marital Status				
Married	23	66	3	5
Living Together	9	26	1	2
Separated	-	-	5	8
Divorced	-	-	3	5
In a Relationship	-	-	1	2
Engaged	3	9	-	-
Never Married	-	-	43	67
Undetermined	-	-	8	12

[a] Families in which mothers entered the shelter with male partners.
[b] Families in which mothers entered the shelter without male partners.

The Children

Numbers of children per mother present in the shelter was similar
for mothers in couples and single mothers (Table 5-5). Thirty seven
percent of women in couples and forty-one percent of single mothers
had one child with them in Baghdad Inn. Slightly over one-quarter of
the women in couples and single women had two children with them
in the shelter. A differing point between mothers in couples and
single mothers was the number of mothers in couples having three
children with them in the shelter. Fourteen percent of mothers in
couples versus only five percent of single mothers had three children
with them in the shelter.

Single mothers (19 percent) were more likely to have children
living elsewhere than were mothers in couples (15 percent) (Table 5-
5). Some mothers with children living elsewhere had children

TABLE 5-5

**Number and Living Arrangements of Children of Mothers
Attending Parenting Classes at Baghdad Inn
and Starlight Inn in the Late 1980s**

	Couples[a] (n=35)		Single[b] (n=64)	
	Number	Percent	Number	Percent
Number of Children in Families				
Living in the Shelter				
1	13	37	26	41
2	9	26	17	27
3	5	14	3	5
4 or More	2	6	3	5
None	-	-	6	9
Living Elsewhere				
1	-	-	6	9
2	3	9	4	6
3	-	-	1	2
4 or More	2	6	1	2
Undetermined	3	9	1	2

[a] Families in which mothers entered the shelter with male partners.
[b] Families in which mothers entered the shelter without male partners.

removed from their home by Child Protective Services for offenses, i.e., drug abuse, alcoholism, or endangerment. For example, Beth had her two older children placed with her mother by Child Protective Services, because of her estranged husband's drug abuse. Other mothers may ask relatives to care for their children rather than bring them into the shelter. Marjie left her sixteen year old daughter in the custody of her mother in order for the daughter to have a stable environment. During one especially hot summer, another mother allowed her ex-husband to take custody of their toddler, because the shelter was too hot for the baby to rest comfortably at night.

Children living in the shelter tended to be aged one to nine for mothers in couples and single mothers (Table 5-6). Thirty percent of children in couples' families were aged one to four, while fifteen percent were five to nine years old. Fifteen percent of children in families with single mothers were aged one to four with an additional fifteen percent aged five to nine. Sixteen percent of children in couples' families were under the age of one compared to thirteen percent for single mothers. Sixty-one percent of children living with their mothers and her male partner (mothers in couples) and forty-three percent of children living with their single mother in the shelter were under the age of ten.

Children living elsewhere tended to be older than children living in the shelter. None of the mothers living in couples or single mothers had children under the age of one living somewhere else (Table 5-6). Mothers in couples were more likely to place older children (11 percent) than were single mothers (2 percent).[6] For mothers in couples, children placed were most likely to be fifteen to nineteen-years-old. Two children placed by single mothers were both over five years of age.

Fathers in Parenting Classes

Single fathers in this sample were too few to allow any conclusions to be drawn regarding the general nature of single homeless fathers. However, they did make up a facet of the picture of homeless families and for this reason should not be ignored.

In this study only four single fathers attended parenting classes. Two were white, and two were African American. All four men were divorced or separated from their spouses when they entered the shelter. Three of the fathers had one child each and one father had two children. Children of these men were older than children of mothers in parenting classes with only one child being eighteen months. Two of the children were three years old while the final child was six. One of the fathers had placed his six-year old son with his ex-wife to protect the child from life on the streets and to provide the child a safer environment. The other three fathers had kept their children with them in the shelter.

Summary

Mothers in Baghdad Inn were more likely to enter the shelter as single mothers than to enter with male partners. Mothers, whether they were single or in couples, were most likely to be white. However, African-American mothers, single or in couples, did represent a significant proportion of the sample. Mothers in couples were most likely to report being married at the time they were in the shelter while single mothers were most likely to report having never been married.

TABLE 5-6

**Ages and Living Arrangements of Children of Mothers
Attending Parenting Classes at Baghdad Inn and
Starlight Inn in the Late 1980s**

	Couples[a] (n=67)		Single[b] (n=104)	
	Number	Percent	Number	Percent
Age of Children				
Living in the Shelter				
0-5 Months	7	10	11	11
6-11 Months	4	6	2	2
1-4 Years	20	30	16	15
5-9 Years	10	15	16	15
10-14 Years	5	7	5	5
15-19 Years	3	4	1	1
20+ Years	-	-	1	1
Undetermined	4	6	31	30
Living Elsewhere				
0-5 Months	-	-	-	-
6-11 Months	-	-	-	-
1-4 Years	1	1	-	-
5-9 Years	1	1	1	1
10-14 Years	2	3	-	-
15-19 Years	4	6	1	1
20+ Years	1	1	-	-
Undetermined	5	7	19	18

[a] Families in which mothers entered the shelter with male partners.
[b] Families in which mothers entered the shelter without male partners.

Most mothers in couples and single mothers had only one child with them in the shelter. Single mothers were more likely than mothers in couples to have children living somewhere other than Baghdad Inn. Children living in the shelter tended to be younger than children who were living elsewhere. Children in the shelter tended to be younger than nine years old. Conversely children from couples' families living elsewhere were more likely to be older than nine years. Children from single mothers' families living elsewhere were five years or older.

This chapter has presented a demographic portrait of the homeless individuals who lived at Baghdad Inn and descriptions of parents who attended parenting classes. The next chapter describes how families found their way to the Inn.

Notes

1. Educational levels of shelter population were calculated by Askagrant (1990a) using the entire population of the shelter (8,617 homeless persons) from 1987 to 1990 including infants and young children. Seven percent (603 residents) of the residents of Baghdad Inn from 1987 to 1990 are school age or younger. Therefore, to make Askagrant's data comparable with educational attainment of the State population, infants and children currently of school age needed to be removed from Askagrant's data. Educational attainment was then calculated using those individuals aged 20 years and older.

2. Unfortunately, information as to how Mr. Askagrant selected his sample of 132 individuals was not available from the report. Since publication of the report, Mr. Askagrant had been terminated from the shelter staff, and I was unable to locate him for clarification of his research methods.

3. As a result of the larger number of mothers in comparison to the number of fathers with whom I had contact, discussion of the sample was couched in terms of women. Information regarding fathers is presented in the text but their numbers were too small to be of value in understanding male parents.

4. Eight women were classified as "undetermined." They were women who came to one parenting class, left during the break, and never returned. Therefore, because brief contact provided only the most limited field notes, many characteristics were not recorded.

5. Five mothers in couples consistently reported being married over several meetings. However, other mothers in the shelter informed me these couples had never legally been married. In spite of the legal definition of their relationship, these five mothers considered themselves married and were included in the category "married."

6. The disparity in numbers of children living elsewhere between Tables 5-5 and 5-6 is due to the inability to ascertain or learn the ages of the single mothers' children (see undetermined in the age category in Table 5-6).

CHAPTER 6

Household Careers of Homeless Families

The preceding chapter, *Shelter Guests*, provided a demographic description of the homeless population of Arid Acropolis, the homeless population of Baghdad Inn, and mothers and fathers who participated in parenting classes at Baghdad Inn and Starlight Inn. This chapter traces household careers of families explaining how they became homeless and the process they followed in efforts to regain a domicile.

Descriptions of paths which families have taken in finding their way to Baghdad Inn provides facets of characteristics missed by demographics discussed in the last chapter. They provide glimpses into the lives and struggles of families prior to coming to the shelter. These paths are not necessarily painless bus rides from apartments or houses to the door step of the shelter. Rather, the stories demonstrate distressing decisions mothers and/or fathers made as they struggled to maintain domiciled existences. The desperation families feel as they open the door to a shelter is reflected through these stories.

Researchers' attempts to delineate routes taken from being domiciled to being homeless have provided only limited glimpses of different paths. These reports suggest no single pathway eclipses all others. Instead, pathways to homelessness can best be described as recurring themes (Cohen and Sokolovsky 1989; Wolch and Dear 1993). Rossi (1989b) and Hope and Young (1986) suggested two or three step processes of (a) losing family domiciles to (b) living with friends or relatives to (c) eventually residing in shelters or on the streets. Bassuk (1986) and Alter et al. (1986) introduced living in welfare hotels or motels as a step between doubling up and shelter or street living. Baum and Burnes (1993, 51) suggest that homeless mothers endure cycles of homelessness that include shelters, hotels, or motels, doubling up with relatives or friends, and in a few cases, sleeping in cars or on the streets." Culhane and Fried (1988) provided the most complex path from disruption in families lives, through efforts to maintain homes, and, eventually, to doubling up. Initial disruption results from business failures, divorces, spousal abuses, job losses, or evictions. Families faced with economic stresses struggle to maintain stability finally moving in with family or friends. Once asked to leave those households, homeless families will live in cheap rented rooms or cars until finally obtaining beds in shelters.

The diverse paths taken by families as they become homeless are represented in Figures 6-1a, 6-1b, and 6-1c. Figure 6-1a are paths most likely to be taken by homeless families even when other alternative paths are available. Families faced with homelessness make valiant attempts to keep themselves and their children off the streets and out of shelters. In efforts to do this, they frequently rent rooms at progressively cheaper hotels, motels, or Single Room Occupancy units. A second alternative is to move in with friends or relatives (doubling up) for as long as possible. This alternative may be attempted immediately after loss of the family home or only after family funds have been exhausted by attempts to remain independent in motel/hotel/SRO rooms. Families who have exhausted their savings or outstayed their welcome in homes of relatives or friends are faced with the prospect of living in shelters. The first shelter to which they are introduced is an emergency shelter. From here it is the goal to move them to a transitional shelter where they can eventually gain temporary housing. Temporary housing may eventually develop into stable housing as families begin to recover financially. Unfortunately, it is plausible that families will lose temporary housing because of job loss, loss of benefits from governmental programs, or other financial setbacks and once again enter an emergency shelter.

Figure 6-1b represents paths taken by homeless families when other alternatives are not available. A result of doubling up could be the ability of families to save funds needed to rent homes of their own. Therefore, some families may never get admitted into the shelter system. Additionally, although less probable, after having spent time in hotels, motels, or SROs, families are able to rent apartments or houses and move directly into stable housing. In addition, families who have been doubling up may find themselves moving to motels, hotels, or SROs when they are no longer able to remain with friends or relatives and no other alternative is readily available. Families who have lost temporary housing may also find themselves doubling

Figure 6-1a

Household Careers of Homeless Families

**Movements most likely to be made by homeless families
even when other alternative paths are available**

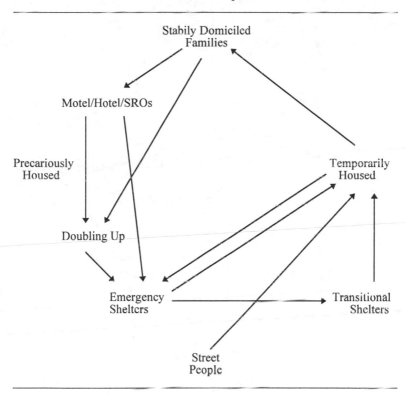

Terms:

Precariously Housed: Motel/Hotel/Single Room Occupancy Motels/
'Doubling Up'
Emergency Shelters: Public Shelters/Private Shelters/Winter Shelters
(Armories)
Street People: Autos/Tents/Parks/Empty Lots/Under Bridges
Transitional Shelters: Public Shelters/Private Shelters/Pocket Shelters (run
by Churches)
Temporarily Housed: Doubling Up/HUD-Sponsored Housing/Section 8
Housing

Figure 6-1b

Household Careers of Homeless Families

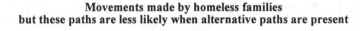

**Movements made by homeless families
but these paths are less likely when alternative paths are present**

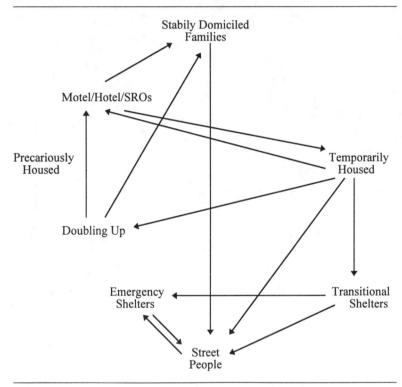

Terms:

Precariously Housed: Motel/Hotel/Single Room Occupancy Motels/ 'Doubling Up'

Emergency Shelters: Public Shelters/Private Shelters/Winter Shelters (Armories)

Street People: Autos/Tents/Parks/Empty Lots/Under Bridges

Transitional Shelters: Public Shelters/Private Shelters/Pocket Shelters (run by Churches)

Temporarily Housed: Doubling Up/HUD-Sponsored Housing/Section 8 Housing

Figure 6-1c

Household Careers of Homeless Families

Movements which are possible for homeless families to make but are highly implausible because of restricting factors such as agency policies and loss of family assistance

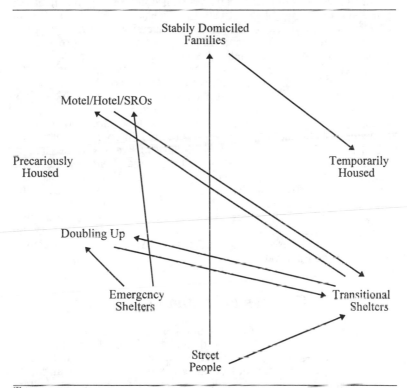

Terms:

Precariously Housed: Motel/Hotel/Single Room Occupancy Motels/ 'Doubling Up'

Emergency Shelters: Public Shelters/Private Shelters/Winter Shelters (Armories)

Street People: Autos/Tents/Parks/Empty Lots/Under Bridges

Transitional Shelters: Public Shelters/Private Shelters/Pocket Shelters (run by Churches)

Temporarily Housed: Doubling Up/HUD-Sponsored Housing/Section 8 Housing

up with family and friends or moving into motels, hotels, or SROs. Another possibility for families living in temporary housing is to move onto the streets joining families who have resided in emergency shelters, transitional shelters, or less probable, who have recently been stably domiciled.

The final series of pathways are those which are possible but highly implausible because of restricting factors such as agency policies and loss of family assistance (Figure 6-1c). These pathways include families moving from motels/hotels/SROs, doubling up with relatives or friends, or living on the streets into transitional shelters. Where transitional shelters exist, families are generally required to spend time in emergency shelters while completing intake procedures. These intake procedures help recognize particular needs thereby identifying the transitional shelter best suited to meeting those needs. To be moved immediately into transitional shelters without processing through emergency shelters would be unusual. Just as unlikely is a move from emergency or transitional shelters into unstable housing situations such as living in motels, hotels, SROs, or homes of families or friends. Shelter staff and administrators would counsel against this type of move since it would most likely lead to a return to the shelter. In addition, many families who are living in the shelter system have already doubled up with relatives or friends and have been asked to leave. Additionally, families in the shelter system rarely have the funds available for protracted stays in motels, hotels, or SROs.

These potential paths represent the diversity of possible routes that homeless families take in search for shelters. A sampling of the variety of stories presented by homeless families can be found among the residents of Baghdad Inn.

Household Careers of Baghdad Inn Families

These descriptions of routes from homes to the streets fail to capture the variety of routes from domiciled life to life on the streets or in shelters. Rather, paths to homelessness represent a continuum. Some individuals and families do in fact move from living in homes or apartments to living in automobiles, on the streets, or in shelters specifically designed to aid the homeless population. Many others, however, experience a variety of alternative housing arrangements in efforts to avoid homelessness, as can be seen from Figures 6-1a, 6-1b, and 6-1c.

Precariously Housed

Homeless individuals or families may first use their own funds to pay for temporary housing in a series of motels and hotels of diminishing inhabitability, represented by the Precariously Housed in Figures 6-1a, 6-1b, and 6-1c.

> **Priscilla,**[1] her husband, and two children entered Baghdad Inn after a series of devastating financial blows starting with the loss of their family home. After the family home was lost to fire on Halloween night, the family was placed in a local motel by a charitable organization. This placement was for a period of seven days to allow the family to locate an apartment and obtain the necessary household items. Since the husband was working a forty-hour week, it was left to Priscilla to locate an apartment. During one of her excursions, Priscilla and her eldest son were involved in a car accident which left them both suffering from whiplash. The injuries made it difficult for Priscilla to travel the distances necessary to view apartments. Consequently, the family had not located an apartment at the end of the week. Faced with the loss of the motel room, the family was left with few alternatives. The family left the motel room provided by charity and moved into a motel room provided at their expense. After a single night in this motel room the family sought refuge at Baghdad Inn. This family lived at the shelter for about four months until they were able to find an affordable apartment. The income from the husband's full-time job enhanced their ability to secure housing in such a short time.

As this family demonstrates, believing the homeless condition is temporary, families often rent rooms in hotels or motels until they can find better, more permanent accommodations. Families unable to find alternative housing are often forced to move to a hotel or motel that is less expensive and also less inhabitable. Families may proceed through a variety of such hotels/motels until savings are depleted or further financial problems create a lack of funds. When funds are depleted families are faced with moving in with relatives/friends, moving to shelters, or living on the streets. In a few cases families may be able to qualify for the Department of Housing and Urban Development[2] or HUD-sponsored housing or Section 8[3] supported housing, thereby becoming at least precariously housed in single family homes or apartments.

Faced with these alternatives, some individuals and\or families will "double up." In this strategy families or individuals live with friends or family members as "guests" for an unspecified amount of time. Four alternative strategies are nested within the strategy of doubling up.

First, parents may respond to homelessness by leaving any number of their children with relatives while they search for shelter thereby protecting children from experiences of being homeless and living in shelters or on the streets.

Marjie, a single mother of three children, had attempted to live with her own single mother. Marjie and her mother had frequent conflicts regarding educational goals. Her mother insisted Marjie attend a professional school for an advanced degree; Marjie disagreed. The turmoil finally drove Marjie out of her mother's home and into the shelter. However, Marjie left her teenage daughter in the care of her mother. It was Marjie's belief that her daughter needed to have a stable home and school life during her teens. Marjie's two younger children accompanied her to the shelter.

Second, entire families may reside in homes of relatives. However, this alternative often is beset with strain for both families and often ends with "guest" families moving out of the homes.

Bev, a single mother of two, had entered the shelter after attempting to live in the homes of her relatives. The first home she resided in was that of her mother and father. Her father is an alcoholic who had physically and sexually abused Bev as a child. During the time Bev and her children lived with her parents, her father resumed his physical abuse of Bev. Additionally, during periods of drunkenness, her father would throw all Bev's belongings out on the front lawn. At these times he would threaten to lock Bev out of the house. Fearful for her safety as well as the safety of her children, Bev moved from her parent's home to the home of her grandmother. After a brief time her elderly grandmother was unable to continue providing room for Bev and her children. It was at this time that Bev and her children entered the shelter. Bev continued to use the grandmother's home for periodic short stays. One such stay was a weekend visit following her great-grandfather's funeral.

Bev's weekend stay with her grandmother demonstrates the third alternative of doubling up. The home of the relative is used for short-term refuge of an evening or weekend, such as at Christmas. This provides homeless families with time to perform rituals important to families or with time to physically and emotionally recover from stresses of shelter living or living on the streets.

James, a single father of one small boy, arrived at Baghdad Inn after having lost his house through the financial mismanagement of his estranged wife. He frequently spent a weekend at the home of his mother. James explained his visits were a method of surviving shelter life. "Sometimes I just have to get away. These people [the other people in the shelter] really get to me. I just can't stand it here any longer so I get some food and go to my mother's for the day."

Fourth, persons may use homes of friends or relatives to store material objects for easy retrieval as needed.

Peaches was a single mother with two toddlers. She had lived in two separate shelters prior to coming to Baghdad Inn. Peaches had been evicted from her home when she was unable to pay her bills. She did, however, manage to take some of her belongings with her. These included articles of baby furniture, clothing, and an old television set. Unable to carry these items with her from shelter to shelter, Peaches placed them in temporary storage at a friend's apartment. She retrieved the items as needed and returned them when necessary.

Emergency Shelters

Families and individuals who have been precariously housed are often unable to maintain these arrangements until they can regain permanent housing. At the time they are evicted from homes of family members, friends, or from rented rooms, families must again search for shelter. For some this will be space in emergency shelters.

Others when initially confronted with losses of homes immediately attempt to provide themselves with emergency housing through private charitable sectors, i.e., churches, Salvation Army, or Red Cross (Emergency Shelters in Figure 6-1a, 6-1b, and 6-1c), or public emergency shelters such as Baghdad Inn. A couple with two children were traveling across the country looking for work. Their vehicle became disabled in Arid Acropolis. The couple were able to fix the car, but it required most of their savings. They came to Baghdad Inn in an effort to provide shelter for their children. Within three months both parents had secured employment and had saved enough to allow them to move into an apartment.

Emergency shelters are designed to provide shelter for only short periods of time, usually 30 days. Families at Baghdad Inn are allowed to stay longer as long as they work on goals set out in their case management plan. Two families remained at Baghdad Inn for a year. During this time, the family, with the aid of shelter staff, attempted to find housing and were actively involved in searching for employment. In other words the purpose of emergency shelter systems is to move families to another stage within the career pattern. Families could use a series of emergency shelters before moving to another stage, thus making their stay within this stage short term (at least four families remained in Baghdad Inn for only 2 days) or more extensive (it is possible for families to remain several months at this stage by moving from one emergency shelter to another).

Joanne was a married mother with one teenage child in the shelter. She became homeless when her husband was incarcerated in the State prison. Joanne spent nearly one year in residence at Baghdad Inn during which time she spent only minimal efforts on securing housing. She commented, "I will wait until my husband is home again before I get a house. If I got one now he might not like it and I would just have to leave." When faced with eviction from Baghdad Inn, Joanne did not increase her efforts at securing housing, instead leaving that task to her case manager. In the end the case manager secured her housing in another family shelter in Arid Acropolis.[4]

Transitional Shelters

After initial intake periods at Baghdad Inn, during which shelters are explained to families (for a complete discussion, see Chapter 7), families may be moved into more long-term housing from which it is hoped they will proceed into domiciled existence (Transitional Shelters in Figures 6-1a, 6-1b, and 6-1c).

> **Angela** and **Sam** and their two young girls had spent six months at Baghdad Inn when they were requested to leave. In spite of many failed attempts to secure housing, they faced eviction without a place to turn. Their case manager began a search on behalf of the family and was able to place them in a pocket shelter.[5]

Purposes of transitional shelters, such as pocket shelters, are to provide families with living conditions resembling stable domiciled conditions so families can adopt more traditional family patterns, provide time so one or both parents can obtain employment, provide time to accumulate funds needed to rent apartments, and/or provide time for families to complete necessary paperwork for State and Federal programs, i.e., Section 8 housing, HUD-sponsored housing, Aid to Families with Dependent Children or AFDC payments, food stamps, and so forth. From these types of shelters families are expected to be able to move into their own homes. Angela and Sam had not achieved that goal three months later when this study ended.

Temporarily Housed

Families may move from Emergency Shelters or Transitional Shelters into homes provided through welfare systems (Temporarily Housed in Figures 6-1a, 6-1b, and 6-1c). This housing is subsidized by Federal and State governments through programs such as Section 8 housing where all or portions of rent are paid by the Government. Additionally housing may be subsidized by private parties through HUD programs in which private individuals sponsor families. Under this program families are supplied with houses and private parties guarantee payments of rent and utilities during the families' stays. This type of housing is not permanent although it may become so, especially in cases of HUD-sponsored programs. The purpose is to provide families with housing until such time they are able to provide housing on their own.

> **Judy** was a single mother of two school age children. She was able to benefit from this type of program. Judy was living at Baghdad Inn for three months. In spite of working a full time job, Judy was unable to save enough money to afford rent and, because of the long waiting lists for public housing, could not visualize the day she would be able to leave the shelter. During the Christmas holidays a sponsor became available. It was through the aid of this individual that Judy and her two children were able to move from the shelter into a single family home.

Street People

At any point during the household career these alternatives may disappear, at which time these same families in all likelihood will face life on the streets (Street People in Figure 6-1a, 6-1b, and 6-1c).

> I originally met **Elaine** and **Steve** at parenting classes when I first started my volunteer work. At that time they were residents at the shelter. Shortly after I met them they received some money which allowed them to rent an apartment. After the money was exhausted they lost the apartment and returned to the shelter. This stay was marked by infrequent weekend stays at local cheap hotels with the couple and their small boy returning to the shelter on Monday night when their money was gone. After five months Elaine and Steve were asked to leave Baghdad Inn. At this time they moved into an apartment with some of Steve's friends. It was not long before the friends lost that apartment for not paying their rent. After a couple of nights at a second friend's apartment, Elaine and Steve showed up outside Baghdad Inn living in a car they had purchased. The car had mechanical problems which prevented it from running except on very rare occasions. The car was eventually towed away by the police as an abandoned vehicle (primarily because it had not been moved for over two weeks). As a result of a regulation of Baghdad Inn which requires a year to elapse prior to reentry into the shelter, Elaine, Steve, and their small boy were forced onto the streets. I lost contact with the couple at this point, and my informants were unable to determine what had happened to them.

As this story demonstrates, at this stage families are found living in the family car, a tent city, train stations, bus depots, under bridges, abandoned and/or condemned buildings, or in the open without any shelter.

Some families move back and forth through stages with great fluidity. Presented with changing situations, families select alternatives which appear to provide the best solution to their problems. Families do not follow single direct routes from stable domiciled existences to homeless life on the streets or in shelters but move through various living arrangements in their career as homeless families.

This chapter described steps families may take to avoid homelessness and, once homeless, steps families may take in efforts to regain housing. Included were descriptions of the types of organizations or shelters families may depend on during their struggles. Families entering shelters encounter many problems associated with being homeless and living in shelters with many other families. The next chapter investigates problems and responses to them.

Notes

1. Names of mothers, fathers, and children have been changed and characteristics distorted to protect their identities. Following convention, the names of the mother and/or father are printed in bold the first time they are used in the text.

2. The Department of Housing and Urban Development (HUD) administers a housing subsidy program where low-income families are provided with cash payments to help pay their rents (Ringheim 1990). "Households with incomes at or below 80 percent of the median renter income for a local geographical area are eligible (Burt 1992, 94) to receive the payments "and households below 50 percent of area median (very low income) have priority" (Burt 1992, 94) in having eligibility defined.

3. Section 8 is a federally funded rent subsidy program. It differs from the HUD program in that vouchers are provided to eligible families rather than cash payments. Recipients of vouchers "are required to find housing that meets certain quality standards and that rents for no more than a specified 'fair market rent'" (Carliner 1987, 121).

4. This particular movement from shelter to shelter is called 'shelter hopping' by service providers in Arid Acropolis.

5. Pocket shelters are houses or apartments supplied most often by churches or other charitable organizations to single families or small number of families.

CHAPTER 7

The Shelterization Process

The previous chapter described the many paths that families may take into homelessness. Although paths vary somewhat, all the families in this study eventually stayed at Baghdad Inn or Starlight Inn, where they faced the challenges of living with many other homeless families, finding employment, obtaining homes, and maintaining family life. Responses and reactions of adult family members, when first assessed, appeared to be idiosyncratic. However, upon further study some similarities began to surface. Looking at similarities in characteristics regarding families' homelessness and total time spent in the shelters, similarities began to coalesce into stages. The goal for homeless families is movement toward regaining domiciles, not progression through these stages. The often times bumpy progression through stages results from experiences of families while homeless and sheltered.

"I Really Don't Belong Here"

Upon arrival at Baghdad Inn[1] families begin the shelter's intake process. During this week-long process the family members are assigned beds in appropriate dorms and assigned to case managers. Case managers are available between the hours of eight A.M. and five P.M. Monday through Friday. During these times family case managers meet with incoming families to explain the rules of the shelter. If families enter on weekends or late at night, staff members explain the rules[2] and assign chores to adult family members. Chores consist of housekeeping duties such as sweeping or mopping floors of their dorms, cleaning restrooms, and the family kitchen.

Families meet with case managers for the first time during their first week at the shelter. At this meeting case managers outline rules of the shelter, consequences for violating rules, the appeals process,[3] and the procedures families are expected to follow during their stay. The procedures include meeting with the case manager on a weekly basis, developing a case plan, and working on the specific goals of the case plan. Through this process case managers explain behaviors that are expected from family members as well as those behaviors which are not tolerated.

Activities of families during the first week are focused on adjusting to shelter life (Figure 7-1). Families must not only memorize official rules of the shelter but mothers must master unofficial rules of other mothers residing at the shelter. They learn which mothers are willing to furnish information regarding service agency location, explain how to fill out forms required by these agencies, supply locations of clothing and food banks, and provide emotional support. Furthermore, new mothers learn which mothers can not be relied upon for information or support and which mothers prefer to be left alone.

During this first week families who had never lived in homeless shelters express confidence that the current shelter (homeless) situation will exist only for a short time before they will be in homes of their own. They feel the only obstruction keeping them from being housed are the lack of jobs.

> **Laura**, a single mother accompanied by one child, arrived at the shelter reluctant to accept help. This was her first episode of homelessness, and she intended it to be her last. She expressed humiliation in having to ask for a place to stay and made it clear through her statements to me that she did not want any additional help. She expressed confidence in her ability to gain employment, and once employed to be able to afford her own apartment. True to her word, Laura did begin a new job while in the shelter and moved into an apartment within three months of our first meeting.

When I met families for the first time they went to great lengths to explain the circumstances which brought them to the shelter. When introduced to Maria, she explained she had left her home in an effort to escape an abusive husband. After she left home she attempted to enter a domestic violence shelter but found them to be full. Rather than return home Maria came to Baghdad Inn with her two children looking for assistance.

Figure 7-1

**Graphic Representation of Stages and
Movement Between Stages**

Homeless families enter the shelter.

Stage 1

"I Really Don't Belong Here."
Families are assigned beds, learn rules of the shelter,
and have first meetings with case managers.

Families realize how long it will take
to get redomiciled.

Stage 2

"Why Doesn't Someone Help?"
Families experience anger when they realize case
managers and shelter staff do not see they are different
from other homeless families.

Families accept that it is going to take
time to complete paper work and
receive housing vouchers. They
recognize the importance of case plans
in obtaining goals and feel they are
in control of their futures.

Stage 3

"Following the Steps Will Get Me Out of Here."
Families actively attempt to meet case plan goals by
filing paper work, attending GED classes, and
applying for jobs. Attempts made to find time to
interact and communicate as a family.

Families see other homeless families
receive housing subsidies and move
out of the shelter. Also, they
experience lack of success in finding
employment.

Figure 7-1

(Continued)

Stage 4

"No Matter What I Do I Can't Get Out."
Families work on case plan goals as a matter of
routine. Adults are compliant with rules and demands
of the shelter and shelter staff.

> Families experience a sense of
> rejection from potential employers,
> shelter staff, and relatives. Families
> have lost close contact with relatives.
> They have experienced one or more
> episodes of homelessness.

Stage 5

"I Guess This is Home for Now."
Case plans are not seen as a means of escaping
homelessness, rather as a means of remaining in the
shelter. When faced with shelter eviction, families
depend on case managers to find them alternative
housing.

As described in Chapter 6, **Priscilla** arrived at Baghdad Inn with
her husband and two children after suffering a series of
devastating financial crises. At the time of our introduction,
Priscilla offered the complete story of her passage from renting a
house to living in the shelter. At first she dominated the
conversation, but she became subdued when she had explained
the desperate attempts her family had made in an effort to remain
in a home of their own. She admitted being impatient with other
mothers and staff of Baghdad Inn, and she relentlessly pushed her
husband to save enough money so they could move into a new
home.

As demonstrated by the stories of Maria and Priscilla, explanations of their presence at Baghdad Inn are offered when introduced to someone new, generally without prompting.

Time spent relating stories seems to be an effort (a) to explain they are not living in the shelter by choice, nor is it their fault they are in the shelter, as demonstrated by the stories of Maria and Priscilla, (b) to support their belief the shelter stay will only be temporary, that with the first employment check they will be leaving the shelter as illustrated by Laura's narrative, and (c) to separate themselves from the negative image the listener may have of welfare and/or homeless families. During parenting classes, Maria kept reminding members of the class she should be living in a domestic violence shelter and not a shelter for homeless families since, in her words, "I am not homeless."

"Why Doesn't Someone Help?"

After the first week has passed, families enter the second stage of activity at the shelter (Figure 7-1). It is assumed by shelter staff and case managers that families understand the rules and duties while staying at the shelter.

In the second week families must have their second meeting with case managers. At these meetings adult family members attempt to isolate personal problems that plunged them into homelessness and ultimately brought them to the shelter. Once these problems have been identified case managers assist families in developing case plans. The purpose of case plans are to provide steps designed to move families from shelters to domiciled existences. Case plans focus on immediate causes of homelessness, i.e., personal problems identified earlier. Case plans may include treatment for adult family members who exhibit alcohol or drug abuse problems, job training for adult members, and/or GED classes for members who lack high school education. In addition to these goals, case plans also include directives for conducting job searches, enrolling children in school, attending parenting classes, applying for federal and state assistance, i.e., welfare, food stamps, or AFDC, and requesting housing assistance.

Families frequently lose important records as they move from domiciled lives to shelters and a homeless existence. Therefore, families are requested to fill out forms requesting duplicates of official documents, i.e., birth certificates, immunization records for children, social security cards, disability forms from physicians, and marriage licenses or divorce decrees where applicable. These records are required by various agencies to prove eligibility for programs, obtain jobs, or enroll children in schools. In addition, families are busy setting appointments to meet with welfare and housing officials in order to begin processes required to receive aid. As a result, during the second and third weeks, families begin to gather a myriad of forms needed in order to obtain assistance.

Faced with the prospect of filling out overwhelming numbers of forms, mothers began to express anger and resentment toward society, shelter administrators and staff, and other mothers. Mothers expressed anger in parenting classes by not providing any information to Babette[4] or myself regarding themselves or their children and spent class time with arms crossed in angry defiance. When I pressed them to provide their names, they did so reluctantly.

> I met **Toni** during her second week in the shelter. In the introductions at the beginning of class Toni introduced herself as Mr. Clancy's wife. Only after encouragement did she provide us with her first name. At this time she expressed intense anger at having to be in class and informed the facilitator and myself she could not be forced to participate. Therefore, I was unable to gain any information regarding her children or her history.

Families express anger that the society in which they have worked and to which they feel they have contributed appears to be uncaring; living in the shelter for so long is the result of its neglect.

> **John** and **Joan** lived in Baghdad Inn with their two children. They were in their late 40's thus making them older than the average resident at the shelter. During a conversation regarding shelter life, John expressed anger over having to live in a shelter. He had been a truck driver prior to coming to the shelter and felt betrayed by a country he felt he had served well. "A man works most of his life and pays taxes, doesn't ask for much, and when he needs help he has to come to a place like this. I think it's a crime."

Resentment is frequently expressed. The objects of resentment are many--shelter staff, any professional from outside the shelter (i.e., State health services case managers, welfare workers, special workshop instructors, and volunteers), and other families and individuals in the shelter and on the streets. I was included in the list of offenders. In parenting classes I explained to mothers the research I was conducting. After one introduction, Janice confronted me by stating, "We are tired of being studied. People are always studying us. Quit studying us and buy me a home! Then you will be helpful!"

> **Peaches** expressed frustration by angrily denouncing the required participation in parenting classes. In the early part of the parenting class meeting, she frequently informed the facilitator and myself that she did not need parenting classes and should not have to attend. In addition, it was not uncommon for her to verbally attack other mothers in parenting classes for their views

on topics being discussed. Peaches didn't hesitate to denigrate comments of other mothers as frivolous.

Donna K. was a single mother with two children. When she first appeared in class she would not give us her real name, instead she provided the parenting class facilitator and me with several different first names, never a last name. After four class meetings she finally provided us with her real name explaining that she trusted no one and preferred for no one to know her. During classes Donna sat straight-backed in her chair with her arms crossed, participating only when there was no escape. During her first class meetings, Donna frequently complained shelter staff had been unfair in correcting behaviors of various residents. Additionally, she complained bitterly that shelter administrators were not performing their duties in providing for the needs of residents.

This phase of adjustment is short-lived, lasting, on the average, two weeks. During this phase it is difficult to gather information concerning the mothers' relationships or contacts with family or spouse. The end of this phase or stage is marked by adults' willingness to follow case plans developed in cooperation with case managers.

"Following the Steps Will Get Me Out of Here"

As mothers began to recognize case plans as a directive for obtaining homes of their own, they began to follow the steps set forward in those plans (Figure 7-1). The first step for most families is to fill out all the forms they have acquired. Once the forms are completed they are returned to the various agencies.

The process of returning the forms necessitates mothers making appointments at appropriate agencies, arranging for bus tokens or other forms of transportation, arranging for childcare if children are not in school or daycare, and traveling from one agency to another, meeting with one official after another. Mothers experience frustration since they usually must wait at each agency to be seen by appropriate officials. Once in the offices they are asked additional questions. While attempting to answer questions, officials make notes in the margins of applications. Upon completion of the meeting, officials normally tell them it takes three to four weeks to process applications and that they will hear from the agency as to eligibility. Mothers leave frustrated, exhausted, and facing a bus trip back to the shelter. Time spent traveling to agencies and waiting for appointments reduces the number of agencies mothers are able to visit to one or two a day. Thus, the process of returning all paperwork and meeting with officials may take two or more weeks to complete.

Adults also attempt to meet additional requirements of case plans by going to Learning Centers and enrolling in GED classes, registering for job training programs, attending parenting classes, signing up at the job placement office located at the shelter, and/or filling out job applications. During this process, adults meet with case managers on a weekly basis[5] to report progress and solve problems they have encountered.

Mothers of families at this stage desperately attempt to keep family life as normal as possible by arranging family meetings and family time somewhere outside the shelter. They energetically work at including husbands (who are living downstairs in separate shelters) in decisions concerning the children. Additionally, families have difficulty adjusting to shelter living and experience stresses of shelter living in forms of depression.

> **Charlene** was living in Baghdad Inn with her husband and two teenage children. Since the husband had been able to secure employment, the family was waiting for his next paycheck, which would allow them to move into their own apartment. As the time spent waiting in the shelter lengthened, Charlene began to experience problems related to stresses of waiting and commented to me, "I almost lost it last night. I thought I was going crazy. If it had not been for the other mothers, I'm not sure what I would have done. We have to move out of here and soon."

> A husband and father of two commented he had to get his seven year old son out of the working men's dorm "no matter what the cost." His son was not able to sleep and had requested that his father stay awake in order to protect him from other male shelter dwellers.

The process of filing the proper paper work makes adults aware of the complexity of tasks before them. Prior to this point, mothers expressed certainty they would not have to remain in the shelter long. Once paperwork is completed they are sure they will be moving from the shelter. However, as they traveled from agency to agency and were informed of the length of time required to process requests for assistance, mothers became aware that their stay in the shelter would be longer than they originally assumed.

> **Twila** had been a resident at Baghdad Inn for three months at the time I met her. She had received a voucher for housing supplied by a program which worked with individual community sponsors. This program matches an individual sponsor from the community to a homeless family. The sponsor agrees to provide a home for a homeless family free of charge or at minimal expense to the homeless family. The sponsor guarantees payment of utility bills and taxes on the dwelling for a period of two years. Upon

receipt of the voucher in November, Twila immediately began looking for a suitable home. She had initially expected to move into a home of her own by the first of December. As December approached and Twila had been unable to locate a house that met the sponsor's requirements, she expressed frustration and anger but still maintained the belief she would be in a home by Christmas. After celebrating Christmas at Baghdad Inn, she commented she was getting tired of trying to meet the sponsor's demands and was getting frustrated with the length of time the process was taking. At this time, after having located several homes and having the sponsor turn down the dwelling for a variety of reasons, Twila began paperwork to receive Section 8 housing. This brought more frustration as she learned how long it would be before she would receive a Section 8 voucher. Fortunately, she was able move into a house approved by the community sponsor the following March.

As Twila's story demonstrated, the waiting time before receiving housing became apparent to adult family members as they began the formal process. Prior to returning completed forms, many families continued to hold the belief that it will only be a week or two before they are able to move from the shelter into houses or apartments. After learning of the length of the waiting lists for housing vouchers as well as the length of time it takes to process applications, families became more cognizant of the amount of time it takes before they would be able to move from the shelter.

Additionally, adult members recognized difficulties they faced in finding employment with salaries adequate enough to afford housing.

Betsy, a single mother with one child, frequently complained that many of the "good jobs" had already been filled before she was able to fill out the application form. On those occasions when she was early enough to fill out an application, she felt she was disadvantaged by the condition of her donated clothing or by her disheveled appearance which resulted from riding a bus and then walking several blocks in the heat. Betsy was concerned she would not be able to find employment and would have to remain in the shelter for an extended period.

Families at this stage often have frequent contacts with extended family. Homeless families often use extended family homes as places for weekend visits or holiday retreats from shelter life. James, who was described in Chapter 6, frequently retreated to his mother's home when stresses of shelter life became too great. At these times James took his young son and some food to his mother's and spent the weekend enjoying the peace and quiet of a private home.

Many families stayed in homes of extended family members prior to coming to the shelter and may still have children placed in homes of relatives (most generally grandparents of the children).

Marjie, the young, vivacious mother of three, described in Chapter 4, lived with her mother in another state until tensions became more than she could bear. After fighting with her mother regarding educational goals, Marjie moved out of her mother's home and out of the state taking two of her three children with her. As mentioned previously, Marjie had arranged for her teenage daughter to continue living with her mother until Marjie could provide a home. This arrangement helped relieve the stress on Marjie by reducing the number of children she needed to provide for as well as assuring Marjie that her daughter would have some stability during her high school years.

Lynette and **Roger** never lived with Lynette's mother but arranged for the mother to care for two of Lynette's three children. The third child was born while Lynette and Roger lived at Baghdad Inn and remained with them in the shelter. After the birth of this third child Roger called his mother to report the birth and to inform his mother that they had been homeless for almost half a year. Both Lynette's parents and Roger's mother lived in other states. Therefore, Lynette kept in contact with her parents by telephone and by exchanging letters. Roger initiated contact with his mother by telephone.

Parents additionally used homes of extended families as places to recuperate from illnesses or as daycare for sick children (daycare at the shelter did not accept sick children). Ties to extended family were used to aid homeless families in adjusting to shelter living and efforts at acquiring homes. When extended families did not live in the area, as illustrated in the stories of Marjie and Lynette and Roger frequent contacts are maintained through letters and telephone calls. These methods of contact allowed extended families to be utilized as sources of family information.

In some instances extended families may be used for placement of children to prevent their homelessness or for financial help; for example, Loren and John used John's brother as the source of money for bus tickets which allowed the homeless family to move to Pennsylvania. This move allowed Loren, John, and their children to be closer to John's family and continue their search for work.

"No Matter What I Do I Can't Get Out"

Life for families who had been in the shelter two months or longer developed into an established routine dictated by case plans and case managers. Families received duplicate documents requested in the first three weeks of their shelter stay. Mothers began receiving food stamps, general assistance payments, and/or supplemental income payments. Adult family members continued attending parenting classes, GED classes, and job training sessions. Paperwork for housing assistance was completed and families were awaiting notification of eligibility.

Mothers at the shelter the longest may have already received Section 8 certificates, HUD vouchers, or placement in low-income housing projects. As some families received notice of eligibility and began searching for homes, other families had moved into homes. Mothers left behind in the shelter expressed feelings of frustration (Figure 7-1). They expressed anger toward what they viewed as the case manager's lack of diligence in obtaining housing for them. They blamed delays in receiving certificates or vouchers for housing on the ineptness of personnel at the various agencies. Jill, a divorced mother of three, complained bitterly about Section 8 housing personnel, "They lost all my paperwork so I had to start all over. That's the second time too. I think they don't want to be bothered and just throw it away."

At this stage adult family members attempted to secure employment by filling out applications and interviewing with prospective employers. Adults who were successful in job searches moved from the shelter. Adults who remained in the shelter viewed their lack of success as rejection. They felt employers were rejecting them because of their homeless situation and appearance. Betsy, after unsuccessfully applying for half a dozen positions, protested her futile efforts resulted from her appearance and not from any personal deficiency. She complained she had to interview in donated clothing that made her look poor and unreliable and, due to a lack of adequate transportation, often arrived at interviews soaked with sweat and her hair hanging in her face. In spite of feelings of rejection, they must continue to apply for employment in order to fulfill requirements of case plans and so remain in the shelter.

Additionally, mothers began to complain that case managers hadn't time to meet and discuss problems they encountered in fulfilling requirements of case plans. LuAnne reported her case manager had not been able to meet with her for two weeks. She felt the case manager was trying to help too many people and simply did not have time for her. As a result LuAnne turned to other mothers for help with forms and other agencies for bus tokens. Faced with the same dilemma, Jolene felt the case manager had lost interest in her problems and, despite having time for an appointment, refused to see her.

At this stage then families performed tasks in routinized manner. Expectations of shelter staff and tasks have not changed dramatically. However, families experienced failure in efforts to remove themselves from the shelter. Families translated failures in obtaining employment, obtaining housing, or meeting the demands of case plans into statements about their homeless condition. They questioned whether society, in the form of employers or landlords, would ever allow them to rise above homelessness. Additionally, they doubted their ability to rise above problems and challenged the purposes of case plans.

The zealous approach to case plans manifested in earlier stages transformed into forms of hopeless resignation. At this point families began to spend less time working on case plans and, instead, began to identify Government subsidized housing as the solution to their problems.

> **Crystal** had been in the shelter five months before she received a certificate from the Government for Section 8 housing. Prior to getting formal notification of qualification for housing, Crystal frequently began statements concerning her future goals with "When I get my house. . ." Crystal believed housing, in terms of "her house," was the solution to her problems. Once she was able to move into a house of her own all other problems would be resolved or would simply disappear.[6]

Like Crystal, you often hear mothers making comments, i.e., "When I get my house, then I will 'look for a job,' 'get my GED,' 'get special training at a trade school,' or 'go to school/college.'"

> **Donna L.** was a fun-loving single mother with one child in the shelter. During conversations she remarked she intended to take steps necessary to acquire a GED once she got into her home. When it was suggested she attend the Learning Center and work towards the GED while in the shelter, she commented, "It's too distracting here. I couldn't find a place to study. No, it would be better to wait 'til I have my own house." Donna was also delaying getting any special job training until she moved into her own home.

> **Lucy** spoke frequently of wanting to learn to sew in order to make "beautiful clothes" for her two daughters. It was during these conversations she would share her dream of designing women's clothing. When asked why she did not take steps toward accomplishing her dreams, she remarked she needed to wait until she moved into her house. Immediately prior to moving into her apartment, Lucy took money she managed to save and purchased an inexpensive sewing machine. After she purchased the machine, three of the mothers in the shelter offered to teach her how to sew. However, she continued to delay learning until she moved.

Stories of Crystal, Donna, and Lucy helped demonstrate how mothers delayed beginning anything new until they moved from the shelter. It was as if the move into houses or apartments would provide them with the promise of a stable future. This stability would provide them with the support they needed to risk entertaining new activities and challenges such as acquiring the GED, getting job training, or learning to sew.

Families who had adult members with higher levels of education or skills which allowed them to find employment quickly (within a month or two) generally did not experience this sense of resignation. These families were also most likely to have moved from the shelter prior to entering this stage. Unfortunately, successes of families who are able to move out may serve to deepen the sense of resignation of families left behind in the shelter.

Families that have reached this stage and have been homeless longer than one or two months often have not maintained ties with family and friends that were as close as ones described in earlier stages.

> Elaine and Steve were an unmarried couple who often had heated arguments during classes. Both had been in and out of shelters several times. Elaine was pregnant with Steve's child at the time I met them. Steve never mentioned any family during the time I knew him. Elaine had a mother and sister who lived in New York. Elaine's contact with her mother and sister was limited to infrequent telephone calls. She rarely asked them for help except in extreme emergencies. One such instance was when Elaine called her sister requesting that she adopt Elaine's unborn child. Elaine's purpose for this request was to provide the child with a stable family life and to prevent Steve from seeing his child.

As Elaine and Steve's story demonstrates, families have limited contact with extended family members. Extended family members may be used as sources of family gossip or an afternoon (rarely longer) away from the shelter. Even afternoon visits were less frequent than in earlier stages. Mothers depended on shelter services and other mothers in the shelter for help, i.e., daycare, emotional support, and answering childrearing questions. Extended families are called on to provide these services in cases of extreme emergency. Homeless mothers were often unsure their families would help them. Lucy related that she had difficulty making childcare arrangements for her youngest daughter, Tasha. When asked why she did not call her mother, Lucy remarked, "I suppose I could ask her but I'm not sure she would do it. It would probably be a waste of time to ask." Contacts with extended family members may be maintained but are not seen as very supportive or reliable.

"I Guess This is Home for Now"

Families were expected to work on goals of case plans for the time they are in the shelter. It was an assumption of case managers that with accomplishment of the goals, families would obtain employment and/or a house or an apartment, and would then leave the shelter. However, there were families who after six months or more at the shelter had not realized their goals. Case managers attempted to

pressure these families to satisfy demands of case plans.   Adult
families members conversely sought to avoid case managers.   Thus,
meetings with case managers were infrequent.

These families were not consistently seeking employment or a
residence (Figure 7-1). They most likely quit attending GED classes
or job training sessions. They attended parenting classes irregularly.
Adult members customarily spent time engaged in social activities
with other homeless families residing at the shelter or in their room (if
they were residing at Starlight Inn).   Any effort to find housing
commonly occurred after meetings with case managers where eviction
from the shelter was threatened.   Attempts tended to be brief with
adult family members quickly resuming lives of relative inactivity.

If inactivity continued, families were evicted from the shelter.
Families evicted for this reason from Starlight Inn denied the need to
search for housing relying instead on reversal of case managers'
decisions to evict. These families delayed moving until case managers
forced them out of the shelter by providing assistance to physically
move them to new locations. These moves were most likely to other
shelters where case managers were able to find rooms for the families.

Families who had been in shelters on several occasions before and
who seemed detached from their own lives appeared to adjust quickly.
These families did not seem to go through stages of anger and
resentment that other families experienced. Rather these families
shared past experiences much as if they were war stories and
explained to the listener how to manipulate various welfare programs.

> **Rebecca** was a single mother who was currently in a relationship
> with a man named Martin living in the shelter. She was quite
> aggressive and tended at times to intimidate other mothers
> generally overpowering them to achieve her goals. Rebecca had
> been in the shelter twice before. She adjusted quite easily to life
> in the shelter and became the group leader for mothers, often
> directing them to attend parenting classes, meet with their case
> managers, perform their shelter tasks, or participate in some
> shelter activity. She adhered to the very letter of the rules of the
> shelter and expected other mothers to do the same.   Prior to
> coming to Baghdad Inn, Rebecca tried living with her sister but
> reported they could not seem to get along. Since that time she
> has had only minimal contact with her sister. She had seen her
> mother only once in five years. Rebecca's first contact with her
> occurred recently when she phoned her mother "just to talk."
> Rebecca spent a year in Baghdad Inn before being placed in an
> apartment. She found leaving the shelter difficult and delayed the
> move for as long as her case manager would allow.   After
> Rebecca moved into her apartment she sought employment at the
> shelter as a floor supervisor. She was hired by the shelter and
> began to spend the majority of her day at the shelter, bringing her
> daughter to the daycare, doing her laundry at the shelter during
> her shift, and frequently staying later in the evening gossiping

with other mothers. Rebecca did not seem to have any goals beyond her job at Baghdad Inn. As her relationship with Martin became more strained, she seemed to rely on the shelter staff and residents more heavily for support and companionship.

Adult members of these families usually look for work or attend school or training classes primarily so they may remain in the shelter. Therefore, these activities are performed more because they are part of the case plans rather than something which will have a lasting effect on future security.

> **Rachel** had mothered two children before entering the shelter. Neither of the children were with her in the shelter. One child had been placed in foster care and the second child lived with her ex-husband. Rachel had been in Baghdad Inn or one of the other shelters in Arid Acropolis a total of five times and had been in two more shelters since leaving Baghdad Inn. Rachel did not express any goals for the future. She remarked looking for a job was a waste of time since she would not be able to find one that paid enough. She mentioned she placed applications on occasion in order to satisfy her case manager and keep from being harassed or evicted. Rachel was also enrolled in classes to prepare her for the tests to qualify her for a GED. However, she performed this activity for the purpose of satisfying case managers; she did not have any plans of ever taking the exam. Her only concern was to remain in the shelter for as long as the shelter staff would allow.

Mothers of these families can explain how best to work the welfare system. A mother who had been in the shelter twice and on welfare most of her life explained to me how you could live in project housing and still remain on Section 8 or HUD housing lists as a homeless family in spite of the fact the family was no longer officially homeless.

Rachel, upon introduction, gave a detailed account of the various shelters where she had lived. She gave information on the length of time you were allowed to stay, the rules, and the positive and negative aspects of living in that shelter. It was common for these families, when met for the first time, to tell you of the other shelters in which they had lived.

They are unlikely to tell you how they originally became homeless even upon probing.

> As described in Chapter 6, **Joanne** was living in the shelter while her husband was in prison. In a conversation with her prior to class time, I asked her how she became homeless. Joanne gave me a blank stare for a couple of minutes and then began to describe a different shelter and its rules. It was only over the course of 12 to 15 class meetings that enough information came to light to allow me to piece Joanne's story together.

When families at this stage were asked how they became homeless, they tended to react in a manner similar to Joanne's which suggested they did not (a) consider this information important, (b) understand the question and its relevance to the current situation, or (c) no longer remembered or cared to remember circumstances which led to their current situation.   However, they generously offered information concerning rules of other shelters, location of free food pantries, location of used clothing outlets, and other aspects of "street knowledge."

Families at this stage had only the most limited contact with extended families. Peaches frequently complained she was unable to talk to her mother without arguing. She felt her mother was too critical of her and her choice of male friends. As a result their relationship had been strained for several years. Therefore, because of the tensions between herself and her mother, Peaches was able to use her family for little more than storage room for her material possessions, i.e., her small television set, baby clothes, and a few household items. Peaches' visits to her mother's apartment were usually limited to times she retrieved items from storage or returned items. Similarly, Angela and Sam's visits to Angela's father and brother were limited to special holidays. Prior to holidays, i.e., Christmas or Easter, Angela began a series of telephone contacts with her father in efforts to coax an invitation from him. If an invitation was not extended, Angela, Sam, and their two daughters had to make other plans for celebrating the holidays.

These families generally limited contact with their extended families. Families are used for limited purposes such as storage of personal possessions, as in the case of Peaches, or the location of important family rituals, as demonstrated by the story of Angela and Sam. However, extended families cooperation in these uses are not automatic nor certain. As a result most associations and friendships of these families seemed to be focused on the shelter and street environment. Families were, therefore, of more limited utility and were more likely to function as reinforcement agents to the identity as homeless persons.

Stories of families living in Baghdad Inn related a process of "shelterization" similar to the process described by Sutherland and Locke in 1936.[7] During this process homeless families began to lose contact with extended family members and strengthened friendships among other homeless individuals. In the initial stages, homeless families limit the contact they had with their family until tensions created by circumstances such as doubling up and disagreements over the choice of a spouse, had been reduced. However, within the first month of residence at shelters, homeless families usually initiated contact with kin and began a period of relatively intense interaction which included, frequent afternoon visits, phone calls, over-night stays, and holiday visits. Homeless families called upon family to help in instances of sickness or other crises. As the length of stay at the shelter increased, contacts with family lessens. Families relied on friends in the shelter to provide for needs and called upon family less often. Homeless families were not able to reciprocate extended family aid. However, they were able to reciprocate aid of other homeless families by taking turns at watching children, providing information about housing, clothing, and household items, or taking the side of other families in disputes with other shelter residents or shelter staff. For needs homeless families in the shelter cannot meet, i.e., financial assistance, housing assistance, or legal aid, homeless families turned to the appropriate governmental agency rather than non-homeless family members. Thus, the contact homeless families had with extended families was limited to holiday rituals, aid in emergency situations (transportation to funerals), or providing family gossip.

Summary

Stories of families residing at Baghdad Inn delineated five separate stages in the shelterization process (for graphic representation of stages, see Figure 7-1):

1. **Stage One--Intake.** At this initial stage adults in families may be characterized by compliance to shelter rules and demands of shelter staff, uncertainty, and feelings of humiliation. Homeless families have only limited contact with extended families because of humiliation, tensions created by circumstances prior to homelessness, i.e., doubling up, not repaying loans, arguments, or desire to pull themselves out of homelessness without help.

2. **Stage Two--Non-compliance.** This stage is characterized by anger, frustration, and resentment. Contact with extended families are difficult to determine because of adult members angry resistance to interaction with non-homeless individuals.

3. **Stage Three--Adaptation.** At this stage families begin to accept life in Baghdad Inn. It is characterized by energetic approaches toward families' case plans, general attitude of hope, goal setting and planning activities, and expressed anticipation for the future. Homeless families begin to initiate contact with extended families through telephone calls, letters, recurrent afternoon or overnight visits, and attendance at family rituals. The extended family can be depended upon for childcare, financial aid, and opening homes to provide quiet havens.

4. **Stage Four--Withdrawal.** This stage is characterized by frustration and resignation. Family ties become more limited with homeless families restricting visits to short stays such as an afternoon. Homeless families begin to rely more upon other homeless families and staff of Baghdad Inn than extended families to meet their needs.

5. **Stage Five--Resignation.** Families at this stage have histories of long periods of homelessness with numerous stays in one or more shelters. Families exhibit feelings of hopelessness linked with a sense of detachment from life and everyone around them. These homeless families have the most limited contact with extended families. Contact is generally restricted to storage of personal items, sources of family gossip, or locations to perform the most important family rituals. However, this last function is neither certain nor automatic, but instead requires extended families to invite homeless families to attend these rituals.

Hence, as stories of families from Baghdad Inn elucidate, the longer homeless families live in shelters, the more limited their contact with extended families. As contact with extended families becomes limited, homeless families begin to depend more upon other homeless families, service providers, and governmental agencies than extended families for support.

The lengths of time families live in shelters and numbers of episodes of homelessness are not suitable variables to determine placement of families within particular stages. Rather than progressing smoothly through Stage One to Stage Five, families seemed to fluctuate between stages. Some families regressed to earlier stages, while other families skipped stages. A more complete discussion of this phenomenon is presented in the following chapter.

Notes

1. Families may be moved to Starlight Inn after the family has completed the week of intake at Baghdad Inn. Starlight Inn has room for twenty families, therefore not all families who initially enter Baghdad Inn move to the Starlight Inn. Some families remain at Baghdad Inn until they are able to move into houses or apartments.

2. One case manager supervises all families residing at Baghdad Inn. Due to this overwhelming caseload staff members frequently explain rules to families during week days.

3. As noted earlier, staff members may also explain rules to families. Apparently, there are times when the case manager and staff assume rules were explained by their counterparts. Consequently, this duplication of duties results in families not receiving proper notification of rules and appeal procedures of the shelter. Twelve mothers complained during parenting classes they were unaware of the rules.

4. Babette is the primary facilitator for parenting classes presented at Baghdad Inn and Starlight Inn.

5. Meetings may be more frequent than once a week since case managers provide bus tokens or cab vouchers.

6. After six months in Baghdad Inn, Crystal received a house of her own. She lived in this house for less than three months when she experienced a financial setback and was unable to pay the reduced rent. Therefore, she lost the house and returned to the shelter. At this time she told me she realized that the house had not been the solution to her problems. Unfortunately, she did not know what the solution might be.

7. The term "shelterization" has been borrowed from the study by Sutherland and Locke (1936).

CHAPTER 8

The Erlyouts, Uphills, and Lukles

On any given night Baghdad Inn registered on average two families who came seeking shelter (Annual Report 1989, 1990). These families learned of the shelter from social workers, police, religious leaders, or managers of other shelters or services. They came with expectations of what shelter life holds for them and their families and the length of time they need to stay in the shelter. This chapter introduces us to three hypothetical families and follows them through their stay at Baghdad Inn. These families and their stories are composites developed from stories of families who lived at Baghdad Inn.

Stories of hypothetical families provide "ideal" examples which demonstrate how families experience shelter life and the impact of those experiences on future capabilities of maintaining permanent housing. Being ideal examples, the families' stories provide descriptions of linear movement through stages thereby providing descriptions unclouded by outside influences that affect movement of "real" families. Variations in movement through stages is discussed in Chapter 9. Hypothetical families are used to illustrate three types of experiences and outcomes of shelter stay. We will see how the families experience the shelter and follow them through the stages of shelterization.

Introduction to the Families

On the night of November 28, two families checked into Baghdad Inn. One family, Mr. and Mrs. Erlyout and their two children (a female 9 years old and a male 13 years old) were brought to the shelter by a police officer who had found them trying to sleep in their car. After Mr. Erlyout lost his job in the middle of November, they left their home in Rusty Metropolis seeking one of many jobs they had heard were waiting in Arid Acropolis. Their car broke down and it had taken most of the money they had to get it fixed and drive the rest of the way. They arrived in Arid Acropolis on November 28 with no money or housing.

While the Erlyouts waited to be assigned beds, Mrs. Erlyout noticed another family of four being admitted to the shelter. Mrs. Erlyout was amazed at the calm manner in which the woman dealt with the paper work and questions that were part of the intake interview. Finished with all the forms the woman sat down next to Mrs. Erlyout and introduced herself as Mrs. Lukles. Mrs. Lukles smiled and told Mrs. Erlyout she was lucky, this was one of the better shelters in the city. The others had rules that made Mrs. Lukles feel as if she were living with her mother again, "You know, the kind that makes you feel like a stupid kid. Like you don't know what you need to do."

For the past three months Mrs. Lukles and her family lived in one of the other shelters in Arid Acropolis, and this was her second stay at Baghdad Inn. She referred to Mr. Lukles as her husband but they were not officially married. She met Mr. Lukles in the serving line at a local soup kitchen. They had lived together since then, about three weeks. Mrs. Lukles' two female children were aged 18 months and 3 years old. The children's father left them right after the youngest child was born. Unable to afford rent Mrs. Lukles moved into Baghdad Inn. From there she was placed in an apartment but was evicted from it when she could not pay the rent. She then moved into the Central Avenue shelter. That shelter allowed families to stay for a period of ninety days. At the end of the ninety days Mrs. Lukles had not found an apartment for her family. She and Mr. Lukles had then been referred to Baghdad Inn.

After receiving bed assignments Mrs. Erlyout said goodnight to her husband and 13 year old son and went upstairs. She was anxious about what awaited her in the dorm where she and her daughter would stay. She wished she and her husband could have stayed together, but rules do not allow men and male children over seven years of age in the family dorm. Instead, her husband and son had been assigned to the men's dorm on the first floor. Her anxiety was increased by her worry over what awaited her husband and son. The staff member who escorted her upstairs showed her into the dorm, pointed to the area she and her daughter would sleep, and introduced her to the woman sitting on the bed next to hers.

The woman, introduced as Ms. Uphill, turned and gave her a welcoming smile. She told Mrs. Erlyout that she had been in the shelter for three weeks and would try to answer any questions. She told Mrs. Erlyout that she would not be in the shelter much longer since she had just received notification she would receive her Section 8-housing voucher soon. "I'll be out of here and in a home of my own by Christmas. My kids will be able to spend Christmas in their own home." Her excitement was contagious and Mrs. Erlyout began to feel hope for the first time since she had arrived at the shelter.

As Mrs. Erlyout and her daughter arranged their few possessions in the small dresser provided by the shelter, Ms. Uphill continued her dialogue about her life and family unabated. She explained to Mrs. Erlyout that she is a single mother with three children, a male aged four and two females aged 2 years and 6 years. She had never been married. She became pregnant with her oldest daughter when she was 17. She finished high school and tried to find work. Her children were the result of romantic relationships with two men. The fathers of her children have not provided any childcare. In fact, Ms. Uphill admitted she did not know where either father lived.

Ms. Uphill is an independent woman who tried to maintain a residence on her own. She had received food stamps before she came to the shelter. She had been employed in a variety of minimum-wage jobs and was currently employed. Unfortunately, the combination of food stamps and minimum-wage employment did not provide enough financial resources to allow her to pay rent, childcare, and utilities. Ms. Uphill had family living in the area but explained that her two brothers and a sister were still living at home. Her mother and father simply could not afford to support her and her child. Therefore, when she was unable to pay the rent the first of November, her landlord evicted her, and she was forced to move to the shelter.

These are the three families which are followed through their experiences in Baghdad Inn. The stories are divided into a series of time frames relevant to challenges families face and reactions to their experiences. The story of the Erlyouts, because we met them on the first night of their shelter stay, deals in depth with the first two weeks of their stay. This will be followed by a brief discussion of the second two weeks and the second month of their stay. Since the Erlyouts will be able to leave the shelter after ten weeks, their story will conclude with their move from the shelter (Moving Out). The story of the Uphills follows the same time sequence, with a three-part discussion--the first two weeks, the second two weeks, and the second month of their stay in the shelter. However, since the Uphills spent a total of five months in the shelter, subsequent months in the shelter need to be discussed. The conclusion of the Uphills' story involves their move from the shelter. The Lukles family have a different series of time sequences discussed. So that we understand the experiences of the Lukles family, we must discuss their previous experiences with homeless shelters. Due to earlier homeless experiences, Mrs. Lukles reacted to entering the shelter differently from Mrs. Erlyout, thereby necessitating a discussion of the Lukles' first night. This will be followed with discussion of experiences of the first month, subsequent months, and their move out of the shelter. We shall begin with the Erlyouts, then the Uphills, and finally, end with a discussion of the Lukles.

The Erlyouts

First Two Weeks

After a long, sleepless night Mrs. Erlyout and her daughter rose to the noise of the other mothers and children readying themselves for the day. Ms. Uphill explained the rules to Mrs. Erlyout, telling her she would receive cleaning duties for the dorm later that day. Ms. Uphill suggested the first step was to contact the family's case manager. Mrs. Erlyout and her daughter dressed and went into the single women's lounge for breakfast brought to the shelter by a local soup kitchen. They could barely eat the donuts provided. Other mothers suggested they buy milk and cereal.

Mrs. Erlyout and her daughter went down to the main floor after breakfast to meet her husband and son. At that time they learned that the two males had to walk to the local soup kitchen and stand in-line for breakfast. After exchanging brief comments concerning shelter facilities and their breakfasts, Mrs. Erlyout nervously suggested they go meet with their case manager.

Once inside the case manager's office Mrs. Erlyout relaxed slightly. She regarded the case manager as nice and seemingly genuinely interested in their case. Mrs. Erlyout explained to the case manager how the family came to live in the shelter. The case manager agreed the circumstances which brought them to the shelter were not their fault. However, she pointed out this information was irrelevant to the Erlyouts getting a new home, and they needed to begin with the paper work. Mrs. Erlyout left the case manager's office with several forms that needed filling out and returned to the appropriate office in order for the family to qualify for housing, medical assistance, food stamps, and general assistance.

The Erlyouts were told their children needed to attend school. They could either attend the school for homeless children or enroll in a local public school. Since it was so close to the end of the term, it was decided the Erlyout children attend the school for homeless children, at least in the beginning. The case manager made a call to the school and told the Erlyouts their children were enrolled and would be taken to school the next morning.

The case manager informed the family that parenting classes met once a week for three hours and, as part of the requirements of the shelter, one of the parents had to attend the classes. Mrs. Erlyout said she would attend since she was positive her husband would get employment soon. Mr. Erlyout was told he needed to hunt for employment and was told of the job search service available in the shelter. Mrs. Erlyout assured the case manager her husband would have no trouble finding employment. After all, her husband had received some training in carpentry at the Rusty Metropolis Community College. She said she would also look for employment since she had received nurse's aide training at the same community college.

When they left the case manager's office, the family members hung their heads looking at the ground so they would not have to meet anyone's eyes. Silently each member of the family felt the embarrassment of being homeless and wondered how they had come to this low point. Shelter rules did not allow them to re-enter the shelter until late afternoon. Therefore, the family wandered the area around the shelter attempting to find a place out of the sun and where they were not visible to individuals walking by on their way to work.

During the next two weeks the Erlyouts tried to gain an understanding of what was expected of them, remember all the shelter's rules, learn how to get along with other shelter residents, and find some family stability. Mrs. Erlyout attended the parenting classes where she told her story for what seemed the thousandth time of how her family came to the shelter. It was important to Mrs. Erlyout that people understood she and her husband did not want to live off welfare but found themselves in a difficult financial situation and nowhere to turn for help except the shelter. Mrs. Erlyout did not say much more at the meetings the first couple of weeks. She heard many mothers complain about parenting classes at night after the children were asleep. Unlike the complaining mothers she enjoyed the meetings since they broke the monotony of shelter routine and could talk to someone who still lived in a home.

Every weekday morning Mr. Erlyout got up early so he could be one of the first at the job service. He liked to be out looking for employment by mid-morning. The men in the shelter told him employers did not like to hire homeless men, because it was felt they could not be trusted to show up for work. Mr. Erlyout hoped by being one of the first to fill out an application employers would overlook his current housing situation. After a day of searching Mr. Erlyout came back to the shelter withdrawn and angry.

Mrs. Erlyout saw her children off each morning on the school bus. The children did not mind going to the school for homeless children, but she noticed they became quieter--they did not seem to share as much with her as before. Mrs. Erlyout suspected her son was frightened most of the time he was in the shelter but would not confide in her. She did know her daughter had difficulty coping with the lack of privacy. Both children seemed angry more frequently now than when they had lived in Rusty Metropolis.

Second Two Weeks

During the first two weeks Mrs. Erlyout convinced herself they would not be in the shelter long. She became angry the longer the family was in the shelter and she began sensing her family pulling away from one another. She found herself screaming at her daughter at night for no apparent reason. She was irritated at her husband for taking so long at finding employment and not helping her more with the endless agency forms. Mrs. Erlyout occasionally talked to her husband about contacting relatives in Rusty Metropolis and asking for aid. After a heated discussion they decided their family was too far away to be of help. Secondly, the relatives were financially incapable of assisting them. She became resentful toward shelter staff and leaders of the parenting classes, often not speaking to them even when asked a direct question. She was sure no one really cared about her or her family, so why should she involve herself in their lives and silly classes. What was really irritating was the other mothers did not appear to notice her anger.

Second Month

Eventually, the anger subsided and Mrs. Erlyout found the routine of the shelter almost comforting. Her husband continued to look for work but came home at night more withdrawn than before. She often complained bitterly in parenting meetings that Mr. Erlyout no longer seemed to take an interest in her or their children. When they attempted to share their day with him, he simply turned and walked off without a word to anyone. Mrs. Erlyout worried that if the family remained in the shelter too much longer, her marriage to Mr. Erlyout would suffer irreparable harm. To attempt to remedy the problem, Mrs. Erlyout began looking for employment. She spent a great deal of energy filling out welfare forms, going to appointments at the welfare agencies, and applying for jobs. She pressured her family to take time for family discussions at night after evening meals and on weekends.

The Erlyouts lived in the shelter approximately eight weeks when Mr. Erlyout got a job at a local factory. Mrs. Erlyout received employment at a local hospital the same week. The family planned to save two pay checks from each job and with the aid of housing assistance be in a home of their own. The time between employment and moving out of the shelter seemed to progress at an unbearably slow rate. The family finally received low income housing assistance, found an apartment that met requirements, and planned on moving within a week. However, the wait became too much for Mrs. Erlyout. About four nights before they planned on moving, Mrs. Erlyout returned to the family dorm after the evening meal and began to cry. She was not able to stop crying. The other mothers comforted her and talked with her throughout the night. She felt if it had not been for their caring she would have gone insane. The decision was made that night for the family to move immediately into their new apartment.

Moving Out

The Erlyouts moved into their new home the next night. With the aid of friends in service organizations, charities, and shelter staff, the Erlyouts were able to find beds enough for the family. They were also given sheets, some dishes, utensils, pots, pans, glasses, and a few towels. Not nearly enough to properly begin housekeeping but Mrs. Erlyout was determined to make it work. She did not want to return to the shelter for even one more night. Since the Erlyouts' move from the shelter, the leaders of parenting classes have visited the home once. The Erlyouts were able to reconstruct their lives as a family and with the aid of the two jobs and welfare maintain their home. They were determined: Baghdad Inn would never be their home again!

Summary

The Erlyouts are typical of families that are homeless for the first time when they move into the shelter. As with most such families the Erlyouts experienced embarrassment of being homeless and found it necessary to explain to everyone they met just how they became homeless (Stage One). They hoped to convince people their homeless state is not the result of frivolous spending or laziness, but instead, results of circumstances they were unable to control. Additionally, the Erlyouts and similar families view themselves as not being any different from domiciled families. Therefore, they identify most closely with shelter staff and administration. It is important these representatives of the domiciled population understand their situations and accept homeless families as equals. By explaining that their current circumstances were brought about by events out of the family's control, the Erlyouts set themselves apart from other homeless families who may be seen by shelter staff as undeserving of assistance.

At the end of two weeks the Erlyouts entered Stage Two in which they experienced anger at society and those around them (a) for forcing them out of their home and then (b) for forcing them to remain in a place like the shelter. Much of the anger felt by family members emanated from perceived failure of shelter staff to recognize their family was different from other homeless families. Shelter staff and agency workers adopted methods of interaction in which the Erlyouts were treated the same as other homeless families. This perceived failure of the staff to recognize the potential of the family and the differences between them and other families resulted in the anger demonstrated by Mrs. Erlyout.

After a couple more weeks the Erlyouts worked through most of their anger and focused on the tasks that would enable them to move out of the shelter (Stage Three). At this stage the family still identified with shelter staff but not as strongly as in prior stages. They began to acknowledge their temporary status as homeless and identified with the other homeless families to the extent they were sharing a common "residence." They understood the staff viewed them as similar to other homeless families because of their presence in the shelter. However, families at this stage attempted to distinguish between themselves and other homeless families by having aggressively worked on fulfilling requirements of their case management plan. By exhibiting an honest desire to secure employment and move into a home they hoped to confirm they were more like the staff than the other homeless families and thereby gain the recognition of the staff as equals.

Once employment and assistance were obtained they quickly located an apartment, made arrangements to move, and moved as quickly as possible. They were then able to maintain housing through assistance and employment. Based on visitation to the Erlyouts' home as well as the absence of reports of similar families having returned to Baghdad Inn, Starlight Inn, or other shelters in the area, it appeared families like the Erlyouts are more likely to regain stability in their lives and not to experience homelessness again.

The Uphills

The second family to be discussed is Ms. Uphill and her children. They were in the shelter before the Erlyouts had arrived so we begin their story with entry into the shelter.

First Two Weeks

Ms. Uphill spent several sleepless nights prior to moving to the shelter attempting to find alternative housing. Eventually, she realized her resources were depleted, her family of orientation was unable to help, and her paycheck was too small to meet housing needs. As a result she stored some of her personal household items at her parents' house and moved her children to Baghdad Inn. Ms. Uphill was embarrassed about being at the Inn. She explained the reasons for her homelessness to staff at the shelter several times. Ms. Uphill always ended her story with assurances she would move into her own apartment the moment she obtained a better-paying job. In parenting classes she insisted she was not like other mothers and she did not wish to live on welfare.

Second Two Weeks

After living in the shelter for ten days Ms. Uphill found herself being angry and resentful. When she was not searching for better employment she spent as much time as possible by herself. Ms. Uphill verbally attacked other mothers during parenting classes in her third week at the shelter, calling them "lazy street walkers who only want to sit at home and draw welfare payments." She did not really mean it and was not sure why she got so angry at them. She spent the rest of that class and the next one in stony silence.

Second Month

Around the fifth week Ms. Uphill began feeling more energetic and less angry. She turned once more to the task of getting better employment and finding a home. She filled out paper work with zeal and pressured agency workers to process her forms as quickly as possible. Ms. Uphill began participating frequently in classes and became a friend and confidant to several of the mothers living in the shelter. The staff frequently turned to her as an advisor to the new mothers. She took great interest in her children's progress in the shelter's daycare and her eldest daughter's progress in the school for homeless children. Ms. Uphill frequently took her children to her parents' home for weekends as a retreat from the rigors of shelter living. Holidays were spent with her family.

During the last week of November Ms. Uphill, who had been in the shelter for three weeks, was informed she would receive one of the next available Section 8-housing vouchers. Her case manager explained the number of vouchers available each time they are issued are limited so it may be a few weeks before she actually received the certificate. However, she was allowed to undergo the introductory interview, fill out the necessary paper work, and begin looking for a home. Ms. Uphill was confident that she would be in her new home by Christmas.

Once the interview was completed Ms. Uphill immediately began looking for a house or apartment. She became aware of problems she faced in finding an apartment with the right number of bedrooms. Since she had two girls and a boy all over the age of six months, Section 8 housing required that she have an apartment with three bedrooms. There were not many three-bedroom apartments or houses available in the nicer areas of Arid Acropolis. By mid-December, after receiving her official Section 8 certificate, Ms. Uphill located an apartment with the requisite number of bedrooms in a nice clean neighborhood. She filled out the form requesting on-site appraisal of the apartment, filed it with the agency, and waited.

The week before Christmas the agency reported the apartment did not meet its specifications concerning wiring and the landlord refused to correct the problem. Ms. Uphill would have to continue her search. Ms. Uphill reacted with anger, complaining that the agency personnel just did not want to see her have a home. She told parenting class leaders she had been told by other mothers that these personnel took pleasure in making families stay in the shelter over Christmas. She threatened to report workers to their supervisors and to sue the agency for her inconvenience.

Subsequent Months

After five days when Ms. Uphill's anger was spent, she became resigned to the agency's decision and began looking for another apartment. However, the search was not conducted with the excitement Ms. Uphill had exhibited previously.

Ms. Uphill began to help more with new families moving into the shelter. She befriended several of the families currently in the shelter and spent much of her spare time in their company. She spent afternoons or entire days with her parents returning to the shelter at night. Visits to her parents became less frequent than was her previous routine. Occasionally Ms. Uphill included one or two of the other families in her family home visits.

Ms. Uphill began depending upon mothers in the shelter rather than her parents for childcare when she had to work late. She became close to several mothers, sharing her fears and frustrations with them. She would comment in parenting classes that mothers in the shelter understood what she was feeling and experiencing. She did not feel her parents could provide useful advice since they had neither lived in a shelter nor experienced the frustrations of searching for Section 8 housing. Additionally, she began to depend more on shelter staff and other service providers for answers to questions she might have for direction and support.

Moving Out

In early March Ms. Uphill located a house that was approved, and she moved from the shelter. She received aid from shelter staff in moving what possessions she had in the shelter. Private charities provided her with furniture and other essential household items. A private contributor paid the utility deposits for her house. She was thrilled to finally be in a home of her own and invited the mothers who were close friends to visit her.

After moving from the shelter Ms. Uphill kept in close contact with mothers still in the shelter, shelter staff, and leaders of the parenting classes. After living in her apartment for one month Ms. Uphill came to parenting classes seeking advice. She learned the shelter would not provide her with daycare after she had moved into her house. In seeking welfare assistance she learned there would be a thirty day delay between the time of her application and the time she would receive assistance. This meant she would be without daycare for a month and unable to pay for daycare on her current salary. Ms. Uphill did not feel she could turn to her parents for help because she felt they had already done more than she could repay. She was concerned because if she was unable to secure daycare she would have to quit her job to stay home with her children. Without the salary from her job she would be unable to pay her utilities or her portion of the rent. Fortunately, the shelter's case managers were able to locate temporary financial assistance which allowed Ms. Uphill to purchase daycare until welfare provided the needed funds.

Summary

Ms. Uphill is representative of families who are not able to move from the shelter as quickly as the Erlyouts. Like the Erlyouts, Ms. Uphill experienced embarrassment upon becoming homeless. She attempted to forestall the move to a shelter as long as possible. Once in the shelter she experienced humiliation and the need to explain how she could possibly have become homeless (Stage One). Ms. Uphill, like Mrs. Erlyout, identified closely with staff of the shelter at this stage. She saw her family as a domiciled family caught in an embarrassing series of events ending with temporary homelessness. After a couple of weeks in the shelter Ms. Uphill experienced anger at being homeless (Stage Two). She expressed anger by verbally attacking mothers in parenting classes, explaining how she was different from them and sitting in silence during classes. Once again like Mrs. Erlyout, Ms. Uphill saw herself as different from other mothers in the shelter. She became angry when staff insisted on treating her like other mothers rather than recognizing the difference. Additionally, other homeless mothers did not grant Ms. Uphill any deference in their interactions with her that demonstrated a recognition of her different status. Hence, Ms. Uphill angrily insisted she was not like them; that she was not a "welfare mother."

Once Ms. Uphill had worked through the anger, she began tackling the task of moving out of the shelter (Stage Three). During this period Ms. Uphill recognized her presence at the shelter made her appear to be similar to the other homeless mothers in the shelter. However, she did not identify closely with the other mothers and during parenting classes insisted she was not like them.   In one particular class Ms. Uphill complained the shelter staff referred to her as a homeless mother during a phone conversation with an official of another agency.   She protested, "I know I'm homeless, they don't need to keep rubbing my nose in it by telling everyone in front of me!"

Through persistence Ms. Uphill was able to secure a Section 8-housing voucher quickly.   She tirelessly visited apartments and houses until she found one that met the requirements of Section 8-housing regulations and met her needs.   After having this apartment rejected by the housing agency she again experienced anger.   She became angry with the staff because they continued to treat her like a homeless mother even though she had found an apartment and planned on moving.   Ms. Uphill felt by locating an apartment she proved she was not like other mothers and should receive treatment more in line with respect offered to shelter staff or parenting class facilitators who had homes.

When the anger subsided this time it was replaced by a sense of resignation (Stage Four).   Ms. Uphill continued to follow shelter rules and involved herself in the operations of the shelter.   She reduced the amount of time spent with her family, becoming more dependent upon mothers in the family dorm.   Thus, as Ms. Uphill entered Stage Four of the shelterization process, she began to identify more closely with other homeless mothers in the shelter.   She began to recognize similarities between herself and other mothers and began to view homeless mothers as victims of circumstances similar to those that brought her to the shelter.   On the other hand she felt staff who had not experienced these devastating events could not understand what it meant to be homeless.   At this point Ms. Uphill realized other mothers could empathize more closely with her feelings of frustration than shelter staff.   As a result she turned more frequently to these mothers for support and assistance and less to the staff, who she felt could no longer identify with her problems.

Because of the delay in finding housing, Ms. Uphill also represents families who have progressed through the fourth stage of shelterization.   Ms. Uphill became more dependent upon governmental agencies and other homeless families for assistance rather than her relatives.   Therefore, the Uphills, like similar families, remain marginally housed depending upon assistance.   Her experience in needing but being unable to afford childcare demonstrates the precarious nature of her housing.   If any of the forms of assistance becomes unavailable Ms. Uphill is likely to become homeless again.

The Lukles

The last family discussed is the Lukles. This family arrived at the shelter the same night as the Erlyouts. In spite of this the history of the Lukles as a homeless family started several months earlier. Therefore, a brief sketch of the family history prior to entry into Baghdad Inn on that night in November will first be provided. This sketch is followed with a description of the family's experiences in the current shelter stay.

Previous Experiences

Mrs. Lukles had been housed in Baghdad Inn on a previous occasion. She spent four months at the shelter before finding employment. She became acquainted with a man living at the shelter during this time. By combining their incomes and public assistance, the couple was able to rent a small apartment in an older section of the city.

This arrangement worked well for several months. In the end the man moved into an apartment with another woman, leaving Mrs. Lukles alone with her children. Without the combined incomes Mrs. Lukles was unable to pay rent and was evicted. She packed her belongings, and along with her children, moved into the Central Avenue shelter. This shelter allowed families to live in the shelter for ninety days. At the end of this time the family was expected to move into an apartment of its own or to find other arrangements. While at the shelter Mrs. Lukles participated in the case management plan and applied for assistance. Her efforts were complicated by the loss of much of her paper work, the loss of the children's birth certificates, and the need to apply for social security numbers for the children. Notwithstanding her efforts, Mrs. Lukles was unable to find housing within the prescribed amount of time. Faced with eviction from this shelter Mrs. Lukles had to find other quarters. The case manager suggested she and her family move to Baghdad Inn. With the case manager acting as advocate, the staff of Baghdad Inn voted to allow Mrs. Lukles to re-enter the shelter with her family. As a result Mrs. Lukles, her new boyfriend,[1] and her children re-entered the shelter on the same night as the Erlyouts.

The First Night

Mrs. Lukles went ahead of Mrs. Erlyout up the steps and into the family dorm. She did not take time to say good night to Mr. Lukles. She gathered up the children and her belongings, told Mr. Lukles she would see him tomorrow, and started upstairs.

Once she was assigned a bed she began to settle into her area.
Upon entering the dorm the two girls sat down in the midst of other
children and began playing. Mrs. Lukles quickly unpacked 'most of
her belongings and placed them in the dressers provided. She began
introducing herself to other mothers in the dorm. After she
introduced herself to everyone she became involved in a conversation
with two mothers she met on her previous stay at Baghdad Inn. They
spent most of the night comparing notes on various shelters and
discussing changes that had taken place at Baghdad Inn.

Mrs. Lukles did not tell anyone how she originally became
homeless. She already shared her story of becoming homeless with
several staff members and mothers in the early days of her first stay at
the Inn. She considered it a waste of time since it had not provided
any solutions to her problems. Instead she discussed her relationship
with Mr. Lukles, how they met, their plans for the future, and how he
treated her children. She was quick to offer newer mothers
information concerning the myriad of forms that must be completed,
answers which are most likely to result in assistance, location of
clothing and furniture banks, and location of the best food banks and
soup kitchens.

The First Month

Mrs. Lukles promptly settled into the routine of the shelter. During
parenting classes Mrs. Lukles reminisced about her first stay at
Baghdad Inn. She recalled innumerable times she explained how she
came to be homeless, commenting, "I think the whole world knows
my story." She laughed when she remembered how desperately she
looked for an apartment and applied for welfare during her first stay
at the Inn. She commented it had felt as if she had spent every
waking hour looking for employment or a home. She believed her
life during that first stay became easier when she finally accepted she
was homeless and began relying on help from other mothers.
Recalling frustrations she felt regarding the rules and her attempts at
finding a home and a job, Mrs. Lukles remembered following the
rules of the shelter even though they did not seem to relate to her life.
This time Mrs. Lukles was determined not to repeat the same
mistakes. Mrs. Lukles continued to regard the rules of the shelter as
irrelevant to her life or her current situation. In her opinion her life
would continue much the same as it had in the past. When staff or
parenting class facilitators protested about her pessimistic convictions,
she smiled and told them they would have to be homeless to
understand.

The changes in staff members and the few rule changes that
occurred since her last stay provided some inconvenience, but Mrs.
Lukles rapidly adapted even to these changes. She began attending
parenting classes, actively participating with other mothers and

leaders of the classes. She did not feel the need to explain her presence in the shelter; she felt it was irrelevant. What was important was she was homeless and living in the shelter. She was quick to answer questions concerning the shelter and its rules, questions concerning welfare or housing assistance, and questions concerning other service organizations. At times she recalled how quiet she had been the first couple of classes during her first stay. She would laugh and say to the class leaders, "I'll bet you wish I was that quiet now."

The second and third week brought only slight changes in Mrs. Lukles' attitude. She complained the staff showed favoritism to some of the other mothers (usually those not attending parenting classes). She urged the mothers to complain about these staff members in efforts to get them dismissed. She was quick to point out how other mothers were wrongly treated, even if the victim did not feel persecuted. Mrs. Lukles was demonstrating anger, but it was unlike the anger experienced during her first stay. She recalled her anger during the first stay being focused on how people could let anyone remain in a homeless shelter. She remembered sitting in parenting classes seething with anger and not wanting to talk to anyone. This anger was limited to shelter staff and administrators. Rather than expressing anger over being homeless as she did during her first visit, Mrs. Lukles was angry that staff treated her like a new mother constantly reminding her of the rules. She felt they should recognize she was familiar with the rules (Often quipping, "I probably know them better than they do.") and felt she should be given special privileges.

Mrs. Lukles spent much of her time at the shelter. She looked for work during her first month at the shelter but complained that prospective employers would not hire homeless persons. Neither she nor Mr. Lukles graduated from high school. Therefore, one of the goals developed in their case management plan was for them to earn GEDs. To this end they went to the learning center and enrolled in the GED preparation courses taught there. Mrs. Lukles attended classes the first week and then missed the rest, having scores of excuses to explain her absences. Mr. Lukles never attended GED classes, claiming he was looking for employment when the classes were offered. Mr. Lukles had not been able to secure employment.

Mrs. Lukles explained to leaders of parenting classes she did have family in the area but was uncomfortable asking relatives for help. She was not sure they would help even if asked. Mrs. Lukles admitted she spent more time with relatives when she lived at Baghdad Inn the first time. But even then, after living in the shelter three months, Mrs. Lukles decreased family visits. However, afterwards, when she moved into her apartment, the number of visits to her parents increased, spending enjoyable afternoons and evenings with them. Upon becoming homeless again she once more restricted her visits when she moved into the Central Avenue shelter and, because of their dislike for Mr. Lukles, severely limited her visits shortly before her second move to Baghdad Inn. She admitted feeling awkward in going to their homes now because they did so much previously. She resented their interference and felt they expected a lot from her in return. "It's just not worth it. I feel like I'm begging! Don't get me wrong, I still love them, we just don't have much to talk about anymore." Therefore, Mrs. Lukles limited contact to phone calls and only rarely stopped at their houses for an hour or two. She mentioned calling her sister more frequently lately, "just to talk." Mrs. Lukles hoped her sister will invite her and her children for Christmas. If an invitation does not come, Mrs. Lukles hopes to organize a party at the shelter for Christmas.

Eventually, Mrs. Lukles resolved her difficulties with shelter administrators and staff and found her special niche in the residents' social structure. By the end of the first month at the shelter Mrs. Lukles had became leader of the mothers. In this capacity she saw it as her duty to cajole mothers into attending parenting classes, remind mothers of appointments with case managers, resolve conflicts between residents or between mothers and shelter staff, and remind mothers of their assigned chores.

Subsequent Months

In January the shelter assigned Mrs. Lukles the duty of resident volunteer worker. The shelter volunteer supervisor felt Mrs. Lukles demonstrated adequate knowledge and understanding of shelter rules and regulations and possessed natural leadership abilities with other mothers. Staff got along easily with Mrs. Lukles. She rarely presented any discipline problems and encouraged other mothers to follow the rules of the shelter precisely. Mrs. Lukles seemed to thrive in this new position of authority and responsibility.

Mrs. Lukles stopped looking for employment or attending GED classes. She told her case manager she was too busy working at the shelter to work on those aspects of her plan. The case manager threatened to evict Mrs. Lukles and her family from the shelter unless she and Mr. Lukles finished the paper work necessary for housing assistance, continued GED classes, and looked for employment. In response to the threats Mr. Lukles applied for a couple of jobs, and Mrs. Lukles filed Section 8-housing forms. Mr. Lukles took various jobs at the day labor office for about seven days but then quit, complaining he was unable to find steady employment if he kept working at day labor.

Moving Out

Mr. and Mrs. Lukles continued living at the shelter, working on various aspects of their case management plan only when their case manager threatened them with eviction. Eventually, Baghdad Inn staff determined the shelter was not helping the Lukles family by allowing them to stay, and the decision was made to force them to find an apartment and leave. The Lukles family was given a date by which they were expected to move out of the shelter. As the date of eviction drew near Mr. and Mrs. Lukles still had not taken any steps toward finding housing. When the case manager became concerned they would be on the streets, she made a number of phone calls to the Section 8-housing office in their behalf. As a result the case manager was able to secure them a Section 8-housing certificate and to locate a suitable apartment. With the aid of shelter staff the Lukles family moved into their new apartment by the deadline.

Two months after the Lukles' moved into their apartment, one of parenting classes leaders saw Mr. and Mrs. Lukles coming out of the Homeless Outreach office. Mrs. Lukles explained they were searching for help in paying utility bills. She further explained they had just come from the blood bank. Money from the sale of their blood would be enough to pay their portion of the rent for the next month. Mrs. Lukles told the worker her two children were doing well in school and were happy. Several months after this meeting, Mrs. Lukles and her children arrived at Baghdad Inn again seeking shelter. Mr. Lukles had left, and she had been unable to pay the rent and utilities on the apartment by herself. Therefore, she was requesting permission to move into the shelter again until she could get her GED certificate, find employment, and find an apartment she could afford. The staff was reluctant to override the shelter's regulations and allow her to move back into the shelter. However, they finally consented. They knew Mrs. Lukles would not present any problems for the staff. In addition, the staff liked her and did not want to see her and the children living on the streets.

Summary

Mrs. Lukles and her family are typical of families who have a long history of homelessness or have stayed one or more times in shelters. As such, the history of the family's experiences in the various shelters needs to be investigated to understand through which stages they have progressed and where they are currently situated within the pattern of shelterization. As her history and her reminiscing elucidates, Mrs. Lukles and her family had experienced the first four stages of shelterization during previous stays at Baghdad Inn and the Central Avenue shelter.[2] Mrs. Lukles experienced humiliation and attempted to make herself invisible during the first two weeks of her first shelter stay. Determined not to let people think she became homeless through her actions, she told her story to many of the people working at the shelter and other mothers (Stage One). As with the Erlyouts and Uphills, Mrs. Lukles identified closely with the domiciled population and wanted to be sure others saw her as worthy of assistance and that she was not the cause of her homeless condition. Mrs. Lukles experienced anger during both of her stays at Baghdad Inn. In the course of her first stay, she felt angry at the shelter administration, shelter staff, other mothers, and society in general. During this difficult time she withdrew even more, refusing to answer questions or interact with other mothers (Stage Two). This expression of anger was the result of shelter staff's failure to see she was different from other mothers. Since the staff continued to treat her like the other mothers, Mrs. Lukles alternated angry outbursts with silence. Anger at the time of the second stay was different in that it was focused. Mrs. Lukles found herself angry at shelter staff and administration for the way they treated her. She did not mind living in the shelter as much as being treated as if she were not aware of the rules and regulations--as if she were a new mother who did not understand the process. She was angry because she felt her prior stay should have gained her an elevated status--one with special benefits, i.e., a volunteer worker position. At this point Mrs. Lukles felt she deserved deferential treatment, not because she was different from other homeless mothers, but because she knew the rules of the shelter as well as many of shelter staff. Due to this special knowledge she identified with the staff, not as a domiciled person but as a shelter insider. She felt this insider position should bring increased benefits and special recognition. Mrs. Lukles became angry when shelter staff failed to recognize her insider status.

Mrs. Lukles experienced Stage Three when, as she recalled later, she worked on her case management plan with a vengeance. She spent days looking for employment and looked at a dozen apartments before she settled on one as perfect. Additionally, during this time, Mrs. Lukles increased her contact with family frequently asking for favors. Like the Erlyouts and Uphills, Mrs. Lukles viewed herself as dissimilar from other mothers and set about to prove that fact to shelter staff.

After observing other families move from the shelter while she remained and re-submitted several of the housing forms (the originals were misplaced), Mrs. Lukles became frustrated and began to follow rules with little thought of purpose or consequences of her behavior. She followed her case management plan with less energy than before and felt her life was simplified by accepting her situation. Additionally, she began to restrict contact with relatives feeling they made demands she could not meet (Stage Four). Mrs. Lukles began spending more time with other mothers in the shelter, sharing gossip, taking turns caring for the children, and providing as well as receiving emotional support. At this stage Mrs. Lukles, like Ms. Uphill, began to identify closely with other homeless mothers seeing their fates as similar.

Mrs. Lukles entered Baghdad Inn the second time feeling homelessness and shelter living was all she could expect from life. These feelings of resignation and hopelessness were not eradicated by protestations of parenting class facilitators or shelter staff. She limited contact with family to a few short visits or phone calls and waited and hoped for invitations to family holiday activities. This was partially due to the family's dislike for Mr. Lukles. Limited contact also resulted from a desire to be independent from the family. She felt they could not understand what it was like to be homeless and she would end up owing them too much if she continued a close relationship. Her sense of detachment from the world became apparent in her protestations that the only people who could fully understand her were other individuals who themselves were homeless. Thus, Mrs. Lukles saw herself as homeless and quite unlike the domiciled population. In her view shelter staff as well as the domiciled population could not understand what it meant to be homeless. Therefore, she turned to other homeless parents for empathy and understanding. This sense of isolation from the domiciled world was expressed in the words of a single woman who was episodically homeless for five years, "All my friends are down here [meaning the area around Baghdad Inn where homeless people tend to congregate]. Maybe that's why I can't get off the streets."

At this stage of shelterization Mrs. Lukles seemed not to acknowledge her responsibility for finding housing and establishing financial stability. Instead she acted as if they were problems to be solved by others. Therefore, she allowed her case manager to take charge of her eventual eviction and find her housing assistance and an apartment. She did not see these activities as important in her daily life.

Her life after leaving the shelter continued to be marked with dependence upon welfare agencies, charities, and other people. When faced with problems Mrs. Lukles found agency workers who could help her. Problems were left for them to solve while Mrs. Lukles followed their prescriptions without question. Additionally, the third and eventually fourth stay in the shelter illustrated instability within Mrs. Lukles' family life. Without Mr. Lukles present she did not have resources to maintain an apartment. The only solution was to once again move into the shelter. This provided support and resources she needed to continue.

Summary

This chapter presented the shelter histories of three families. The Erlyouts represent families that remain in shelters for a brief time then move into a home and regain family stability. The Erlyouts are least likely of the three families to experience homelessness for a second time. Unlike the Erlyouts who experienced only three of the stages of shelterization, Ms. Uphill progressed through the fourth stage of the shelterization process before she was able to move out. Her history illustrates how she was able to move into a house but was unable to gain the same level of family stability as the Erlyouts. The Lukles family progressed through all five stages of shelterization. Due to their experiences they were unable to regain a stable family life. Instead they become dependent upon government agencies and agency workers to solve problems and meet their needs. Therefore, they are most likely to endure homelessness again after moving into a house or an apartment.

Histories of these hypothetical families demonstrate changes that occur in the lives and relationships of homeless families the longer they remain in shelters. Families enter the shelter with hope for their futures. They are convinced they will be domiciled after only brief stays. These hopes gradually succumb to understanding of time they may have to spend in the shelter before they are able to find housing and employment. Eventually family members become resigned to their situation and begin to lack enthusiasm for activities which will allow them to move from the shelter. If they remain in the shelter (or a series of shelters) for an extended time, families perceive life as continuing unaltered. They feel little hope for the future and feel helpless in resolving their own problems without assistance from agencies and social workers.

In conjunction with loss of hope families undergo change in identities. In the first two stages of shelterization families consider themselves unlike other families living in the shelter. They view themselves as domiciled families temporarily without homes. In the first stage of shelterization adult family members expend much energy attempting to maintain this identity while convincing shelter staff they are unlike other homeless families. The second stage of shelterization was marked by anger when staff failed to recognize differences between their family and other homeless people.

By the time families enter the third stage of shelterization, adult members have begun to identify themselves as homeless, at least temporarily. Families have become cognizant of the length of time required for the process of applying for housing assistance and, upon approval, locating appropriate housing. As a result they resign themselves to living in the shelter until the process of receiving housing is completed. In efforts to shorten the time spent in shelters they work diligently on case management plans. Additionally, families at this stage participate in activities which serve to reinforce the shrinking number of dissimilarities between themselves and other homeless families, such as strengthening ties with relatives and emphasizing interests and values they have in common with shelter staff. In addition, they see case management plans as the method by which they can regain full standing in the domiciled population and remove the stigma of homelessness.

The fourth stage of shelterization is marked by a more complete identification with other homeless families. Families begin to view themselves as most like homeless families and least like staff. By the time they have entered the fifth stage of shelterization, families have lived several months to several years in homeless shelters. They have experienced strained relationships with relatives and domiciled friends, lost jobs and housing, and have been rejected by potential employers and other members of the general public. As a result adult family members completely identify themselves with other homeless families in the shelter. They believe the staff cannot understand their experiences and feelings, only other homeless families can truly empathize with their situation. Thus, the longer families remain in shelters, the more completely adult family members identify with homeless families, sensing important differences between themselves and the staff as well as the general domiciled population.

Additionally, the longer families remain in shelters the more likely they are to avoid contact with relatives. Families in stage four begin to reduce the amount of interaction with relatives by limiting length of visits and reducing the number of visits to relatives' homes. By stage five visitations with relatives have ended except on rare occasions when homeless families are invited by domiciled relatives to participate in family holidays. Homeless families do not depend on relatives for assistance at this stage. Comprehending their inability to fulfill reciprocal obligations in continuing to accept assistance from relatives, families experience a loss of dependence. They begin to sense relatives' hesitation at continuing to provide aid when they have not received reciprocal payments. In efforts to avoid further demands on relatives, homeless families withdraw from family activities and assistance.

These hypothetical family histories demonstrate stages in ideal form. Experiences of homeless families will vary. This diversity contributes to variations in how families experience and progress through the stages. These differences are discussed in more detail in the following chapter.

Notes

1. Mrs. Lukles' boyfriend will be referred to as Mr. Lukles for convenience and to assist the reader in linking him with the Lukles family.

2. For graphic representation of the stages of shelterization and movement between the stages, see Figure 7-1.

CHAPTER 9

Discussion and Conclusions

This chapter's purpose is to provide brief summaries of previous chapters, to describe fluctuations that occur in movement between stages of shelterization, to outline limitations of the study, and to suggest some questions which remain. This book has presented demographic information regarding individual and family homelessness, accounts of homeless mothers gathered during participant-observation of parenting classes, and findings derived from these accounts. Previous chapters also presented discussions concerning types of assistance provided by extended families to needy members and factors which determine who can expect to receive assistance as well as pathways to homelessness taken by homeless families and individuals. In this chapter I first summarize the preceding chapters. Second, I outline how all factors previously discussed create environments in which homeless families suffer the consequences of shelterization.

Stages and Identities

This book examines movements of homeless families through stages of shelterization as well as changes of self-concept which occur in conjunction with this movement. Past studies demonstrated elements of the impact of separation from family and friends on actions and self-concepts of people (see Glaser 1964; Goffman 1961). Glaser (1964) in his study of men in prison found separation and isolation leads people to develop new friendships in order to meet needs previously met by others. The men gradually began to rely more heavily on new relationships than upon relationships they enjoyed prior to institutionalization. This change in importance of relationships to prisoners takes the form of a U-curve. According to Glaser, new relationships made while in prison began to lose importance as men approached their release dates. As these dates approached, inmates began to stress relationships with families and friendships which existed prior to incarceration. By following the process of the U-curve, men in prison change support groups according to groups of individuals they felt are most likely to understand their problems. Thus, relatives and friendships prior to incarceration provided important sources of support for the men when they are out of prison or close to entry or exit dates. However, during incarceration, fellow inmates are seen as providing the most effective support.

Goffman (1961) recognized the impact of isolation experience upon entry into a total institution. He suggested total institutions (e.g., mental hospitals and prisons), by nature of the degree of isolation imposed on patients or inmates, attacked and altered residents' self-concept. Goffman called this process mortification. Mortification occurs in institutions where all aspects of residents' lives are controlled by institutional administrators.

Kübler-Ross (1969) in her study of the process of grieving, found separation from a loved one brought about by one's own death or death of another, can be viewed as a five-stage process. These stages are defined by emotional and behavioral changes through which individuals proceed as they accept the death. Individuals will initially react with (a) denial, followed by (b) anger, succeeded by (c) efforts to negotiate for divine intervention to save the dying person, (d) gradually resigning themselves to the eventuality of death, and finally (e) attaining acceptance. According to Kübler-Ross, individuals may experience difficulty in progressing to the stage beyond their current position. If this "roadblock" cannot be overcome, grieving persons continue experiencing depression and, possibly, anger over the death. Only by reaching the final stage and accepting the death can people hope to regain a healthy mental state.

Sutherland and Locke (1936) studied homeless men in Chicago and suggested these men experienced changes in identities as the result of association with other homeless men. They called this process of change "shelterization." Once in shelters men in their study gradually adopted the unique language, values, and beliefs of other homeless men. Homeless men adopted an identity in which they felt close affiliation with other homeless men. At the same time men in their study began to feel isolated from the general domiciled population of

Chicago. Thus, Sutherland and Locke, like Glaser and Goffman, found when people are isolated from relatives and friends, they develop closer affiliations with others in their closed world and experience weakening of affiliations to people they knew before entering this closed world.

These studies with their descriptions of how people react to isolation and separation do not fully explain what happens when families become homeless. Families who enter homeless shelters are certainly separated from relatives and friends but are not isolated from them as they would be in a total institution. Therefore, extrapolating from the findings of Glaser (1964), Goffman (1961), or Kübler-Ross (1969) to suggest how homeless families change spheres of support is hazardous. My study demonstrates through use of data collected from homeless families just what changes they do experience and how support networks and relationships change with lengths of stay in homeless shelters.

Additionally, Glaser's (1964) U-Curve was developed within a population which would know the exact date of release in advance of that date. However, unlike prison inmates, homeless families when they move into a shelter do not know dates they will be able to move from the shelter into a home. Most families know only the week before the actual move. Therefore, they do not have the time prison inmates have in which to reestablish ties to relatives and pre-shelter friends. Hence, once ties to relatives and pre-shelter friends are broken, it may be a permanent break that cannot be reestablished once families move into their own homes. Once again using Glaser to extrapolate effects of living in homeless shelters on ties homeless families have to relatives and friends would be little more than a guess. This study, however, provides data which suggests these ties when broken are not easily repaired (and may never be reestablished).

This study of homeless families does expand the study of Sutherland and Locke (1936). The study explains stages of shelterization as experienced by homeless families rather than just the homeless men of Sutherland and Locke's study. It also provides more distinct characteristics of each stage than did Sutherland and Locke. Sutherland and Locke suggested men gradually adopted the culture of homelessness as they interacted with other homeless men and lost contact with relatives and domiciled friends. This study suggests as homeless families progress through stages of shelterization, adult members begin to identify closely with other homeless families. Concurrently, they begin to feel distinct and isolated from domiciled extended family members as well as the general domiciled population. They become convinced relatives are unable to understand their homeless plight and, as a result, cannot be of meaningful assistance. Thus, this study serves to update Sutherland and Locke's concept of shelterization by demonstrating it may be successfully applied to contemporary homeless families.

In addition this study demonstrates how Goffman's (1961) explanation as to how persons' self-concept changes can be applied to families living in homeless shelters. Goffman suggested total institutions controlled all aspects of individuals' lives. Thus, activities such as eating, sleeping, playing, and working were all under the control of the institution's administrator. Goffman felt complete control within total institutions combined with limited contact with the outside world set up a situation in which residents' self-concepts were attacked and eventually altered. He called this process mortification. The result of mortification is to undermine the patients' senses of autonomy and to create a dependence upon institutional staff. Goffman suggested mortification is something staff of institutions attempt to establish since it makes patients easier to control and order easier to maintain.

Like Goffman, this study finds homeless families who move through four of the five stages of shelterization become dependent upon shelter staff or other government agency employees to resolve their problems. Like patients of a mental institution, homeless families become easier to control and order easier to maintain as adults of families reach the fourth stage of shelterization, only to be increased in the fifth stage. Conversely, homeless shelters cannot be considered total institutions since it is not possible to closely restrict contact with the outside world.[1] In fact, stated goals of homeless shelters are to provide support to families so they will be able to reenter the domiciled world. Therefore, isolation of homeless families from relatives and friends is not one of the goals of homeless shelters. However, as this study demonstrates, loss of contact with relatives and domiciled friends is a result of extended periods of homelessness. Consequently, this study expands the concept of mortification to an institution which is not the total institution of Goffman's studies.

In summary this study, by describing how families experience life in homeless shelters, contributes to literature represented by Glaser (1964), Goffman (1961), Kübler-Ross (1969), and Sutherland and Locke (1936). By examining homeless families this study demonstrates how they move through a series of stages. Location of families within these stages has important consequences upon self-concept of families as well as their chances of remaining domiciled once housing is acquired. Families who closely identify with other homeless families are less likely to have sources of support that will assist them in solving problems they face when in their own home or apartment. This study, then, provides an important description of life for families in homeless shelters, a description which could not be extrapolated from other studies mentioned above.

Roles of Extended Families

Roles of extended families in prevention of homelessness has its source in the views of the functions of families as an institution and an historical role of the traditional family.   Meyer Fortes (1969) suggested family members have an obligation to provide assistance to needy family members. Historically the family was viewed as having the ultimate responsibility to care for members who do not have homes and/or are unable to work.   Studies by Cavan and Ranck (1969), Farmer (1970), and Stack (1970) demonstrated how families can assist their members in times of need. Individuals who are unable to live with their families are generally found to have been separated from families by deaths of relatives (such as occurred during the Black Plague) or through personal problems (i.e., alcoholism or mental illness) that may force families to expel the members. (For a more complete discussion of the history of homelessness and antecedents to homelessness, see Chapter 2.)   As they lost contact with family and friends they became dependent on local governments and later the Federal Government for assistance.

There is a prevailing controversy over whether the current homeless population maintains ties with domiciled family and friends. Traditional assumption is homeless individuals are disaffiliated and/or alienated from family (Bahr 1973; Bogue 1986; Roth 1989; Wright 1989).   Following this traditional assumption, some researchers suggest homeless individuals lose meaningful contact with extended family (Cohen and Sokolovsky 1989; Committee 1988; Lee 1989; Rossi and Wright 1987; Roth 1989; Shinn, Knickman, and Weitzman 1991; Wright 1989). Conversely, other studies demonstrate homeless individuals have ties of varying strengths with domiciled extended families (Bassuk 1992; Committee 1988; Hoch and Slayton 1989; Jones, Gray, and Goldstein 1986; Lee 1989; Miller 1991; Molnar et al. 1991; Piliavin, Sosin, and Westerfelt 1988; Rossi 1989a).   Recent studies by Allatt and Yeandle (1986), Firth, Hubert, and Forge (1970), Parish, Hao, and Hogan (1991), and Pearce and McAdoo (1984) suggest level of assistance provided by families to their needy members is limited mainly by inability to provide aid. Recent studies of homeless individuals (Bassuk 1992; Committee 1988; Hoch and Slayton 1989; Jones, Gray, and Goldstein 1986; Miller 1991; Molnar et al. 1991; Rossi 1989a) have found homeless individuals do have contact with their families.   Strengths of family ties range from having fragmented and limited contact to having substantial and frequent contact. (For a more complete discussion of arrangements of assistance, see Chapter 3.)

Presence of extended families is an important factor in the ability of families who are marginally-housed to remain domiciled.   After becoming homeless emotional support provided by extended family members may enhance abilities of homeless families to extricate themselves from the homeless condition. This study found homeless families living in shelters in Arid Acropolis do have contact with extended families. However, not all homeless families can expect to receive support from relatives.

The Study

This study evolved from observations of a group of homeless men that challenged my assumptions regarding their social behavior. Upon learning more about homelessness I became curious about how families adjusted to homelessness in efforts to maintain family structure. This study was undertaken to gain an understanding of homeless families and how they adapt to being homeless.

The results reported in this study ensue from data collected through participant-observation, interviews, and interactions with adult members of homeless families. In an early phase of the study I interviewed administrators and staff of agencies providing assistance to homeless families so as to obtain information concerning various shelters located in Arid Acropolis and to determine which shelter would best meet the needs of this study. As a result of these interviews I decided to collect data from families residing at Baghdad Inn and participated in parenting classes offered there. I participated in parenting class meetings held at Baghdad Inn and Starlight Inn shelters as a volunteer aide. My association with parenting classes lasted for two years. In addition to data gathered through parenting classes I collected data through informal interviews of parents who were willing to discuss family goals and relationships with extended families.   Through participant-observation of "gossip sessions" involving mothers before and after parenting class meetings, I was able to gather unguarded reactions to shelter life, other families, and to their homeless situation. Chance encounters with parents in areas close to Baghdad Inn and other agencies serving the homeless population provided me with information concerning interactions between homeless mothers and between mothers and shelter staff at times when I could not be present in the shelter.

Parenting classes are offered by Arid Acropolis Homeless Outreach for purposes of introducing homeless parents to alternative parenting practices, i.e., methods of disciplining children, improving communication with spouses and children, planning, goal setting, and goal achievement. The first two months of the study were spent quietly observing class meetings. Mothers are suspicious of strangers. They fear possible repercussions from shelter authorities for disclosures concerning the shelter and its administration. Therefore, time had to be taken for mothers to become comfortable with my presence and my role as researcher. After the first two months I began to fully participate in discussions and class exercises.

The mothers[2] eventually accepted my presence in the classes and included me as a member of their group. (For a more complete description of mothers and their children, see Chapter 5.) I was included in gossip sessions when I arrived early for class meetings. Informal visiting between myself and parents could occur wherever we happened to meet, such as during time I spent at the homeless services offices located in the area of the shelter. (For a more complete discussion of methods used in this study, see Appendix.)

Family Life in the Shelters

Baghdad Inn is a large shelter capable of sheltering 30 women and children (except male children over the age of seven), 44 single women, 88 working men and men with male children over the age of seven, 244 single men, and 200 adults in tents. Families in which both spouses are present must separate, with men in the men's shelter on the first floor and women and children housed on the second floor.

Baghdad Inn does not offer rooms which would provide families with a place of privacy. The only room available to families for common activities is the day room which can be used by anyone sheltered at Baghdad Inn and, until the late 1980s, individuals living on the streets of Arid Acropolis. This room does not provide a private space in which families can discuss family concerns or can attend to family rituals, i.e., birthday parties or religious observances. As a result families must leave the shelter in order to find privacy. This often means walking to a local park or sitting in the family car (or a borrowed car if the family does not have one) on cold or rainy days.

Starlight Inn is a shelter designed to house families in shared living quarters. After an initial stay at Baghdad Inn families can be moved to Starlight Inn where entire families live in a single motel room. In spite of the crowded conditions of the room, married couples prefer Starlight Inn because it allows them to live together and provides some privacy to the family. One important feature of Starlight Inn for adult family members is the ability to place personal items in a room, lock the door, and keep the key. Starlight Inn does not have a larger common room available where families could entertain extended family. Additionally, families are unable to cook meals because of lack of kitchen facilities and rules do not allow any cooking in the rooms. Thus, families are limited in their abilities to reciprocate assistance provided by friends and extended family members.

Shelters have rules designed to provide organization to the individual's life and encourage activities which build self-esteem and stimulate search for employment and housing (Typesalot 1989). Moreover, these rules help maintain order in living situations in which strangers are required to live in close proximity.

Consequently, rules of the shelter cover all aspects of families' lives. Rules inform parents (a) at what times they are expected to be in the building, (b) at what times they are to be in their dormitories, (c) the times they are not allowed to be in the building or the dorms, (d) when men are allowed on the second floor and in the family dorm, (e) what constitutes acceptable and unacceptable discipline for their children, (f) the chores mothers are expected to perform and when chores must be completed, (g) bedtimes for children, (h) how late they are able to sleep in the morning, and (i) who may baby-sit for their children.

> **Wanda**, a single mother of three, frequently complained her children would not obey her. When she made demands on them or corrected their behavior, they would tell her, "I won't do it. And if you spank me I'll tell the staff and you will get in trouble."

> **Carla**, a mother of an adolescent boy, reported that when she tried to discipline her son, he ran down the hall toward the staff's table shouting, "You can't do that! I'm telling."

Parents feel their children no longer view them as the authority figure in their lives but instead see the parent as similar to an older child. When conflict occurs children use shelter staff and rules in attempts to win arguments. Hence, parents feel their roles as parents have been usurped by shelter rules. This only further damages relationships within families.

Lack of privacy for families in both shelters is a source of complaint for many mothers. They resent not being able to spend time alone with their husbands or boyfriends. Married couples feel their marriage suffers from lack of privacy, with some mothers complaining their husbands seem to lose interest in their children's lives and family concerns. Moreover, lack of a common room eliminates possibilities for families with extended family living in the area to be able to entertain family members, to help care for family member's children for an afternoon, or to cook family meals. Thus, ability to reciprocate aid received from extended family members is limited by the physical structure of the shelter. As a result many families are unwilling to accept much aid from extended family members because of the inability to reciprocate. Hence, many homeless mothers turned to one another for assistance.

Paths into Homelessness

The stories of families disclose desperate attempts to keep themselves and their children domiciled. Paths to homelessness families take represent a continuum. These range from a linear path (e.g., families moving from living in homes or apartments to living on the streets, in automobiles, or shelters designed to aid homeless people) to far more complex paths which involve several steps carrying families through a variety of shelter forms. The paths families have taken in finding their way to Baghdad Inn are discussed more completely in Chapter 6.

Homeless individuals or families may first live in a series of hotels and motels of diminishing conditions of inhabitability. These rooms are most likely obtained with use of families' own funds. When savings are depleted families are faced with choices of moving in with friends or relatives (i.e., doubling up), moving into shelters for homeless people, or moving to unsheltered existence on the streets. In a few cases families may qualify for government subsidized housing, i.e., HUD-sponsored housing or Section 8-supported housing, thereby remaining at least precariously housed.

Homeless or near-homeless families may use relatives' homes in varieties of ways. One way is for homeless families to move into homes of relatives. Frequently this is only a temporary solution. Pressures of two families residing in a residence meant for one family create tensions that can strain family relationships. Tensions produced between two families can intensify to degrees where both families agree it is best for the guest family to leave. Further, these tensions, often resulting in arguments, can erode extended family relationships resulting in limitations of accessibility of host families in providing assistance to homeless families in the future. Additionally, a host family, in providing for two families, may see its own financial resources stretched beyond its ability to survive. When faced with financial collapse or eviction the host family will evict the guest family. As a result doubling up, even though it appears to be a logical step in avoiding homelessness, may have the reverse consequence of restricting or eliminating an important source of support and assistance for the homeless family. Thus, homeless families enter shelters or arrive on the street with strained family relationships, depleted crises resources and goodwill available from family and friends, and with few additional resources on which to call for aid. (For a complete discussion of how the homes of relatives may be used by homeless families, see Chapter 7.)

When families are evicted from homes of relatives, they are faced with few alternatives, one of these is moving into a shelter. The two shelter types most available to families are emergency shelters and transitional shelters. Emergency shelters may be sponsored by private charitable organizations, i.e., the Salvation Army, Red Cross, local church, or it may be public shelter like Baghdad Inn. The purpose of the emergency shelter is to provide a haven until families or individuals can be moved to transitional shelters or to more permanent housing (i.e., Section 8 housing) or into low-rent housing. Therefore, the length of stay allowed by emergency shelters tend to be short, normally 30 days. However, because of a general shortage of transitional shelters, government-subsidized housing, and low-rent apartments, families and individuals may find themselves spending long periods of time in shelter facilities designed for short stays.

Since families and individuals are not expected to reside in emergency shelters for long, shelters such as Baghdad Inn and Starlight Inn are not equipped with kitchen facilities where families can prepare their own meals. Furthermore, the structure of Baghdad Inn as an emergency shelter requires the male family members (fathers and male children aged seven years and older) to be housed separately from female members and male members under seven years of age. This separation effectively splits families and makes familial communication more difficult. The number of families demanding shelter and the shelter's attempt to accommodate as many families as possible creates crowded conditions in the dormitories. The open room dormitory-style sleeping quarters of Baghdad Inn, while housing more people, further reduces privacy available for mothers and their children or for fathers and their older male children. The crowded conditions, lack of privacy, inability to interact as a family, and separation of spouses, fathers from children, and mothers from older male children, linked with the stresses of homelessness and the stressed relationships with extended family members creates an environment where the dissolution of the family may easily occur.

> **Lynette** and **Roger**, the young couple described in Chapter 7, had returned a second time to Baghdad Inn after being evicted from their low-rent apartment. During a parenting class Lynette complained bitterly that Roger did not understand they were homeless and that he was not trying to get a job. Roger countered by saying Lynette did not understand his problems and that she refused to recognize his efforts. She retorted, "What efforts?" Two weeks later Lynette reported in a parenting class that she and Roger were separated and seeking a divorce.

Lack of communication and the stresses and insecurity of being homeless acted in unification to create a situation for Lynette and Roger where divorce seemed the most reasonable solution to their problems. It is only through the persistence of family members that the family is able to maintain communication and continuity in interaction in order to continue functioning as a family.

Stages of Shelterization

Sutherland and Locke (1936) described a process they called "shelterization" in their study of homeless men. As a result of shelterization men, new to homelessness and shelter life, underwent a process during which they adopted mannerisms, language, and beliefs of men who had been in the shelter longer. Stories of families living in Baghdad Inn and Starlight Inn relate a process of "shelterization" which is similar to that presented in the Sutherland and Locke study. The shelterization process to which families are subjected has five separate stages. (A complete description of the stages of shelterization can be found in Chapter 7 and Chapter 8, and a graphic representation of the stages of shelterization and the movement between the stages can be seen in Figure 7-1.)

The first stage is characterized by compliance, uncertainty, and feelings of humiliation (see Figure 9-1). Homeless families in this stage have only limited contact with extended families because of humiliation, tensions created by circumstances prior to homelessness, or desire to pull themselves out of homelessness without help. Adult family members quickly assure shelter staff, facilitators of parenting classes, and other homeless mothers they are not at fault for their present lack of housing. Their identity is most closely attached to non-homeless personnel of the shelter and other agencies.

The second stage is characterized by anger, frustration, and resentment (see Figure 9-1). During this stage adult family members sit in angry defiance refusing to interact with any of the parenting class members. Contact with extended family is difficult to determine because of resistance to answering questions or participating in any conversations. The adult members' anger results from a feeling of being rejected, of being left unaided in a horrible situation. They feel abandoned; that no one cares about where they are living or the conditions in which they must live. Mothers during the first stage have consistently attempted to identify with the domiciled population in their interactions with shelter staff, agency personnel, and parenting class facilitators. However, various agency personnel consistently treat mothers in the same manner as those who have been homeless much longer. The mothers view this refusal to see them as different as a form of rejection and as a verification of their status as homeless.

As mothers begin to accept their homeless status they enter Stage Three (see Figure 9-1). This stage is characterized by an energetic approach toward the case plan, a general attitude of hope, goal setting and planning activities, and an expressed anticipation for the future. Mothers begin to reestablish contacts with extended families by visiting, telephoning, or writing letters. Extended families can be depended upon for childcare, financial aid, and opening their homes to provide quiet havens. Adult family members have resolved the identity conflict of Stage Two and have marginally accepted their status as homeless. They do not view the status as permanent and believe their actions and efforts can remove them from homelessness and restore their status as domiciled citizens. Therefore, in an effort to obtain a domicile as quickly as possible, they become energetically

Figure 9-1

Summary of Characteristics Exhibited by Homeless Families in Each Stage of Shelterization Depending upon Activities of Families, People with Whom they Relate, Self-concept of Homeless Families, and Factors that Precipitate Movement Between Stages

Stage	Shelter Activity	Relations Within Families	Shelter Staff	Relatives	Self-concept	Factors Precipitating Movement
❶	Families are adjusting to shelter life. Activities are learning shelter rules, meeting other parents, and attending first meeting with case managers.	Families are first faced with separation required by shelter. It is their first experience with crowded conditions of dormitories. Children often express confusion and fear.	Families spend time convincing shelter staff they are not like other homeless families. They attempt to be cooperative.	Family relations are strained from previous demands for assistance, i.e., doubling up.	Adults identify with domiciled population. They see themselves as homeless through circumstances beyond their control.	Families realize how long it will take to get redomiciled. They adapt to shelter living at least for a short stay.

Figure 9-1
(Continued)

Stage	Shelter Activity	Relations Within Families	Shelter Staff	Relatives	Self-concept	Factors Precipitating Movement
❷	With assistance of case managers families develop case plans. They replace missing records such as birth certificates, health records, and social security cards.	Without reports from individuals it is difficult to determine what is happening within families at this stage.	Adults are angry because shelter staff fail to see them as different from other homeless families. Shelter staff often become objects of resentment.	Unknown– However, I suspect there is little contact with relatives.	Adults identify with domiciled population but experience anger over the fact that no one else (namely shelter staff and workers) appears to recognize this identity.	Families accept that it is going to take time to complete paper work and receive Section 8- housing vouchers. They recognize importance of case plans in obtaining goals and feel they are in control of their lives.

Figure 9-1
(Continued)

Stage	Shelter Activity	Relations Within the Families	Shelter Staff	Relatives	Self-concept	Factors Precipitating Movement
❸	Adults fill out forms for Section 8-housing certificates, welfare payments, AFDC, food stamps, and healthcare. They look for employment and begin GED training classes where necessary.	Adults work diligently to maintain family structure by finding time and places where they can have some privacy. Mothers work to include fathers in decisions concerning children. Children express fear of sleeping (especially young boys in the men's dorm).	Adults become cooperative with shelter staff in meeting case plan goals. They pressure shelter staff and workers to quickly process paper work so they can move from the shelter as soon as possible.	Actively involved with relatives on weekend visits, family rituals, and use relatives for childcare.	Adults recognize homeless situation but still feel they have control over their futures. They can remove themselves through activity. They still identify with domiciled population.	Families see other homeless families receive housing subsidies and move out of the shelter. Adults are experiencing a lack of success in finding employment. Families who have received housing vouchers will return to the self-concept of Stage 1.

Figure 9-1
(Continued)

Stage	Shelter Activity	Relations Within the Families	Shelter Staff	Relatives	Self-concept	Factors Precipitating Movement
❹	Life becomes routine. Adults look for jobs and work on GEDs but only to stay in the shelter. Families begin receiving welfare payments, AFDC, food stamps, and healthcare. Some families may have received housing certificates.	Relationships between spouses seem to be strained for some. Some families have separated and are discussing divorce. Children challenge the authority of parents using shelter rules to threaten them.	Adults are cooperative with shelter staff but no longer pressure staff to quickly process their forms for housing and assistance. They are compliant with staff's demands.	Families restrict amount of time spent with relatives. Visits are reduced to afternoons and important holidays. with no overnight stays.	Adults strongly identify with other homeless families rather than the domiciled population, looking to them for assistance and answers.	Families experience rejection from potential employers, shelter staff, and relatives. They lose close contact with relatives. They have experienced one or more episodes of homelessness. Families with housing vouchers at this stage may return to Stage 3.

Figure 9-1
(Continued)

Stage	Shelter Activity	Relations Within the Families	Shelter Staff	Relatives	Self-concept	Factors Precipitating Movement
❺	Adults work on case plans only when case managers threaten eviction from the shelter. At that time they do only enough to maintain their residence at the shelter.	Some families have separated by this stage. Families see homeless shelters as home. They see no other future. Children consider the shelter as home.	Adults avoid shelter staff. They no longer work on case plans. When faced with eviction they expect case managers to find them new living quarters.	There is very little contact with relatives. Homeless families can only hope for invitations to important family rituals and holidays but cannot assume they will be invited.	Adults most completely identify with other homeless families. They feel relatives and shelter staff cannot relate to their problems because they are not homeless.	Families at this stage may exhibit some characteristics of earlier stages when they once more move into a shelter after being domiciled.

involved in all the activities they feel will assist them in achieving their goal. These adults identify themselves with the domiciled population but recognize their temporary change in status. With continued residence in the shelter adult family members advance to Stage Four.

Stage Four is characterized by frustration and resignation (see Figure 9-1). Family ties become more limited as homeless families restrict contact with extended families. As homeless mothers withdraw from interaction with extended families, they begin to rely more heavily upon other homeless families and staff of Baghdad Inn and Starlight Inn for assistance. Families become more closely identified with homeless individuals. They feel they have little in common with individuals who have a house and feel more closely allied with the homeless population. As a result of their failure to acquire a home or employment, they no longer believe they can extricate themselves from homelessness purely through their own actions. Instead they sense they are at the mercy of case workers who review their applications and make decisions. They now accept the status of homeless and feel that only through the benevolence of their case manager will they be declared suitable for a home. Therefore, they become compliant to the demands of agency personnel and make efforts not to anger anyone who they feel have the power to assist them in obtaining housing. As a result of their identification with the homeless status and other homeless individuals, families who have progressed to Stage Four and who have become domiciled are more likely to again become homeless in the future than any of the individuals who moved out of the shelter prior to reaching Stage Four. If they do not receive housing these families are likely to progress to Stage Five.

Stage Five is characterized by family histories of long periods of homelessness with numerous stays in one or more shelters, feelings of hopelessness, and a sense of detachment from life and everyone around them (see Figure 9-1). Families who have progressed to this point have the most limited contact with extended families. Contact is generally restricted to storage of personal items, a source of family gossip, or location to perform the most important of family rituals. However, this last function is not automatic and requires an invitation from the extended family. Families at this stage most closely identify with other homeless individuals. They have few friends who are domiciled. Most of their acquaintances are other homeless families and individuals. The stigma of being homeless appears to no longer cause any discomfort for members of these families. They have accepted the status of being homeless and see no resolution to their homeless dilemma. They generally feel they have been abandoned by society and will continue to live in shelters far into the future. If families who have reached Stage Five are able to move into houses or apartments, they are most likely of all the groups to become homeless again. They depend on shelter staff, personnel from other agencies, and facilitators of parenting classes to meet all their needs and to assist them in solving any problems that may appear.

Thus, as stories of families from Baghdad Inn and Starlight Inn help to elucidate, the longer homeless families live in shelters, the more limited their contact with extended families become and the more closely they identify with being homeless.

Fluctuations in the Stages

Families may not progress smoothly from Stage One to Stage Five of shelterization. Instead some families appear to regress to earlier stages while others appear to skip stages. This is the result of factors other than shelter structure which influences strength of families' identities as homeless.

Disappointment is one factor that can cause families to skip stages or regress to previous stages. Families who have obtained apartments or houses but experience problems that delay moving from the shelter may regress to a previous stage, especially to Stage Two re-experiencing its anger. Knowing they will eventually be able to move provides some comfort. However, frustration of meeting added requirements by agencies or sponsors or having to complete additional paperwork before being allowed to move provokes anger. In parenting classes they again sit in angry defiance refusing to talk or if they do talk it is to verbally attack the other mothers, shelter staff, and agencies or persons they feel are preventing their move.

> **Twila** (first introduced in Chapter 7) had spent several months engaged in locating an apartment which met the requirements of her private sponsor. Finally she found an apartment the sponsor had approved, and Twila had set the date she would move. Three days prior to moving problems with having the water and lights connected at her new apartment were discovered. Without utilities the shelter would not allow her to move. After learning of this new barrier she came to a parenting class and began angrily berating the shelter, shelter staff, and her sponsor. Spiced with many expletives Twila explained what had happened and then sank into a stony silence. As mothers in the parenting class suggested possible solutions to her dilemma, Twila sat sulking, not acknowledging any of the suggestions. Rather than recognizing this as a problem common to moving, Twila saw the incident as a way of reminding her she was homeless, as a form of rejection. Twila had previously been in Stage Three but, with the disappointment of delaying her move from the shelter, she slipped back into Stage Two.

This return to Stage Two resulted from feeling shelter staff and others failed to recognize that one's own family is different from other families in the shelter. Families who acquire homes and are preparing to move begin to identify once again with the domiciled population. When denied this move and forced to remain in the shelter, they feel they should be treated differently because they are no longer homeless. When shelter staff treat them the same as before finding homes they become angry. They see staff treatment as a denial of their new status as domiciled.

Families who experience frustration of thinking they have found apartments or homes only to have the appropriate government agency not approve them have two options. First, they regress from the stage they are currently in back to Stage Two and anger. Like Twila's reactions this anger is the result of the family feeling different about themselves and identifying more closely with the domiciled population. After resolving this issue families in this situation may return to the stage where they were originally or may skip to an even later stage. The skip to a later stage is the result of increased feelings of hopelessness and increased sense of being at the mercy of various agency personnel and rules. This creates a sense of increased social distance between themselves and the domiciled population while decreasing social distance between themselves and other homeless families. Second, upon loss of apartments or houses, they move into later stages where they begin to identify even more closely with homeless people around them. Again this results because families feel more at the mercy of various agency personnel than before. Therefore, they begin to identify more closely with homeless individuals around them and less with the domiciled population.

Families who have previous experience with homelessness will appear to skip stages upon entering shelters. Previous experiences have supplied these families with an identity of homelessness that they bring with them into shelters. Therefore, they do not exhibit characteristics of Stage One and may not experience the anger of Stage Two. Rather these families quickly identify with other homeless families and assume roles expected of them while in the shelter. As the number of times families have been homeless increases, chances increase they will skip Stages Three and Four as well. Thus, it is possible for families to enter a shelter exhibiting characteristics of Stage Five.

Conversely, previous experience of living in poverty does not prepare families for life in homeless shelters. It does provide them with more extensive knowledge concerning various welfare agencies, rules of welfare agencies, and food and clothing banks. However, families living in poverty who are domiciled do not identify with the homeless people they see on the streets. Therefore, when they enter shelters they do not skip the first stages but begin with Stage One.

Strength of ties homeless families have with extended families can function to reduce the impact of shelterization. However, if extended families refuse to provide aid, homeless families, feeling rejected, may first move into Stage Two and then to later stages. Adult members begin to perceive other homeless families as reliable sources of assistance and extended families as unreliable. Thus, homeless families begin to identify more closely with other homeless families and individuals than domiciled extended families. This sense of rejection by relatives propels them through earlier stages into later stages of shelterization.

Additionally, marital status and strength of marital relationships can effect progression of families through stages. Families consisting of married couples may halt at Stage Three not progressing into Stages Four or Five regardless of the length of time spent in shelters. This results from strong emotional ties between spouses which provides support for families' identities as domiciled. Thus, families are able to resist the impact of shelters and remain closely identified with domiciled individuals with which they come in contact. If marital relationships do not provide this support, families progress through stages of shelterization, slowly adopting an identity of homelessness. Likewise, single parents, who do not have the identity support provided by spouses, progress through the stages.

Interestingly, husbands and wives may not experience each stage of shelterization at the same time. Of families who participated in this study, husbands lagged behind wives in advancing to next stages. This is especially true for progression from Stage One to Stage Two and then from Stage Two to Stage Three. When wives accepted the homeless situation and entered Stage Three, husbands still denied the homeless situation and did not identify with other homeless people.

> In the case of **Lynette** and **Roger** (first introduced in Chapter 7), Lynette accepted the homeless situation and took steps to obtain housing. During the same time, Roger spent considerable class time trying to convince the facilitators he was not homeless. This difference in progression through stages created conflict. Lynette frequently was angry at Roger for his unwillingness to face the situation and find employment so they would be able to afford a house. Lynette informed the parenting class she and Roger quarreled frequently. After several weeks Lynette expressed her belief that she had a better chance of getting and keeping a home without Roger.

> Similarly, **Charlene** (first introduced in Chapter 7) was concerned when her husband, Bradley, progressed into Stage Four and subsequently identified closely with other homeless men in the Working Men's Shelter. With this identification Bradley withdrew from the family and did not wish to take part in efforts to find housing or to move from the shelter.

If Lynette had not resisted Roger's refusal to accept their homelessness, the family would not have found the apartment and Lynette would have digressed back to Stage Two or possibly Stage One. Likewise, if Charlene had not defiantly resisted her husband's progression into Stage Four, the family would not have been able to move as quickly as they did. It was Charlene's refusal to identify closely with other homeless mothers that kept her in Stage Three and diligently working to find a home for her family. However, not all families have adult members who are able to resist the pull of spouses towards later stages.

> When I first met **Angela** and **Sam** (see Chapter 6 for more of their story), Angela expressed frustration and resignation of Stage Four. In spite of feeling resigned to being homeless, she frequently voiced hopes of attending a trade school in order to obtain employment and move into a home. Sam, demonstrating the complete resignation of Stage Five, ridiculed her for her dreams by telling her, "No one will hire you, you're homeless. They just want to ignore us. What good will training do?" Over the course of several weeks Angela progressed slowly into Stage Five accepting Sam's view of the world and the family's homeless condition.

Angela, unable to resist Sam's pressure toward the next stage, accepted the identity of hopelessly homeless. Rather than working to realize her goals Angela gave up and slipped into Stage Five. As mentioned in Chapter 7 Angela and Sam became dependent upon shelter staff to find them another place to live when they were evicted from the shelter.

Thirty-five families (35 percent) who participated in this study had both parents present in the shelter. Information concerning the father's shelter experiences was available for only seven (20 percent) of these families. These seven families demonstrated the differences in progression through stages noted above with male partners moving into the next stage somewhat later than adult females of the families. Due to availability of only small numbers of families with both partners present, it cannot be determined if differences between men and women in rates of progress through stages is idiosyncratic for these seven families or a typical progression through stages of shelterization for adult members of homeless families.

In summary stages are not necessarily experienced sequentially. Instead families fluctuate between stages as they experience successes and/or failures in realizing goals of obtaining employment and moving into homes. Adult members' reaction to successes and failures influences their sense of identity. If they experience rejection by the domiciled population or do not receive support for their identity as domiciled families, homeless families will proceed to later stages, possibly skipping stages in the process. Conversely, if families feel they are being evaluated as different from other homeless families, they are likely to return to earlier stages or movement through stages will be halted. Thus, movement through stages is not only influenced but is also affected by how strongly families identify with the domiciled population and if they receive support for this identity from representatives of the domiciled population; such as extended families, shelter staff, agency personnel, and parenting class facilitators. In addition to shelter structure, other factors, such as how families feel they are viewed by shelter staff (Are they treated as different from other homeless families?), strength of family ties, strength of marital ties, progression of spouses through stages, and strength of spouses' identification with being homeless, are important influences on how families experience shelter stays and on future potential for remaining domiciled.

Conclusions

Homelessness has some extremely important impacts on families who must endure the situation. First, strength of ties to extended families can be weakened or broken by early experiences of homeless families. The process of becoming homeless often places at-risk families in situations where assistance must be obtained from extended families in order to remain off the streets and out of shelters. Families pride themselves in being able to assist relatives in times of need. In addition, expectations of reciprocation ensures future assistance for families who provide aid. Consequently, extended families offer assistance in variety of forms to at-risk families. One form of assistance is to allow at-risk families to move in with extended families. Frequently, strains placed on familial relationships by this form of assistance commonly leads to the eviction of guest families. Strained family relationships result in guest families moving into homelessness with impaired support systems traditionally provided by extended families. This loss of support may hinder families' abilities to regain stable domiciled lives by increasing chances of proceeding through all stages of shelterization.

Families who enter shelters immediately begin the process of shelterization. Through a series of stages adult family members begin to identify closely with images and realities of homeless people. They become resigned to their lives and lose hope for the future. They progressively turn to agencies and agency workers for resolution of their problems and thus develop more dependence upon outsiders for management of their activities. Factors which influence progression through the stages are length of time families spend in shelters, number of times families have lived in shelters, strength of ties to extended families, strength of marital relationships, if they perceive treatment by others as reinforcing their identity as homeless, progression of spouses through stages, and strength of spouses' identification with other homeless individuals. Therefore, the longer families remain in shelters the more likely they are to adopt an identity of homeless families and the more dependent they become on shelter workers for problem resolution.

As suggested by the demographics of various contemporary studies of homelessness, race or ethnicity of individuals will effect the chances of persons becoming homeless. However, ethnographic data of this study suggest race or ethnicity of individuals does not influence the shelterization process. All mothers participating in this study experienced varying levels of shelterization regardless of race or ethnicity.

Nonetheless, effects of shelterization on families can be accelerated by experiences with failure and/or an ensuing sense of rejection by representatives of the domiciled population, i.e., shelter workers, personnel of other agencies, parenting class facilitators, or extended family. Conversely, effects of shelterization can be reduced or eliminated by presence of strong ties with extended family and/or strong marital ties which support adults' identification with the domiciled population.

Limitations

In conclusion this study investigated the impact of homelessness and shelterization on families who found themselves living in homeless shelters. This represents only half of the shelterization story. The other half, remaining to be studied, is how the structure of shelters impacts people who are employed there. Do shelter employees experience similar forms of shelterization shaping their opinions of homeless people such that they treat residents in manners consistent with attributes that characterize the identity of homeless people?

Many of the staff of Baghdad Inn and Starlight Inn dressed in a fashion that set them apart from men and women living at the shelters. Family case managers wore new clothing, that fit properly, without stains or flaws, and in line with current fashions. Upon entering the shelters, differences in appearance made it easy to identify shelter staff from residents. Staff members also had freedom of movement throughout the shelters which served to separate them from individuals who lived there. Possession of keys and having entry into restricted areas quickly identified individuals as staff. When I began the study the family case manager had a habit of carrying the receiver end of a telephone with her when she visited the family dorm and women's dorms in Baghdad Inn. Since residents had to obtain permission to use telephones in the shelter, this became a symbol of her position as staff.

Behaviors and mannerisms demonstrated by Baghdad Inn and Starlight Inn staff suggest questions regarding the manner of interactions between staff and residents and barriers constructed by staff need to be investigated. Accordingly, do shelter employees unconsciously adopt manners of interaction which places protective barriers between themselves and shelter residents thereby protecting their identity as domiciled? What devices do employees use to insure protection of a non-homeless identity, and how do these devices influence residents' identities? Do these adaptations to staff's manners of interaction reinforce homeless residents' sense of identity as distinct from the domiciled population? By answering these questions a more complete description of shelterization will emerge. One in which impact on staff members as well as families who must reside in shelters can be determined. The impact of the shelter system structure currently used to assist homeless families can be investigated to determine if it contributes to the continued dependence of homeless families upon shelters and other agencies.

Additionally, this study was unable to determine effects of adults' progression through stages of shelterization on their children. During the first hour of parenting class meetings, mothers discussed problems experienced with their children. Mothers reported their children hitting or biting other children for the first time after moving into the shelter. They also reported their children experienced difficulties going to sleep and sleeping through the night as well as loss of appetite. Many of these behaviors suggest children experienced anger, frustration, fear, and insecurity. I was unable to determine from the mothers' reports which behaviors existed prior to moving into shelters and which were results of homelessness and/or living in shelters. Additionally, service providers, such as Ron Askagrant (1990b) and Babette Pinstripe (1990), expressed concern that children in shelters were learning to think of homeless shelters as home. They feared these young people would grow up to be second generation homeless people giving birth to a third generation of homeless people.

As a result of mothers' reports and concerns of service providers, a series of questions regarding impacts of homelessness and shelter living on children of homeless families need to be investigated. What perceptions do children have about their homelessness?--How do these perceptions affect their behavior and self-concept? Do children experience shelterization the same as adults? Do children of homeless families see their place in the family changed because of shelter experiences? Answers to questions just posed may provide descriptions of how children experience shelter life as well as what to expect from these children in the future. This information can help to assess the impact of the homeless experience on the life chances of the youngest of the homeless population.

These and other questions remain unanswered. The answers may provide important information concerning the futures of current homeless families and their children. Additionally, answers could provide important clues as to changes or adaptations that need to be made in existing services as well as suggesting types of new services which need to be provided to homeless populations in the future.

Notes

1. Several studies suggest some characteristics of homeless shelters resemble those of the total institution (Gounis 1992; Hoch and Slayton 1989; Snow and Anderson 1993; Stark 1994).

2. The majority of parents attending classes were women. Men who are accompanied by children do attend classes. Unfortunately the number of men participating is too small to be of value in understanding the male parent generally. (For further discussion of male parents, refer to Chapter 5.)

CHAPTER 10

A Final Word

The discourse thus far has presented demographic information regarding individual and family homelessness, the stories of homeless mothers gathered during participant-observation of parenting classes, and findings derived from the stories. Further, previous chapters have presented discussions concerning (1) types of assistance provided by extended families to needy members and factors which determine who can expect to receive assistance, (2) an historical perspective of homelessness that traces the progression of modern attitudes toward homeless people from antiquity, and (3) pathways to homelessness taken by families and individuals. This chapter presents first an overview of preceding chapters and secondly, a discussion regarding how all factors previously discussed combine to create environments in which homeless families suffer the consequences of shelterization.

From Mendicant to Homeless

Existence of homeless individuals can be traced throughout history beginning in antiquity. Wandering artisans, vagabonds, beggars, and religious mendicants can be found in historical writings dating back to the Greeks and Athenians (Bahr 1973; Butcher and Lang 1906; Cohen and Sokolovsky 1989). Attitudes toward homeless individuals (as discussed in Chapter 2) have fluctuated from tolerance to intolerance.

In early history homeless wanderers were important sources of news and gossip from other, more distant, townships. Homeless individuals, as a result of performing an important function, were provided food and shelter by the community. However, as societies experienced social disruptions brought about by war, famine, plague, and industrialization, attitudes and behaviors of domiciled citizens toward homeless people changed to intolerance. During times of intolerance homeless people were often viewed with contempt having aspects of their lives (i.e., begging, vagrancy, or sleeping in public) mandated as criminal through legislation or decree (Cohen and Sokolovsky 1989). Distinctions between those worthy and those unworthy of receiving assistance were drawn by the domiciled populace and legislation designed to force the unworthy to work or pay penance was enacted (Axelson and Dail 1988; Cohen and Sokolovsky 1989; Miller 1991). Contemporary homeless populations have attempted to eliminate the label of unworthy and gain necessary services through limited activist movements. Additionally, legal challenges to service agency policies have removed some of the obstacles to receiving aid.

Agencies or individuals considered responsible for the care of homeless persons have fluctuated. Traditionally families of homeless individuals were charged with care of the person (Cohen and Sokolovsky 1989; Hoch and Slayton 1989; Miller 1991). However, when families were unable to carry out its duty, care of homeless individuals would fall on the community of residence. As a result caring for homeless people was frequently viewed as a local problem requiring local solutions (Miller 1991; Ropers 1988; Rossi 1989a). In contemporary society charitable organizations responded early to increases in numbers of homeless people seeking assistance by implementing programs, expanding soup kitchens, and opening shelters.

The characteristics of individuals who comprise homeless populations have undergone variations with the fluctuations created by social disruption. Contemporary homeless populations are predominantly male, however, the number of females present in homeless populations have increased in the last decade (Blake and Abbott 1989; Koegel and Burnam 1992; Rossi 1989a; Stefl 1987; Wright 1989). Minorities are over-represented in homeless populations of the 1980s and 1990s (Blake and Abbott 1989; Rossi 1989a; Stefl 1987; Wright 1989). Contemporary homeless people are young with an average age in the early to mid-thirties (Blake and Abbott 1989; Rossi 1989a; Stefl 1987; Wright 1989). Additionally, homeless populations of the 1980s and 1990s are predominantly single. However, the fastest growing segment of homeless populations is that of families. The number of homeless people who are part of homeless families have increased in size until they represent approximately one-third of the homeless population (Blake and Abbott 1989; Golden 1992; Lee 1989; Stefl 1987). Whether the current homeless population generally has maintained ties with domiciled families and friends is controversial. There are researchers who suggest homeless individuals have lost meaningful contact with extended families (Cohen and Sokolovsky 1989; Committee 1988; Lee 1989; Rossi and Wright 1987; Roth 1989; Shinn, Knickman, and Weitzman 1991; Wright 1989). Conversely, other studies demonstrate that homeless individuals do have ties of varying strengths with domiciled extended families (Bassuk 1992; Committee 1988; Hoch and Slayton 1989; Jones, Gray, and Goldstein 1986; Lee 1989; Miller 1991; Molnar et al. 1991; Piliavin, Sosin, and Westerfelt 1988; Rossi 1989a).

The contemporary homeless population most closely resembles the homeless population found wandering the highways of the United States during the Great Depression. These two groups of homeless individuals are similar in the youth of their members, the increased numbers of women present in the population at each time, the increased numbers of intact families who are homeless, and individuals moving about in search of employment. The over-representation of minorities among the contemporary homeless population is a difference from the population of the Depression.

Contemporary American homeless people and homeless wanderers of the Great Depression differ from other periods. Unlike the contemporary homeless population, vagabonds and hobos were characterized as being disaffiliated from families and friends (Bahr 1973; Lee 1989; Miller 1991), females were only rarely found wandering among vagabonds or hobos (Golden 1992; Rossi 1989a),[1] there were fewer families (adults accompanied by their children) among vagabonds and hobos, and the majority of vagabonds and hobos were white (Rossi 1989a).

The high employment rate during World War II served to empty skid-row areas of all people except those incapable of working due to age or disability. After World War II the United States experienced an economic boom which allowed men returning from war theaters to find employment and begin families. Therefore, skid rows during World War II and in the years after the war were occupied by older white males (Alter et al. 1986; Koegel and Burnam 1992; Lee 1989; Miller 1991; Rossi 1989a,b). Rarely were women found living in skid-row hotels or missions (Alter et al. 1986; Cohen and Sokolovsky 1989; Golden 1992). Additionally, men or women living on skid row were single, having lost family ties prior to moving to skid row (Koegel and Burnam 1992).

From the homeless population of colonial United States to the contemporary homeless population, homeless individuals have wandered the country in search of work. Anderson (1923) described five groups of hobos in his study: (a) seasonal laborers, (b) migratory casual laborers, (c) tramps, (d) homeguards, and (e) bums. Of these five groups; seasonal laborers, migratory casual laborers, and homeguards worked and/or were willing to work. Therefore, one common characteristic of homeless populations throughout history is the lack of employment.

Antecedents to Homelessness

Not unlike the wandering homeless groups of the past, the current homeless population reports loss of employment as an antecedent to homelessness (Blake and Abbott 1989; Committee 1988; Hagen 1987a,b; Kunz 1989). Other antecedents of contemporary homelessness (as discussed in Chapter 2) include not only unemployment but underemployment, lack of affordable housing, deinstitutionalization, and personal reasons. Loss of income resulting from unemployment or reduced income from underemployment may spell the loss of home when families become unable to make rent or mortgage payments. Regardless of availability of units, families with reduced or lost income are able to afford only lower rent apartments. The number of families competing for vacant, low-rent apartments places unemployed or underemployed families at a disadvantage in a limited housing market. Faced with shortages of affordable housing, many families are faced with the alternatives of doubling up with relatives or friends or living on the streets or in homeless shelters. Thus, lack of income through unemployment or reduced income of underemployment merges with the lack of affordable housing to place some families and individuals at a disadvantage in the struggle to find adequate housing.

Additionally, lack of affordable housing increases the possibility that families who have lost homes through evictions or natural disasters will have difficulty locating suitable affordable housing (Gioglio 1989; Hirschl and Momeni 1989; Kozol 1988a; Maza and Hall 1988). Families paying more than thirty percent of their incomes for shelter are at risk of becoming homeless (Kunz 1989). Once families have lost housing affordable alternatives may not be available. Therefore, families, faced with the decision to accept housing that places them at risk of becoming homeless once again in the future, live with relatives or friends until affordable housing can be located, or move into homeless shelters, into cars, or onto the city streets. Doubling up with friends or relatives most commonly represents a temporary solution. The financial burden placed on host families along with the stresses of two families living together often create situations where guest families are evicted (Hope and Young 1986). Likewise housing which consumes exorbitant amounts of income places families at risk of returning to homelessness. Any fluctuation in income or unplanned expenses (such as costly medical treatment for family members) means families will not be able to pay rents, thereby potentially leading to evictions (Committee 1988; Hope and Young 1986).

Deinstitutionalization represents a third possible antecedent to homelessness. Researchers suggest efforts to move mental health treatments away from long-term institutionalization and toward community treatment have served to place former institutionalized patients on the streets among homeless people (Committee 1988; Hirschl and Momeni 1989). The inference that the homeless population is composed in large part by mental health patients released from institutions has been challenged by several researchers (Blau 1992; Gioglio 1989; Isaac and Armat 1990; Lamb 1986; Miller 1991; Shore and Cohen 1992; Wright 1989). Solarz (1992) and Bassuk, Rubin, and Lauriat (1986) suggested that presence of mental illness among homeless individuals is the result of stresses associated with lives of homeless people rather than being the cause of the homeless condition. Additionally, adult members of homeless families are less likely to suffer from mental illness than are homeless individuals (Dail 1990; Solarz 1992). Families with mentally ill adult members may disintegrate prior to homelessness leaving families domiciled while mentally ill individuals become homeless (Isaac and Armat 1990; Shore and Cohen 1992). Therefore, the fact that families disintegrate before becoming homeless or evict mentally ill members rather than becoming homeless as families may be one explanation for the apparent mental health of adults living in homeless families. Additionally, adults who are accompanied by their spouse and/or children into homelessness have the advantage of being able to share stresses of homeless life with family members. By sharing and relying on each other family members reduce stresses to manageable levels. If given a test for mental health, adult members of homeless families appear more healthy than isolated individuals because of the stress reduction role performed by family members.

A fourth antecedent to homelessness discussed was personal reasons. There is some controversy in the literature whether personal reasons represent a primary cause or a contributing factor to homelessness. However, personal reasons frequently given by homeless individuals for homelessness include (1) alcohol or substance abuse, (2) domestic violence, and (3) unstable relationships and domestic disruptions. Alcohol or substance abuse may, like mental illness, represent an important antecedent to the homelessness of individuals but may not be an important reason for homelessness of families (Hagen 1987a; Hope and Young 1986). Domestic violence, like unstable relationships, may precipitate homeless episodes because of the lack of stable family ties that could serve to prevent homelessness (Bassuk 1992; Sullivan and Damrosch 1987). Family ties provide resources to near-homeless families or individuals which can be used to prevent homelessness. When ties are absent or weak individuals or families do not have this resource on which to draw in order to prevent or delay homelessness.   Therefore, it may be the isolation of homeless individuals or families from relatives and friends that pushes families or individuals into homelessness.   The presence of mental illness, alcohol or substance abuse, domestic violence, or instability in relationships contributes to homelessness by encouraging breakdown of family ties and loss of sustaining family resources.

Reactions to Homeless People

The history of homelessness elucidates how attitudes and behaviors of the contemporary general domiciled populace had roots in the attitudes and behaviors of people in the past.   The attitude held by the Federal Government that homelessness is a local problem can be traced from the Acts of Settlement of England and the "warning out" procedure of colonial United States.

The role of extended families in prevention of homelessness has its sources in the views of the functions of families as an institution and an historical role of the traditional family.   Meyer Fortes (1969) suggests that family members have an obligation to provide assistance to needy family members.   Historically the family was viewed as having the ultimate responsibility to care for members who did not have homes and\or were unable to work.   Studies by Cavan and Ranck (1969), Farmer (1970), and Stack (1970) demonstrated how the family can assist its members in times of need.   Individuals who were unable to live with their family were generally found to have been separated from their family by the death of relatives (such as occurred during the Black Plague) or through a personal problem that had forced the family to expel the member (such as alcoholism or mental illness).   These individuals became dependent on local governments and later the Federal Government for assistance.   The Reagan administration tended to give low estimates of the numbers of homeless people (Timmer, Eitzen, and Talley 1994), cut budgets for federal housing programs for low income people (Hoch and Slayton 1989; Rosenthal 1994), and suggested that eating at soup kitchens was a way to save money and that homelessness was voluntary (Rosenthal 1994).   Resistance toward providing aid can be traced from The Statute of Laborers in 1351 England, the Poor Laws of Elizabeth, the workhouses of colonial United States, and the Federal Transients Bureau of the United States during the Great Depression to the resistance of the Reagan administration to offer assistance.

The assumption of the view that homeless individuals are disaffiliated is that individuals who are living on the streets, in missions, or in shelters were unable to draw on families resources because homeless members had become alienated from families rather than the result of a limitation of families' ability to help.   However, recent studies by Allatt and Yeandle (1986), Firth, Hubert, and Forge

(1970), Parish, Hao, and Hogan (1991), and Pearce and McAdoo (1984) suggested that level of assistance provided by families to needy members are limited by ability to provide aid. Current studies of homeless individuals (Bassuk 1992; Committee 1988; Hoch and Slayton 1989; Jones, Gray, and Goldstein 1986; Miller 1991; Molnar et al. 1991; Rossi 1989a;) are finding that they do have contact with their families. Strengths of family ties range from having fragmented and limited contact to having substantial and frequent contact.

The prevailing antiquated view of the homeless population as being composed of able bodied men who are unwilling to work, isolated from family and friends, and voluntarily homeless not only has roots in the past but has repercussions in the present. These attitudes have led many domiciled citizens to resist the development of family shelters in their neighborhoods.[2] It has also led to a general lack of accountability of existing shelters by the domiciled population. As long as homeless people do not threaten everyday activities of the domiciled population and are safely housed in an inconspicuous shelter, domiciled people can reassure themselves the needs of the homeless population are being met. This absolves them of any need for concern or action beyond the symbolic efforts at such holidays as Christmas and Thanksgiving. However, shelters do not always meet the needs of homeless individuals beyond limited support mechanisms and shelter from the natural elements. In fact, as this book suggests, shelters may create a dependence which works to sabotage any efforts to get homeless families into houses or apartments and to keep them there.

The process of shelterization delineated in this book sets in motion a progression through a series of stages that for some culminates with homeless families being dependent upon federal assistance for survival and a shelter system for housing. The longer families remain in shelters the more likely they are to suffer isolation from extended families concurrent with reductions in amounts of assistance or support they may expect or accept from domiciled relatives or friends. Additionally, the longer homeless families reside in shelters the more likely they are to identify closely with images and realities of the homeless population. They become resigned to their lives and lose hope for the future. They progressively turn to agencies and agency workers for resolution of their problems and thus develop more dependence upon outsiders for management of their familial activities. A result of the shelterization process is reduced success of families in gaining and maintaining domiciled existences. The longer families remain sheltered the more likely they are to return to homelessness if they do move into apartments or homes. Additionally, they are far more likely than families who have not progressed to the later stages of shelterization to see homeless shelters as "home."

Thus, this book suggests that while homeless shelters are necessary to meet the immediate, emergency needs of homeless families, prolonged stays in shelters only serve to reduce the chances of families (and possibly their children) to regain stable domiciled existences. These findings lead us to an inference that changes such as those described need to be made in shelter systems if they are to accomplish the most often stated mission of assisting homeless families to regain stable housing.

Suggested Modifications

This book points to some changes that, if implemented, could enhance chances of homeless families to regain stabile domiciled lives. The first two suggestions relate to the structure of homeless shelters such as Baghdad Inn and Starlight Inn. First, shelter buildings need to be designed or modified in order to accommodate families in which fathers and/or older sons are present. By providing accommodations which allow families to live together in family units, stresses placed on family structure could be reduced. In situations where families are allowed to live together, family members could provide emotional support and encouragement to one another thereby preventing progression into later stages of shelterization.

Second, homeless shelters should provide common rooms for homeless families in which they could entertain friends and extended families as well as kitchen areas to prepare family meals. These areas would allow families to have meaningful interactions with domiciled relatives and be able to at least partially reciprocate assistance provided by relatives. Strain between homeless families and domiciled relatives may then be alleviated helping to maintain an important resource and an important source of support for domiciled identity.

Third, rules of homeless shelters need to be changed to allow parents to have greater responsibility for correcting their children's behavior and making decisions concerning their family. This alteration must be done carefully so as to preserve rules that protect individuals who live in shelters and allow homeless families to live in close proximity in peace. However, parents need to have more autonomy in decisions and aspects of parenting. In this way homeless parents would not feel they have been stripped of their parenting role.

Lastly, if further study confirms that present behaviors of shelter staff serves to differentiate themselves from homeless families and strengthens families' identities as homeless, then steps would need to be taken to eliminate these barriers. Homeless shelter staff would need to be sensitized to the existence of these barriers and how their behaviors are perceived by homeless families as well as the consequences of these behaviors on families. By reducing distances between staff and families and encouraging homeless families' continued identification with shelter staff, impacts of shelterization could be reduced. This would result in increasing possibilities of families resisting the identity of being homeless and increasing their chances of maintaining domiciled existences once they move from shelters.

Once a complete picture of how experiences of homelessness, living in homeless shelters, interactions with shelter staff, and interactions with extended families is obtained, then the full impact of the shelterization process can be understood. This understanding can lead to alterations or adaptations of homeless shelters in order to maximize the likelihood that homeless families can regain family homes and be able to maintain those homes into the future with the possibility of never having to experience the trauma of homelessness again.

Research Questions

The current study leaves several questions unanswered. These questions are listed at the end of Chapter 9. Based on these questions several hypotheses for future research can be suggested.

This study represents only half of the shelterization study since the other half, how the shelter structure impacts people employed in shelters, remains unstudied. The questions left unanswered revolve around the impact of the shelter structure on its employees. Shelter staff in Arid Acropolis received salaries which placed them barely above the poverty level. The housing and lifestyles afforded by the salaries were little different from those of homeless families once they received housing assistance. One family case manager reported a family from the shelter had been placed in the apartment complex in which she and her husband lived. This lack of demonstrable differences between shelter staff and shelter residents may have created a need by staff to distance themselves in whatever ways were available. Thus, behaviors that served to set staff apart from residents (such as those mentioned in Chapter 9) were observed. Therefore, as staff find it more difficult to distinguish themselves from their homeless clients in meaningful ways, they will develop behaviors that serve to create distinctions. Thus, in order to understand the complete story of shelterization, this research question remains to be investigated.

Second, the current study did not collect data concerning the perceptions of children in homeless families. Therefore little is known about the effects of shelterization on homeless children. It has been suggested by service providers, such as Ron Askagrant (1990b) and Babette Pinstripe (1990), that children living in shelters are beginning to think of homeless shelters as home. They view the homeless existence as the life they can expect in the future. If this is true then homeless shelters may be training successive generations of homeless clients. Research questions concerning the impact of homelessness on children need to be addressed. Do children of homeless families experience the shelterization process the same as adults? Do children perceive shelter rules as affecting their parents' authority over their behavior? Do they begin to view their parents as older siblings to be ignored while shelter rules and staff requests are to be followed (making the shelter and its staff the parent)? How do children perceive their experiences with homelessness and how do these experiences affect future development of homeless children? Does homelessness and shelterization have a lasting and negative impact on children?

These are only a few of the questions that remain unanswered. However, in order to understand all the ramifications of homelessness and to prevent the worst of the impacts of homelessness on future generations, answers to these questions are vital.

Notes

1. According to Golden (1992, 136), the number of females among hobos have been underestimated. She suggests that females in efforts to protect themselves disguised their gender with male clothing and, thus, were counted as male. However, the number of females (6.3 percent) among the hobo population were far fewer in size than the number of females present in the contemporary homeless population.

2. This exclusionist phenomenon is referred to as NIMBY or Not in my back yard (Snow and Anderson 1993).

APPENDIX

Methodology

Carol Stack (1970, ix) writes that she "anticipates curiosity about how a young white woman could conduct a study of black family life."[1] In recognizing the insight of this assertion, I have elected to include an explanation of why I decided to study homeless families in a background segment of this appendix.

The second section of this appendix addresses preparations taken for the field work component of the study. This will be followed with a discussion of (a) the decision to use participant-observation and (b) the role I assumed while attending parenting class meetings. The final section discusses some complications encountered in the field and challenges of participating in class meetings and discussions[2] with families.

Background

During my first two years of graduate study I rented a small house not far from campus. Older, slightly deteriorated single-family homes were predominate structures of the neighborhood. In addition to single-family dwellings there were a few small apartment complexes, several fast food restaurants, and a few bars. The houses and apartments were occupied by university students and working-class families.

A block from my house was a vacant house I often passed while taking a short cut to a local grocery store. During one trip I realized several men occupied this house. I began noticing these men in several other public locations in the neighborhood. The men would meet for coffee and conversation at a local fast-food restaurant every morning after university students had eaten and left. Their conversations were filled with information regarding absent friends, amounts of money they had found in various parking lots in the area, places offering the highest prices for aluminum cans, budding romances, and the drinking party of the previous night. Having read some of the literature written during the Depression which stressed the social isolation of homeless men, I was astonished at the level of sociability these men demonstrated.

In an attempt to understand more about these men, I took notes on their activities, talked with several of them to learn how they provided for their needs, and read much of the current literature about homelessness. I learned from the literature of growing numbers of homeless families found on the streets of the United States. Through my work with Bernard Farber, I had developed an interest in the processes by which families in crisis situations resolve their problems and how they make adjustments necessary for the continued functioning of families. At this point I decided to study homeless families as an example of families in crisis. Having selected the subject of my study I was faced with selecting a method.

Preparing for the Field

The nature of the population, questions to be answered regarding use of extended family, and lack of adequate existing data led me to the classical Chicago School studies and field research that students under Robert Park, Ernest W. Burgess, and others at the University of Chicago had conducted. These studies have served as foundations for field research in sociology and thereby, provide good models for research design. Park and Burgess emphasized use of field research as a means of gathering data from the point of view of the actors. They urged their students to strive for empathy and an understanding of the lives of others (Adler and Adler 1987). Park encouraged his students to gather data first hand. Park defined "getting your hands dirty in real research" as opposed to "grubbing in the library" and utilizing routine records "prepared by tired bureaucrats" (McKinney 1966, 71). He implored his students to "Go and sit in the lounges of the luxury hotels and on the doorsteps of the flophouses; sit on the Gold Coast settees and on the slum shakedowns; . . . In short, gentlemen, go get the seat of your pants dirty in real research" (McKinney 1966, 71). Park and Burgess felt that through field research sociologists could understand the meaning the situation held for the actors.

Accordingly, this understanding allows sociologists to "attain the intuitive empathy necessary to grasp their subjects' perspectives on the social world" (Adler and Adler 1987, 12). Empathy and understanding obtained through the process of "getting your pants dirty" serves to aid sociologists in understanding ways in which research subjects organize their attitudes and behaviors; how actors perceive their world with all its joys and problems (Adler and Adler 1987).

In undertaking a study of homeless families, I wanted to understand how homeless families (families in crisis) structured their lives, viewed their families, and perceived their homeless situation. As a result field research (i.e., going amongst homeless families and listening to their stories) seemed the best approach.

Prior to entering the field I felt it was important to understand more about the homeless population of Arid Acropolis[3] so that I might locate a site where I could meet homeless families. To this end I began contacting various homeless shelters. Administrators of these agencies were contacted by telephone and appointments for face-to-face interviews were arranged. Since most of the administrators complained of being overworked and set time restrictions on the appointments, it was of utmost importance to use the time available to the best advantage. Therefore, I decided to conduct formal interviews for these meetings since this format allowed me to cover the areas of interest within the allotted time. The purpose of the interviews was to determine if the agency might fit into the study. Consequently, I asked questions concerning the agency and it's policies, various attributes of homeless individuals living in shelters, availability of agency documentation and statistical information collected by agencies regarding homeless individuals residing at shelters, and possibilities of conducting interviews with residents within the shelter.

It was not feasible to conduct face-to-face interviews with any of the administrators at one agency, the Baghdad Inn. Nancy Foneghost (1989), the case manager coordinator, expressed a reluctance to set an appointment for an interview. Instead a tour of the facility was arranged. Many of the questions that I would have asked during the interview were answered during the tour. The remainder of questions were answered in telephone conversations with Ms. Foneghost.

It was during a phone conversation with Ms. Foneghost (1989) that I first learned of the Homeless Outreach Parenting Class that was offered at Baghdad Inn and the potential it held for this study.[4] She explained the purpose of the class and suggested it might be the best medium for meeting parents living at the shelter. After visiting a parenting class session and meeting the facilitator,[5] I concurred with Ms. Foneghost that this represented the forum in which to meet homeless families.

Deciding to Participate

Robert G. Burgess (1984) writes that researchers need to consider conditions in field settings in order to conduct effective research. As I became familiar with the research setting through the agency interviews, several factors concerning the conditions of the field surfaced and needed to be considered in determining the most effective method of collecting data: (a) time available to the researcher for data collection, (b) limitations of the setting, (c) willingness of homeless families to be interviewed and their availability for interview appointments, and (d) concerns of homeless families about the research.

The time I had available for data collection was limited by various constraints, including commitments to the graduate program and the time used for traveling to shelters. Times when families might be available served to additionally limit times data could be gathered. This meant that the method of collecting data needed to be efficient in its use of time.

At the beginning of the study I estimated that six months would be needed to conduct formal interviews. As it became clear that informal interviewing and participant-observation would be the primary method used to obtain data about families, the time needed to collect data was expanded to eighteen months. The first two months in the field were spent observing parenting classes with minimal participation on my part. This allowed mothers time to get acquainted with me and accustomed to my presence. After this initial period I began full participation in the classes, including participating in activities and discussions. The first full year was spent exclusively at Baghdad Inn collecting data. Starting the second year parenting classes were offered at a second shelter, the Starlight Inn. Data collection was extended to include this shelter and continued at this location for twelve months. Therefore, actual time spent in the field collecting data was two years.

The setting (i.e., Baghdad Inn and, later, Starlight Inn) placed constraints on the study by limiting times families could be available for interviewing. Shelters (particularly Baghdad Inn) required adult members of families to be out of the shelters from early in the morning until mid-afternoon when children arrived home from school. It proved difficult to make contact with adult members after departure from the shelters since they were leaving for appointments with various welfare agencies or leaving to find places to spend the day. Contact with adults prior to leaving the shelter could interfere with their daily shelter-assigned duties creating problems between adults and shelter staff. Late afternoons were limited because children were present and adult members focused on caring for their children and preparing the evening meal. Additionally, the shelters were unable to provide private locations in which to conduct interviews.

These limitations made contact with families and finding locations in which to meet problematic.

To enhance my understanding of the experiences of these families, it was decided not to use nonparticipant-observation as the only method of gathering data. I felt that observation alone would not give me the needed flexibility to subtly direct conversations into areas of interest. Blumer (1969) writes that the best way to discern the social world is to study that world from the perspective of the members. Heeding Blumer's statement I felt that by merely observing the mothers and their interactions in parenting classes, I would have missed the full meaning of their experiences as homeless parents. Becoming acquainted with parents through interaction enhanced my ability to understand the world of homeless families as seen through their eyes. Furthermore, if I had remained merely an observer, suspicions mothers felt toward strangers would have intruded upon their interactions with one another. This intrusion may have changed behaviors of parents in important ways thereby distorting data. Yancey and Rainwater (1970, 254) suggest obtrusion can be reduced by researchers integrating "the role of observer with roles that are available within the organization or group being studied." Thus, by becoming a participating member of the class I was able to assure them of my honest effort to empathize with them as individuals and my attempt to appreciate the difficult situation they face.

Another method that could have been used to gather data is participation. This method would have necessitated my entry into the shelter disguised as a homeless individual. However, since I would not have had children with me upon intake I would have been housed in the single women's dorm. Placement in a dorm separate from the families' dorm combined with the mothers' intolerance toward single women would have isolated me from the mothers and severely restricted my capability to gather necessary data. This method would have limited my ability to ask questions that would have been seen as unusual and possibly threatening.

On a more ethical note it is possible that by entering the research setting in the covert manner required of full participation, discomfort or pain would be caused to the families living in the shelter. In considering this method I needed to "weigh the scientific and social benefits of that procedure against its possible cost in human discomfort" (Erikson 1967, 368). One such discomfort would have been the loss of a bed for a woman who depends upon the shelter to provide haven from the streets. Therefore, knowing I would displace a homeless woman and that other methods of data gathering were at my disposal, I chose not to use this method.

Early in the study I had considered formal interviewing of adult members of families as my primary method. I tried to set up interviews with four mothers I had met through the parenting classes. On the appointed day I would drive to the shelter only to find the mothers not available or absent from the shelter. The mothers explained that they had either forgotten the appointment or they had a prior commitment they could not forego. In an effort to improve communication I tried giving the mothers a business card listing a telephone number to call in the event they needed to cancel the appointment. Recognizing their financial difficulties I attached a quarter to the business card in order to eradicate any cost to the mother. This method failed because the mothers would spend the quarter on other things or would simply forget to call me.

Robert Burgess (1984) and Rosalie Wax (1971) argued that field workers need to maintain flexibility in conducting research. That is, "if he finds himself in a field situation where he is limited by a particular method, theory, or technique, he will do well to slip through the bars and try to find out what is really going on" (Wax 1971, 10). In order to remain flexible and take advantage of any possible interview situation, I undertook a method of group-focused interviewing when I was called on to lead one of the parenting class meetings in the first three months of my volunteer work. During this class I asked the mothers some direct questions regarding problems they faced in caring for children while living in the shelter. The mothers' answers to these questions tended to be evasive. They quickly changed the subject, talked amongst themselves, or gave me a cold stare. The mothers made it clear that they resented this blunt intrusion into their personal lives even by someone they knew.

Reactions of the mothers to my questions demonstrated the depth of concern about their roles in a research project. The parents[6] in Baghdad Inn and Starlight Inn were often suspicious of people they did not know. Out of fear of possible repercussions from shelter authorities for disclosures concerning shelter procedures and living conditions, the parents tend to limit their conversations to trivial matters concerning their lives in the shelter (such as when they are scheduled to do laundry). Barriers of silence are quickly erected and take substantial time to overcome.

While the effectiveness of conducting formal interviews was looking bleak, it became clear that the discussions during parenting class meetings would provide the information I was seeking. A method needed to be adopted which would allow parents to become familiar with me and become comfortable with my role as researcher. Participant-observation seemed to be the method that met this qualification while being flexible enough to work within the framework of time and setting limitations. By providing me with a role which allowed me to participate in the activities of parenting classes and to have meaningful interactions with the parents, participant-observation promised to be the best method of gathering data. Use of a method of interviewing which was informal and unstructured (a method characteristic of Park and Burgess and used by Anderson (Bulmer 1984)) aided in reducing parents' suspicions and surmounted barriers of silence I had experienced. Additionally, by enlisting Babette Pinstripe's[7] help, class topics could be focused on areas of particular interest.

In the Field

The families' stories which provided data for this study came from my participant-observation in parenting classes. An entry into the world of homeless families was gained by becoming a volunteer aide for parenting class meetings, which were offered weekly at Baghdad Inn and Starlight Inn.   As a volunteer aide I was expected to participate fully in the classes by becoming involved in discussions, offering suggestions, relating experiences from my past, and on occasion leading class discussions.

My role as participant-observer was well suited for this study. The role of volunteer provided me a natural entrance into the shelter world of the families. In addition it gave me a purpose for being in the shelters at class meeting times as well as at other times, i.e., before and after classes. Classes dealt with features of family life that were of importance to the study, i.e., parents' relationship with their extended family, hopes for the future, and views on living in the shelters or being homeless. Consequently, the necessity of asking questions about these matters was reduced. Conversations frequently could be directed into areas of interest with a little gentle probing. Furthermore, since parents' attendance was required for the case management plan, the parenting class provided an ideal setting in which to meet all the parents staying at both of the shelters.

Classes were structured to include time for personal introductions at the beginning. Introductions were performed most specifically during classes in which several new parents were present. It was at these times I introduced myself and explained my role as a researcher interested in homeless families and their shelter experiences. Therefore, parents were aware of my role as a researcher. This role was reaffirmed with periodic introductions as new parents attended classes.

In the beginning parents attending parenting class meetings demonstrated some reluctance in divulging information out of mistrust and fear. Therefore, parents were not pressured to give information or relate personal histories in class. Class members could participate in discussions to the degree they felt comfortable. They gave only information they chose to reveal. However, as I became a fully participating group member and started sharing my personal history and fears, parents began treating me as a class member rather than a researcher.

Class meetings with parents presented a problematic situation for note taking. Parents tended to be apprehensive of people they perceived as officials.   They feared eviction from the shelters, removal of their children, or embarrassment.   Their comments to officials tended to be guarded and included only information they felt officials wanted to hear.   Therefore, in an effort to put parents at ease with my presence in parenting classes, I chose to dictate notes into a tape recorder after leaving the shelter.   This reduced the parents' feelings of having to weigh each word they uttered.   By not taking notes or recording sessions, obstacles to my acceptance by the families were reduced.   Families could begin to think of me as a member of the group and not primarily a researcher.

Furthermore, I dressed in well-worn clothing and used language devoid of academic jargon as a way to reduce resistance to my presence in the classes.   Additionally, I adopted a role that was a mixture of friend and researcher; much like what was employed by Liebow (1967) and Whyte (1955) in their studies.   This role has been labeled buddy-researcher by Snow, Benford, and Anderson (1986). In line with being a buddy this role involves both receiving and giving on the part of the researcher.   As a result I was frequently called on for advice concerning problems mothers experienced in their interactions with various agencies.   In addition I provided mothers with small loans (given without the expectation of being repaid) for the purchase of sandwiches or sodas.   The role of being a friend also carried the reverse expectation of receiving gifts.   Therefore, I accepted repayment of loans as well as learned to graciously accept food and sodas from mothers even though I knew it worked a hardship on them.

As I became an accepted class member my presence in the shelters at other times was not questioned.   When I arrived early I was included in conversations occurring between mothers.   During these chats I frequently would be informed of special news, i.e., arrival of Section 8-housing certificates,[8] receipt of federal assistance, accomplishments of children, and, of course, the latest shelter gossip.[9]

Informal visiting and sharing extended beyond the shelter walls. Mothers stopped me on the streets outside the shelters or in front of other service agencies to share exciting news or tragedies which had occurred.   Parents with news they felt could not wait for chance meetings or the next class stopped at Babette Pinstripe's office at the Outreach Center or came to stress management classes where I was a volunteer.   Basically, informal visiting between myself and parents occurred anyplace we happened to meet.

Through the parents I learned about late night gossip sessions and conflicts between staff and families which transpired at times I was not at the shelter.   Parents also provided information on families who had left the shelters, i.e., why families had left, if parents had been evicted and why, and where the families had gone.

Leaving the Field and Analyzing the Data

As with any method participant observation was not without some problems. First, in spite of attempts to reduce my identification with the mothers and maintain objectivity, I developed close attachments to several mothers. These friendships made it difficult to maintain objectivity. Gans (1962) recognized that researchers can identify too closely with subjects and that this detracts from the objectivity of the research. Nevertheless, Gans assured the reader that the effects of identification can be "reduced even further in the time which elapses between the end of field work, the data analysis, and the writing of the report" (Gans 1962, 343). Following Gans' advice I took time for decompression between leaving the field and beginning the data analysis. This resulted in reducing the effects of friendships on research objectivity.

Another problem during the study was the guilt I felt each time I left the shelter and returned to the comfort of home. Interaction with women who lived amongst mice and roaches, struggled with securing housing and food for their children while I lived in a comfortable mouse- and roach-free house was disconcerting. The mothers' demonstrations of strength and determination and freely discussing my feelings with Babette Pinstripe and other service providers assisted me in resolving this issue while in the field. Furthermore, decompression time after leaving the field served to dull guilt feelings and replace them with a scientific point of view.

Summary

This study developed from an association with a group of men whose behaviors challenged my assumptions regarding social behavior of homeless men. After learning more about the homeless population, I became curious about how families adjusted to homelessness.

The study utilized participant-observation to gather data on lives of homeless families as they entered, resided in, and left the Baghdad Inn and Starlight Inn over a period of two years. Other data gathering methods, i.e., interviews and observations, were explored but rejected because of limitations or ineffectiveness in gathering data from this particular population.

Interaction with the mothers were informal and unstructured in an effort to reduce the mothers' anxieties. Field notes were taped immediately after the parenting classes. After transcription these notes were organized into family files whereby families could be tracked throughout the study or length of time families spent at the shelters. As previously mentioned I allowed time to pass between exit from the field and analysis of data in order to regain objectivity and overcome possible effects of identification (Gans 1962). Once decompression time was observed notes were analyzed and the report written.

Notes

1. Elliot Liebow (1967) discusses how race acted to distance him from his subjects frequently making him feel like an outsider.

2. The activities I participated in as a member of parenting classes are discussed in detail later in the appendix.

3. The names of the community and shelters where data was collected as well as names of individuals have been changed to protect the identity of homeless families who participated in the study.

4. More thorough descriptions of Baghdad Inn, Starlight Inn, and parenting classes (including a description of their purpose, focus, and organization) may be found in the Preface.

5. The parenting class facilitator was not an employee of Baghdad Inn. The shelter administrator invited the Homeless Outreach office to send a life skills instructor who could introduce parents residing at the shelter to alternative methods of disciplining children.

6. To distinguish parents who participated in the study from parents who did not come to parenting class meetings or elected not to participate in the study, I shall refer to participants as "the parents."

7. The parenting class facilitator's name has been changed to protect the identity of the homeless parents who participated in this study.

8. Section 8-housing certificates are part of a federal government housing program that provides money to disadvantaged families to pay rent. This program is discussed in Chapter 6.

9. After I had been participating in parenting classes for several months, mothers told me they had trouble remembering my name. In order for them to talk about me amongst themselves, they began calling me "that Sandy Duncan lady," because they felt I resembled Sandy Duncan.

BIBLIOGRAPHY

Adler, Patricia A., and Peter Adler. 1987. *Membership roles in field research*. Newbury Park, CA: Sage.

Allatt, Patricia, and Susan Yeandle. 1986. It's not fair, is it?: Youth unemployment, family relations, and the social contract. In *The experience of unemployment*, edited by Sheila Allen, Alan Waton, Kate Purcell, and Stephen Wood, 98-115. London: MacMillan.

Alter, Jonathan, Alexander Stile, Shawn Doherty, Nikke Finke Greenberg, Susan Agrest, Vern E. Smith, and George Raine. 1986. Homeless in America. In *Housing the homeless*, edited by Jon Erickson and Charles Wilhelm, 3-16. New Brunswick, NJ: Center for Urban Policy Research.

Anderson, Nels. 1923. *The hobo: The sociology of the homeless man*. Chicago: The University of Chicago Press.

---. 1940. *Men on the move*. Chicago: The University of Chicago Press.

---. 1975. *The American hobo*. Leiden, Netherlands: E. J. Brill.

Angell, Robert Cooley. 1965. *The family encounters the depression.* Gloucester, MA: Peter Smith.

Annual Report. 1989. Baghdad Inn Shelter: Annual Report.

---. 1990. Baghdad Inn Shelter: Annual Report.

Appelbaum, Richard P. 1988. In *The invisible homeless: A new urban ecology*, edited by Richard H. Ropers, 19-26. New York: Human Sciences Press.

---. 1990. Counting the Homeless. *Homelessness in the United States: Data and issues*, edited by Jamshid A. Momeni, 1-16. New York: Praeger.

Apple, Georgette. 1989. Personal conversation. Teacher, Special School for Homeless Children.

Askagrant, Ron. 1990a. *Characteristics of homeless persons residing at Baghdad Inn: 1987-1990.* Unpublished report.

---. 1990b. Personal conversation. Supervisor of case managers for Baghdad Inn.

Axelson, Leland J., and Paula W. Dail. 1988. The changing character of homelessness in the United States. *Family Relations* 37:463-69.

Bahr, Howard M. 1973. *Skid row: An introduction to disaffiliation.* New York: Oxford University Press.

Bahr, Howard M., and Theodore Caplow. 1973. *Old men drunk and sober.* New York: New York University Press.

Baker, Susan G., and David A. Snow. 1989. Homelessness in Texas: Estimates of population size and demographic composition. In *Homelessness in the United States, volume I: State surveys*, edited by Jamshid A. Momeni, 205-18. New York: Greenwood Press.

Bassuk, Ellen L. 1986. Homeless families: Single mothers and their children in Boston shelters. In *The mental health needs of homeless persons*, edited by Ellen L. Bassuk, 45-53. San Francisco: Jossey-Bass.

---. 1992. Women and children without shelter: The characteristics of homeless families. In *Homelessness: A national perspective*, edited by Marjorie J. Robertson and Milton Greenblatt, 257-64. New York: Plenum Press.

Bassuk, Ellen L., and Lynn Rosenberg. 1988. Why does family homelessness occur? A case-control study. *American Journal of Public Health* 78:783-88.

Bassuk, Ellen L., Lenore Rubin, and Alison S. Lauriat. 1986. Characteristics of sheltered homeless families. *American Journal of Public Health* 76:1097-1101.

Baum, Alice S., and Donald W. Burnes. 1993. *A nation in denial: The truth about homelessness*. Boulder, CO: Westview Press.

Blake, Gerald F., and Martin L. Abbott. 1989. Homelessness in the Pacific Northwest. In *Homelessness in the United States, volume I: State surveys*, edited by Jamshid A. Momeni, 165-280. New York: Greenwood Press.

Blau, Joel. 1992. *The visible poor: Homelessness in the United States*. New York: Oxford University Press.

Blumberg, Leonard, and Robert R. Bell. 1959. Urban migration and kinship ties. *Social Problems* 6(4):328-33.

Blumer, Herbert. 1969. *Symbolic interaction*. Englewood Cliffs, NJ: Prentice-Hall.

Bogue, Donald J. 1986. An introduction to Chicago's skid rows--survey results. In *Housing the homeless*, edited by Jon Erickson and Charles Wilhelm, 190-222. New Brunswick, NJ: Center for Urban Policy Research.

Bott, Elizabeth. 1971. *Family and social network: Roles, norms, and external relationships in ordinary urban families, Second edition*. London: Tavistock.

Breakey, William R. 1992. Mental health services for homeless people. In *Homelessness: A national perspective*, edited by Marjorie J. Robertson and Milton Greenblatt, 101-7. New York: Plenum Press.

Bulmer, Martin. 1984. *The Chicago school of sociology: Institutionalization, diversity, and the rise of sociological research*. Chicago: The University of Chicago Press.

Burgess, Ernest W., Harvey J. Locke, and Mary Margaret Thomes. 1963. *The family: From institution to companionship*. New York: American Book Company.

Burgess, Robert G. 1984. *In the field: An introduction to field research*. London: George Allen and Unwin.

Burt, Martha R. 1992. *Over the edge: The growth of homelessness in the 1980s*. New York: Russell Sage Foundation.

Burt, Martha R., and Barbara E. Cohen. 1990. A sociodemographic profile of the service-using homeless: Findings from a national survey. In *Homelessness in the United States--data and issues*, edited by Jamshid A. Momeni, 17-38. New York: Praeger.

Burton, Linda M., and Peggye Dilworth-Anderson. 1991. The intergenerational family roles of aged black Americans. *Marriage and Family Review* 16:311-30.

Bush, George. 1989. Inaugural address. Washington, DC. *Congressional Quarterly* 47:142-43.

Butcher, Samuel H., and Andrew Lang (Translators). 1906. *The odyssey of Homer*. New York: Macmillan.

Calsyn, Robert J., and Gary A. Morse. 1991. Predicting chronic homelessness. *Urban Affairs Quarterly* 27:155-64.

Carliner, Michael S. 1987. Homelessness: A housing problem? In *The homeless in contemporary society*, edited by Richard D. Bingham, Roy E. Green, and Sammis B. White, 119-29. Newbury Park, CA: Sage.

Cavan, Ruth Shonle, and Katherine Howland Ranck. 1969. *The family and the depression: A study of one hundred Chicago families*. Freeport, NY: Books for Libraries Press.

Cohen, Barbara E., and Martha R. Burt. 1990. Food sources and intake of homeless persons. In *Homelessness in the United States--data and issues*, edited by Jamshid A. Momeni, 39-60. New York: Praeger.

Cohen, Carl I., and Jay Sokolovsky. 1989. *Old men of the bowery: Strategies for survival among the homeless*. New York: The Guilford Press.

Committee on Health Care for Homeless People. 1988. *Homelessness, health, and human needs*. Washington, DC: National Academy Press.

Cooper, Mary Anderson. 1987. The role of religious and nonprofit organizations in combating homelessness. In *The homeless in contemporary society*, edited by Richard D. Bingham, Roy E. Green, and Sammis B. White, 130-49. Newbury Park, CA: Sage.

Coward, Raymond T., and Robert W. Jackson. 1983. Environmental stress: The rural family. In *Stress and the family, volume I: Coping with normative transitions*, edited by Hamilton I. McCubbin and Charles R. Figley, 188-201. New York: Brunner/Mazel.

Culhane, Dennis, and Marc Fried. 1988. Paths in homelessness: A view from the streets. In *Affordable housing and the homeless*, edited by Jürgen Friedrichs, 175-87. Berlin: Walter de Gruyter.

Curtis, W. Robert. 1986. The deinstitutionalization story. *The Public Interest* 85:34-49.

Dail, Paula W. 1990. The psychosocial context of homeless mothers with young children: Program and policy implications. *Child Welfare* LXIX(4):291-308.

Dornbusch, Sanford M., Leonard Drasner, P. Herbert Leiderman, Iris Litt, Hames MacMahon, Hans Steiner, and Marlyn Winkleby. 1991. *The Stanford studies of homeless families, children, and youth*. Stanford, CA: The Stanford Center for the Study of Families, Children, and Youth.

Elder, Glen H. 1974. *Children of the Great Depression*. Chicago: The University of Chicago Press.

Elliott, Marta, and Lauren J. Krivo. 1991. Structural determinants of homelessness in the United States. *Social Problems* 39:113-29.

Erickson, Jon, and Charles Wilhelm. 1986. Introduction. In *Housing the homeless*, edited by Jon Erickson and Charles Wilhelm, xix-xxxvii. New Brunswick, NJ: Center for Urban Policy Research.

Erikson, Kai T. 1967. A comment on disguised observation in sociology. *Social Problems* 14:366-73.

Farber, Bernard. 1974. Structural differences in reciprocity. In *The family: Its structures and functions*, 2d ed., edited by Rose Laub Coser. New York: St. Martin's.

Farmer, Mary. 1970. *The family*. London: Longmans, Green, and Co., LTD.

Ferraro, Kathleen J. 1994. Not that easy: Stories from the streets and shelters. In *Reflections on homelessness in Maricopa County: Preliminary report of the research project for homeless people*, edited by Kathleen J. Ferraro, 1-16. Arizona: College of Public Programs, Arizona State University.

Field Notes. 1992. Personal research notes taken during research involving homeless men living in a city park.

Finch, Janet. 1989. *Family obligations and social change*. Cambridge: Polity Press.

Findaroom, Mike. 1989. Personal conversation. Housing Director for a charities support shelter in Arid Acropolis.

Fiore, Joan, Joseph Becker, and David B. Coppel. 1983. Social network interactions: A buffer or a stress. *American Journal of Community Psychology* 11:423-39.

Firth, Raymond, Jane Hubbert, and Anthony Forge. 1970. *Families and their relatives: Kinship in a middle-class sector of London*. London: Routledge and Kegan Paul.

Foneghost, Nancy. 1989. Personal conversation. Case manager coordinator for Baghdad Inn.

Fortes, Meyer. 1969. *Kinship and the social order: The legacy of Lewis Henry Morgan*. London: Routledge and Kegan Paul.

Gans, Herbert J. 1962. *The urban villagers: Group and class in the life of Italian-Americans*. New York: The Free Press of Glencoe.

Garrett, Gerald R., and Russell K. Schutt. 1989. Homelessness in Massachusetts: Description and analysis. In *Homelessness in the United States, volume I: State surveys,* edited by J. A. Momeni, 73-89. New York: Greenwood Press.

Gioglio, Gerald R. 1989. Homelessness in New Jersey: The social service network and the people served. In *Homelessness in the United States, volume I: State surveys*, edited by Jamshid A. Momeni, 113-30. New York: Greenwood Press.

Glaser, Daniel. 1964. *The effectiveness of a prison and parole system*. New York: Bobbs-Merrill.

Goffman, Erving. 1961. *Asylums: Essays on the social situation of mental patients and other inmates.* Garden City, NY: Doubleday.

Golden, Stephanie. 1992. *The women outside: Meanings and myths of homelessness*. Berkeley: University of California.

Goldman, Howard H., and Joseph P. Morrissey. 1985. The alchemy of mental health policy: Homelessness and the fourth cycle of reform. *American Journal of Public Health* 75:727-31.

Gounis, Kostas. 1992. The manufacture of dependency: Shelterization revisited. *New England Journal of Public Policy* 8(1):685-93.

Hagen, Jan I. 1987a. The heterogeneity of homelessness. *Social Casework* 68:451-57.

---. 1987b. Gender and homelessness. *Social Work* 32:312-16.

Hardey, Michael. 1989. Lone parents and the home. In *Home and family: Creating the domestic sphere*, edited by Graham Allan and Graham Crow, 122-41. London: MacMillan.

Harrington, Michael. 1984. *The new American poverty*. New York: Holt, Rinehart, and Winston.

Hirschl, Thomas, and Jamshid. A. Momeni. 1989. Homelessness in New York: A demographic and socioeconomic analysis. In *Homelessness in the United States, volume I: State surveys*, edited by Jamshid A. Momeni, 131-44. New York: Greenwood Press.

Hoch, Charles. 1987. A brief history of the homeless problem in the United States. In *The homeless in contemporary society*, edited by Richard D. Bingham, Roy E. Green, and Sammis B. White, 16-32. Newbury Park, CA: Sage.

Hoch, Charles, and Robert A. Slayton. 1989. *New homeless and old: Community and the skid-row hotel.* Philadelphia: Temple University Press.

Hombs, Mary Ellen. 1990. *Contemporary world issues: American homelessness.* Santa Barbara, CA: ABC-CLIO.

Hope, Marjorie, and James Young. 1986. *The faces of homelessness.* Lexington, MA: Lexington Books.

Hopper, Kim, and L. Stuart Cox. 1986. Litigation in advocacy for the homeless: The case of New York City. In *Housing the homeless*, edited by Jon Erickson and Charles Wilhelm, 303-14. New Brunswick, NJ: The Center for Urban Policy Research.

Interagency Council on the Homeless. 1991. *Executive summary: The 1990 annual report of the Interagency Council on the homeless.* Washington, DC: U. S. Government Printing Office.

Isaac, Rael Jean, and Virginia C. Armat. 1990. *Madness in the streets: How psychiatry and the law abandoned the mentally ill.* New York: The Free Press.

Jahiel, Rene I. 1987. The situation of homelessness. In *The homeless in contemporary society,* edited by Richard D. Bingham, Roy E. Green, and Sammis B. White, 99-118. Newbury Park, CA: Sage.

Jencks, Christopher. 1994. *The homeless.* Cambridge, MA: Harvard University Press.

Jones, Billy E., Beverly A. Gray, and Deborah B. Goldstein. 1986. Psychosocial profiles of the urban homeless. In *Treating the homeless: Urban psychiatry's challenge*, edited Billy E. Jones, 48-64. Washington, DC: American Psychiatric Press.

Jones, Douglas Lamar. 1975. The strolling poor: Transiency in Eighteenth-Century Massachusetts. *The Journal of Social History* 18(spring):28-54.

Kivisto, Peter. 1989. Homelessness in the frostbelt: The case of Illinois. In *Homelessness in the United States, volume I: State surveys*, edited by Jamshid A. Momeni, 57-71. New York: Greenwood Press.

Koch, June Q. 1987. The federal role in aiding the homeless. In *The homeless in contemporary society*, edited by Richard D. Bingham, Roy E. Green, and Sammis B. White, 216-30. Newbury Park, CA: Sage.

Koegel, Paul, and M. Audrey Burnam. 1992. Problems in the assessment of mental illness among the homeless: An empirical approach. In *Homelessness: A national perspective*, edited by Marjorie J. Robertson and Milton Greenblatt, 77-99. New York: Plenum Press.

Kozol, Jonathan. 1988a. A reporter at large: The homeless and their children--I. *The New Yorker*, January, 65-84.

---. 1988b. *Rachel and her children: Homeless families in America*. New York: Crown.

Kübler-Ross, Elisabeth. 1969. *On death and dying*. New York: Macmillan.

Kunz, Julia S. 1989. Homelessness in Missouri: Populations, problems, and policy. In *Homelessness in the United States, volume I: State surveys*, edited by Jamshid A. Momeni, 91-112. New York: Greenwood Press.

La Gory, Mark, Ferris J. Ritchey, Timothy O'Donoghue, and Jeffrey Mullis. 1989. Homelessness in Alabama: A variety of people and experiences. In *Homelessness in the United States, volume I: State surveys*, edited by Jamshid A. Momeni, 1-20. New York: Greenwood Press.

Lamb, H. Richard. 1986. Deinstitutionalization and the homeless mentally ill. In *Housing the homeless*, edited by Jon Erickson and Charles Wilhelm, 262-78. New Brunswick, NJ: The Center for Urban Policy Research.

Lang, Michael H. 1989. *Homelessness amid affluence: Structure and paradox in the American political economy*. New York: Praeger.

Larney, Barbara E. 1994. Children of World War II in Germany: A life course analysis. Ph.D. diss., Arizona State University.

Lasch, Christopher. 1977. *Haven in a heartless world: The family besieged.* New York: Basic Books.

Leavitt, Jacqueline. 1992. Homelessness and the housing crisis. In *Homelessness: A national perspective*, edited by Marjorie J. Robertson and Milton Greenblatt, 19-34. New York: Plenum Press.

Lee, Barrett A. 1989. Homelessness in Tennessee. In *Homelessness in the United States, volume I: State surveys*, edited by Jamshid A. Momeni, 181-204. New York: Greenwood Press.

Levinson, David. 1974. The etiology of skid rows in the United States. *International Journal of Social Psychiatry* 20:25-33.

Levi-Strauss, Claude. 1969. *The elementary structures of kinship.* Boston: Beacon Press.

Liebow, Elliot. 1967. *Tally's corner.* Boston: Little, Brown.

---. 1993. *Tell them who I am: The lives of homeless women.* New York: Penguin Books.

Litwak, Eugene. 1965. Extended kin relations in an industrial democratic society. In *Social structure and the family: Generational relations*, edited by Ethel Shanas and Gordon F. Streib, 290-323. Englewood Cliffs, NJ: Prentice-Hall.

---. 1985. *Helping the elderly: The complementary roles of informal networks and formal systems.* New York: The Guilford Press.

Litwak, Eugene, and Ivan Szelenyi. 1969. Primary group structures and their functions: Kin, neighbors, and friends. *American Sociological Review* 34:(4)465-81.

Lynd, Robert S., and Helen Merrell Lynd. 1965 [1937]. *Middletown in transition: A study in cultural conflicts.* New York: Harcourt Brace Jovanovich.

Maurin, Judith. T., and Leslie Russell. 1989. Homelessness in Utah. In *Homelessness in the United States, volume I: State surveys*, edited by Jamshid A. Momeni, 219-32. New York: Greenwood Press.

Maza, Penelope L., and Judy A. Hall. 1988. *Homeless children and their families: A preliminary study.* Washington, DC: Child Welfare League of America.

McKee, Lorna. 1987. Households during unemployment: The resourcefulness of the unemployed. In *Give and take in families: Studies in resource distribution,* by Julian Brannen and Gail Wilson, 96-116. London: Allen and Unwin.

McKinney, John C. 1966. *Constructive typology and social theory.* New York: Meredith.

Meltzer, Milton. 1986. *Poverty in America.* New York: William Morrow.

---. 1991. *Brother, can you spare a dime?* New York: Facts on File.

Merves, Esther S. 1992. Homeless women: Beyond the bag lady myth. In *Homelessness: A national perspective,* edited by Marjorie J. Robertson and Milton Greenblatt, 229-44. New York: Plenum Press.

Miller, Henry. 1991. *On the fringe: The dispossessed in America.* Lexington, MA: D. C. Heath.

Modell, John. 1979. Changing risks, changing adaptations: American families in the nineteenth and twentieth centuries. In *Kin and communities: Families in America,* edited by Allan J. Lichtman and Joan R. Challinor, 119-44. Washington, DC: Smithsonian Institution Press.

Molnar, Janice, William R. Rath, Tovah P. Klein, Cynthia Lowe, and Annelie H. Hartman. 1991. *Ill fares the land: The consequences of homelessness and chronic poverty for children and families in New York City, executive summary.* New York: Bank Street College of Education.

Morrow-Jones, Hazel A., and Willem Van Vliet. 1989. Homelessness in Colorado. In *Homelessness in the United States, volume I: State surveys,* edited by Jamshid A. Momeni, 21-38. New York: Greenwood Press.

Murie, Alan, and Ray Forrest. 1988. The new homeless in Britain. In *Affordable housing and the homeless,* edited by Jürgen Friedrichs, 129-45. Berlin: Walter de Gruyter.

Newman, Katherine S. 1988. *Falling from grace: The experience of downward mobility in the American middle class.* New York: The Free Press.

O'Connor, Pat, and George W. Brown. 1984. Supportive relationships: Fact or fancy? *Journal of Social and Personal Relationships* 1:159-75.

Parish, William L., Lingxin Hao, and Dennis P. Hogan. 1991. Family support networks, welfare, and work among young mothers. *Journal of Marriage and the Family* 53:203-15.

Parsons, Talcott. 1968. The stability of the American family system. In *A modern introduction to the family*, rev. ed., edited by Norman W. Bell and Ezra F. Vogel, 97-102. New York: The Free Press.

Patton, Larry T. 1988. Appendix C: The rural homeless. In *Homelessness, health, and human needs*, authored by Committee on Healthcare for Homeless People, 183-217. Washington, DC: National Academy Press.

Pearce, Diana, and Harriette McAdoo. 1984. Women and children: Alone and in poverty. In *Families and change: Social needs and public policies*, edited by Rosalie G. Genovese, 161-76. New York: Praeger.

Peroff, Kathleen. 1987. Who are the homeless and how many are there? In *The homeless in contemporary society*, edited by Richard D. Bingham, Roy E. Green, and Sammis B. White, 33-45. Newbury Park, CA: Sage.

Phillips, Michael H., Neal DeChillo, Daniel Kronenfeld, and Verona Middleton-Jeter. 1986. Homeless families: Services make a difference. *Social Casework* 69(January):48-53.

Piliavin, Irving, Michael Sosin, and Herb Westerfelt. 1988. *Conditions contributing to long-term homelessness: An exploratory study. DP #853-87.* Madison, WI: University of Wisconsin-Madison's Institute for Research on Poverty.

Pinstripe, Babette. 1990. Personal conversation. Parenting class facilitator, County Homeless Outreach Office.

Proch, Kathleen, and Merlin A. Taber. 1987. Helping the homeless. *Public Welfare* 45:5-9.

Question, Roy. 1991. Personal conversation. Case manager at Starlight Inn.

Qureshi, Hazel. 1986. Responses to dependency: Reciprocity, affect, and power in family relationships. In *Dependency and interdependency in old age: Theoretical perspectives and policy alternatives*, edited by Chris Phillipson, Miriam Bernard, and Patricia Strang, 167-79. London: Croom Helm.

Redburn, F. Stevens, and Terry F. Buss. 1986. *Responding to America's homeless: Public policy alternatives*. New York: Praeger.

Ringheim, Karin. 1990. *At risk of homelessness: The roles of income and rent*. New York: Praeger.

Rivlin, Leanne G. 1986. A new look at the homeless. *Social Policy* 16(4):3-10.

Robertson, Marjorie J., and Milton Greenblatt. 1992. Homelessness: A national perspective. In *Homelessness: A national perspective*, edited by Marjorie J. Robertson and Milton Greenblatt, 339-49. New York: Plenum Press.

Ropers, Richard H. 1988. *The invisible homeless: A new urban ecology*. New York: Insight Books.

---. 1991. *Persistent poverty: The American dream turned nightmare*. New York: Plenum Press.

Ropers, Richard, and Marjorie Robertson. 1984. *The inner-city homeless of Los Angeles: An empirical assessment*. Basic Shelter Document, No. 1, 18 January. Los Angeles: UCLA.

Rosenthal, Rob. 1994. *Homeless in paradise: A map of the terrain*. Philadelphia: Temple University Press.

Rosser, Colin, and Christopher Harris. 1983. *The family and social change: A study in family and kinship in a South Wales town*. London: Routledge and Kegan Paul.

Rossi, Peter H. 1989a. *Down and out in America: The origins of homelessness*. Chicago: The University of Chicago Press.

---. 1989b. *Without shelter: Homelessness in the 1980s*. New York: Priority Press.

Rossi, Peter H., and James D. Wright. 1987. The determinants of homelessness. *Health Affairs* 6:19-32.

---. 1989. The urban homeless: A portrait of urban dislocation. *The Annals of the American Academy of Political and Social Science* 501:132-42.

Rossi, Peter H., James D. Wright, Gene A. Fisher, and Georgianna Willis. 1987. The urban homeless: Estimating composition and size. *Science* 235(March):1336-41.

Roth, Dee. 1989. Homelessness in Ohio: A statewide epidemiological study. In *Homelessness in the United States, volume I: State surveys*, edited by Jamshid A. Momeni, 145-64. New York: Greenwood Press.

Roth, Dee, Beverly G. Toomey, and Richard J. First. 1992. Gender, racial, and age variations among homeless persons. In *Homelessness: A national perspective*, edited by Marjorie J. Robertson and Milton Greenblatt, 199-211. New York: Plenum Press.

Schneider, John C. 1986. Skid row as an urban neighborhood, 1880-1960. In *Housing the homeless*, edited by Jon Erickson and Charles Wilhelm, 167-189. New Brunswick, NJ: Center for Urban Policy Research.

Shinn, Marybeth, James R. Knickman, and Beth C. Weitzman. 1991. Social relationships and vulnerability to becoming homeless among poor families. *American Psychologist* 46:1180-87.

Shore, Miles F., and Martin D. Cohen. 1992. Homelessness and the chronically mentally ill. In *Homelessness: A national perspective*, edited by Marjorie J. Robertson and Milton Greenblatt, 67-75. New York: Plenum Press.

Slater, Courtenay M., and George E. Hall, eds. 1992. *1992 county and city extra annual metro, city, and county data book*. Lanham, MD: Bernan Press.

Snow, David A., and Leon Anderson. 1993. *Down on their luck: A study of homeless street people*. Berkeley: University of California Press.

Snow, David A., Robert D. Benford, and Leon Anderson. 1986. Fieldwork roles and informational yield: A comparison of alternative settings and roles. *Urban Life* 14:377-408.

Solarz, Andrea L. 1992. To be young and homeless: Implication of homelessness for children. In *Homelessness: A national perspective*, edited by Marjorie J. Robertson and Milton Greenblatt, 275-86. New York: Plenum Press.

Spradley, James P. 1970. *You owe yourself a drunk: An ethnography of urban nomads*. Boston: Little, Brown.

Stack, Carol B. 1970. *All our kin: Strategies for survival in a black community*. New York: Harper and Row.

Stark, Louisa R. 1994. The shelter as "total institution": An organization barrier to remedying homelessness. *American Behavioral Scientist* 37(4):553-62.

Stefl, Mary E. 1987. The new homeless: A national perspective. In *The homeless in contemporary society*, edited by Richard D. Bingham, Roy E. Green, and Sammis B. White, 46-63. Newbury Park, CA: Sage.

Steinbeck, John. 1991 [1967]. *The grapes of wrath*. New York: Penguin Books.

Stoner, Madeleine R. 1995. *The civil rights of homeless people: Law, social policy, and social work practice*. New York: Aldine De Gruyter.

Stouffer, Samuel A., and Paul F. Lazarsfeld. 1972. *Research memorandum on the family in the depression*. New York: Arno Press.

Sullivan, Patricia A., and Shirley P. Damrosch. 1987. Homeless women and children. In *The homeless in contemporary society*, edited by Richard D. Bingham, Roy E. Green, and Sammis B. White, 82-98. Newbury Park, CA: Sage.

Sussman, Marvin B. 1959. The isolated nuclear family: Fact or fiction. *Social Problems* 6(4):333-40.

Sussman, Marvin B., and Lee Burchinal. 1962. Kin family network: Unheralded structure in current conceptualizations of family functioning. *Marriage and Family Living* 24(3):231-40.

Sutherland, Edwin H., and Harvey J. Locke. 1936. *Twenty thousand homeless men: A study of unemployed men in the Chicago shelters*. Chicago: J. B. Lippincott.

Taietz, Philip. 1970. The extended family in transition: A study of the family life of old people in the Netherlands. In *Readings in kinship in urban society*, edited by C. C. Harris, 321-35. Oxford: Pergamon Press.

Timmer, Doug A., D. Stanley Eitzen, and Kathryn D. Talley. 1994. *Paths to homelessness: Extreme poverty and the urban housing crisis*. Boulder, CO: Westview Press.

Typesalot, Maggie. 1989. Personal conversation. Secretary to Baghdad Inn shelter services manager.

United States Bureau of the Census. 1982. *General population characteristics: Part 1, United States summary, 1980*. Washington, DC: U. S. Government Printing Office.

---. 1984. *Persons in institutions and other group quarters, 1980*. Washington, DC: U. S. Government Printing Office.

---. 1989. *County and city data book, 1988*. Washington, DC: U. S. Government Printing Office.

---. 1991a. *State and metropolitan area data book, 1991*. Washington, DC: U. S. Government Printing Office.

---. 1991b. *Statistical abstract of the United States: 1991* (111th ed.). Washington, DC: U. S. Government Printing Office.

United States Conference of Mayors. 1991. *A status report on hunger and homelessness in America's cities: 1991* (author Laura DeKoven Waxman). Washington, DC: United States Conference of Mayors.

---. 1994. *A status report on hunger and homelessness in America's cities: 1994*. Washington, DC: United States Conference of Mayors.

United States Department of Housing and Urban Development (HUD). 1984. *A report to the secretary on the homeless and emergency shelters*. Washington, DC: Government Publishing Office.

---. 1986. The extent of homelessness in America: A report to the secretary on the homeless and emergency shelters. In *Housing the homeless*, edited by Jon Erickson and Charles Wilhelm, 127-43. New Brunswick, NJ: The Center for Urban Policy Research.

Wagner, David, and Marcia B. Cohen. 1991. The power of the people: Homeless protesters in the aftermath of social movement participation. *Social Problems* 38:543-61.

Walker, Lee. 1988. Homelessness: A case of mistaken identity. *State Government News* 31(June):26-27.

Wallace, Samuel E. 1965. *Skid row as a way of life.* New York: Harper and Row.

Walsh, Mary E. 1992. *Moving to nowhere: Children's stories of homelessness.* New York: Auburn House.

Wax, Rosalie H. 1971. *Doing fieldwork: Warnings and advice.* Chicago: The University of Chicago Press.

Wellman, Barry. 1990. The place of kinfolk in personal community networks. In *Families in community settings: Interdisciplinary perspectives*, edited by Donald G. Unger and Marvin B. Sussman, 195-228. New York: Haworth Press.

White, Richard W., Jr. 1992. *Rude awakenings: What the homelessness crisis tells us.* San Francisco: ICS Press.

Whyte, William F. 1955. *Street corner society.* Chicago: The University of Chicago Press.

Wiclad, Joanne. 1990. Personal conversation. Homeless outreach worker. Women, Infant, and Children Program (WIC).

Wilson, William Julius. 1987. *The truly disadvantaged: The inner city, the underclass, and public policy.* Chicago: The University of Chicago Press.

---. 1991. Studying inner-city social dislocations: The challenge of public agenda research. *American Sociological Review* 56:1-14.

Wolch, Jennifer, and Michael Dear. 1993. *Malign neglect: Homelessness in an American city.* San Francisco: Jossey-Bass.

Wright, James D. 1988. The worthy unworthy homeless. *Society* 25(5):64-69.

---. 1989. *Address unknown: The homeless in America.* New York: Aldine de Gruyter.

Yancy, William L., and Lee Rainwater. 1970. Problems in the ethnography of the urban underclass. In *Pathways to data: Field methods for studying ongoing social organizations*, edited by R. W. Habenstein, 245-69. Chicago: Aldine.

Yeich, Susan. 1994. *The politics of ending homelessness.* Lanham, MD: University Press of America.

Zorbaugh, Harvey W. 1976 [1929]. *The gold coast and the slum: A sociological study of Chicago's near north side.* Chicago: The University of Chicago Press.

INDEX

Numbers in italics refer to tables or figures.

T

Taietz, Philip, 81
total institutions. *See* Goffman
transiency. *See* characteristics of
transitional shelter, 112-6, 120, 173-4
Turner v. City of New Orleans, 59

U

U-Curve. *See* Glaser
Uphills, 143, 145-6, 150-4, 159-60, 162

V

vagabonds. *See* history of
Veteran's Administration, 21

W

warning out. *See* history of
Wellman, Barry, 67-9, 72, 83
worthy and unworthy poor. *See* history of